PRAISE FOR
Babylon Confidential

"An honest, page-turning insight into alcoholism and the road back out."
—NEIL GAIMAN, *New York Times* Bestselling Author

◯

"I was gratified my method of alcoholism treatment could play a part in Claudia's journey from addiction to successful recovery. This vivid and insightful book can help save others suffering from this disease."
—JOHN DAVID SINCLAIR, PhD, Founder,
The Sinclair Method for the treatment of alcohol addiction

◯

"Warning: Once you start reading *Babylon Confidential* you may not be able stop until the last page. Just as with a good novel, whenever I wasn't reading, I found myself wondering what would happen next. *Babylon Confidential* offers mesmerizing insight into the allure of success, the pressures of Hollywood, the pitfalls of love, and the nature of addiction. Despite putting readers through the emotional wringer as it depicts her struggles, Claudia Christian's memoir ultimately emerges as a message of hope."
—REBECCA MOESTA,
New York Times Bestselling Young Adult Author

◯

"*Babylon Confidential* is compelling, horrifying, and uplifting. Claudia Christian has an amazing story of glitz and darkness and ultimately a journey as strange and exciting as any of her films."
—KEVIN J. ANDERSON, *New York Times* Bestselling Coauthor, *Sisterhood of Dune*

◯

"[*Babylon Confidential*] is from the heart, succinct, clear, and gives hope where there is none."
—STEPHEN MICHAEL COX, MD,
President, National Anxiety Foundation

"The dashing and darling Claudia puts herself on the line with her struggles with addiction. Claudia shares and bares it all to help everyone else. . . . A must-read for fans and for folks dealing with any kind of addiction."
—PAT TALLMAN, Actress and Stuntwoman; Author, *Pleasure Thresholds*

∞

"Fearless and inspiring. Claudia not only remembers the torturous calamities of her life, as well as the highs, but she recalls them here with skill, grace, and utterly no apology. If you have an addiction, or know someone who does, you must read this book."
—SHARI SHATTUCK,
Actress; Author, Callaway Wilde novels

∞

"This story is a runaway train on a roller coaster rail. Told with brutal honesty, Claudia Christian takes us on a trip through her life of sex, drugs, despair, betrayal, courage, humor, love, and triumph. She has lived it all and she's inviting us along for the ride. Hold on to your hat!"
—WALTER KOENIG, Actor, Director, and Author

∞

"A wild ride. Claudia's James Frey-like voice reveals the secret life of an alcoholic. Read, laugh, and learn. But most importantly, share—to save a life."
—CLARE KRAMER, Actress

∞

"Claudia Christian shares her darkest secrets and greatest fears in her brilliant new addiction memoir—funny, heart-breaking, engrossing, and brutally honest—a book you won't be able to put down."
—AMY LUWIS, Author, Yoga to the Rescue book series;
Cofounder, AdoptAPet.com and adventuresoftoxicgirl.blogspot.com

BABYLON
CONFIDENTIAL

A MEMOIR OF

LOVE, SEX, AND ADDICTION

CLAUDIA CHRISTIAN

WITH MORGAN GRANT BUCHANAN

BenBella Books, Inc.
Dallas, Texas

BENBELLA

BenBella Books, Inc.
10300 N. Central Expressway
Suite #400
Dallas, TX 75231
www.benbellabooks.com
Send feedback to feedback@benbellabooks.com

Printed in the United States of America
10 9 8 7 6 5 4 3 2 1

Library of Congress Cataloging-in-Publication Data is available for this title.

ISBN 978-1-937856-06-9

Editing by Erin Kelley
Copyediting by David Bessmer
Proofreading by Laura Cherkas and Rainbow Graphics
Cover design by Sarah Dombrowsky
Text design and composition by Neuwirth & Associates, Inc.
Printed by Bang Printing

Distributed by Perseus Distribution
perseusdistribution.com

To place orders through Perseus Distribution:
Tel: 800-343-4499
Fax: 800-351-5073
E-mail: orderentry@perseusbooks.com

Significant discounts for bulk sales are available. Please contact Glenn Yeffeth at
glenn@benbellabooks.com or (214) 750-3628.

*This book is dedicated to my mother, Hildegard.
Her constant love, fierce loyalty, and utter devotion have taught
me that a mother's love is truly incomparable. You are my best
friend, my ballast, and the love of my life, Mama.*

CONTENTS

CONTENTS

BABYLON

CONFIDENTIAL

NO ONE SETS out to become an addict.

When you're a kid and people ask what you want to be when you grow up, you imagine yourself as a doctor or a teacher (or if you're five-year-old me, as an actress or the dictator of a small country), something that involves helping people and making the world a better place. You never consider that one day you'll find yourself sitting at a bus stop on Coldwater Canyon as the morning traffic passes by, your hands shaking as you try to get the vodka-spiked orange juice past your lips. You don't imagine that you'll be close to death in a detox clinic with a total loss of muscle function, dehydrated and hallucinating. No parent gives you advice on how to survive the long walk to the liquor store when the cupboard is dry, though you develop strategies. You ration out sips of vanilla extract (35 percent alcohol) and pray that it will prevent a seizure. It keeps the contents of your stomach down and your shaking legs from buckling under you.

You don't see that coming; I sure didn't when I followed my dream to pursue an acting career in Hollywood. I'd left behind a family wracked by a tragic loss, was betrayed by the people I loved most, and survived a horrific rape. By the time I was eighteen, I was working on shows like *Dallas* and *Falcon Crest* and earning a six-figure income. The Hollywood I found myself caught up in was a whirlwind of beauty, wealth, and power. I made out with stars like George Clooney, Kelly LeBrock, and

Rob Lowe in the hottest hotels and clubs in L.A. and New York, rejected William Shatner, traveled the world on private jets and super yachts with lovers like Dodi Fayed, and, in my break-through role as Commander Susan Ivanova on *Babylon 5*, found millions of fans. My life has been one of extremes. The bounty of love and encouragement from family, friends, and fans is in sharp contrast to the unexpected mix of stalkings, shootings, and betrayals.

By the time I found myself at that bus stop, I was beyond caring if anyone recognized me. The self-aware Claudia was still there inside me, sitting in judgment in the back of my brain, but she wasn't running the show. In the late 1980s I starred in *The Hidden*, a cult classic sci-fi movie. My character is possessed by an alien who steals human bodies to disguise its presence. That was the state I'd reached with my drinking; it was as if another person had taken me over and all I could do was look on like a bystander at a traffic accident.

It took me out of my house at 4 a.m., not caring that Ralph's grocery store couldn't start selling liquor until 6. It had no problem making me stand around for hours, killing time while I waited to buy (or if it wasn't locked up—steal) the first bottle of the day.

I used to camp out at Ralph's. I'd buy bottles of stuff I didn't even like to drink—Grand Marnier, crème de menthe, Drambuie— just so I could tell the checkout clerks that I was making a soufflé and throw them off the scent. One time some pimple-faced kid, half my age, gave me a patronizing smile and said, "A little early for this, isn't it?" He was right; I left the store mortified. I'd get in my car, twist the top off a beer and start drinking. After only a few gulps, I was throwing up all over the parking lot.

I was out of control and more than a little frightened. After finishing my bus stop screwdriver, I went home and looked at myself in the mirror. I barely recognized the puffy, yellow-eyed monster looking back at me. I'd even come to refer to the addiction that overtook me in those terms, as a monster, the monster within me. Even if one of my fans had come and sat down right beside me while I watched the morning traffic, I think my identity would have remained a secret.

I LOVE life. I always have. If I can get that close to utter self-destruction, then there must be other people suffering the same or much worse. I'm writing this memoir for them.

And it's no easy thing—opening the doors to my past—sharing painful and personal memories that I'd hesitate to confide to even my closest friends. But I feel that the story of how I rose to become a star and then came crashing back down to earth at the hands of my addiction is worth sharing—it contains a message of hope.

For over a decade, I lived in a shadow world, one which is easy to enter and not so easy to leave. But I did. I came back. I found a way out of a life filled with shame and despair.

Even at my worst, having gone from working as a successful actress to clinging to a bottle at that bus stop, I never gave up hope that I could reclaim the dream of using my talents to help other people.

ONE

THREE STRIKES

1

UNDER THE INFLUENCE

IT WAS 1973. I was eight years old, and about to learn that fate can be a stone-cold bitch.

That was the year that Shell Oil ordered my dad to pack up our lives and move to Texas. I found myself in the sauna that is a humid Lone Star September with my parents, James and Hildegard, and my three older brothers, Patrick, Jimmy, and Vincent. In place of the beautiful autumn foliage that we'd left behind in Connecticut, Houston greeted us with shrubs, flat-lands, and mosquitoes. None of us was happy about leaving our home back East. There was a palpable tension in the air. My mom had stopped eating and had lost thirty pounds; she'd had a premonition that something terrible was going to happen.

Less than six months later, we would return to Connecticut, having suffered a blow that would continue to impact us until it eventually destroyed our family.

BEFORE THE move to Houston, I grew up in Westport and Weston, Connecticut. That was where we were at our happiest. I would tag along when my brothers built snow forts and tree houses and was appointed the unofficial fourth boy, unless they needed someone to gross out. Then I would revert to being their little sister and be forced to watch while they fed live mice to their pet snakes.

Patrick, my oldest brother, wanted to be Hawkeye from *The Last of the Mohicans*. He beaded things and worked with suede. He used to find dead animals and skin them for his projects. He even made his own moccasins. In the past the Paugusset tribe occupied the land near where we lived, and Pat would lead us in the hunt for old flint arrowheads that were still scattered around the woods.

Some little girls fantasize about being princesses or models. When I read stories about the Pilgrims and their problems, I used to side with the Indians and hope that one day I'd be carried away by a chief to live with his tribe.

Patrick was suitably impressed when, at age five, I landed my first big role: playing Chief Massasoit in a school play. This was a revelatory experience for me. I had three rowdy brothers—I could barely get a word in edgewise—but when I stood on the stage, everyone was quiet, their attention completely focused on me. When I delivered my heartfelt Thanksgiving monologue, I saw adults in the audience listening intently with tears in their eyes, and it astonished me that I could affect them on that emotional level. After that experience, I was hooked. I auditioned for as many plays as I could. The desire to connect with others in that meaningful way, to bring people with me, out of their everyday lives and into another space as I perform, that's exciting and powerful. It has sustained me in my career for over thirty years.

We were close to nature in Westport. The sea was nearby, and if I was good my mom used to let me camp out in the woods and eat Kentucky Fried Chicken with my girlfriends (that being the staple diet of woodland survivalists). Sometimes we'd even spend the night out there, unless someone started talking about murderers or ghosts, which would send us running back to the house, shrieking loudly enough to wake the dead.

So when my dad announced that Shell was transferring us to Houston, land of 64-ounce Slurpees and steaks the size of hubcaps, we were horrified. My brothers threatened to run away from home, I retreated sullenly into my books, and my parents' arguments broke out into full-scale war. The word "divorce" was overheard on more than one occasion, leaving us kids huddled in the corners of the house, drawing straws to see who got to live where. My mom usually got her way, but this time the decision had been made by a higher power—Shell Oil Company—and if my dad wanted to get ahead in his career, then he had to go where they sent him.

So my mom stopped eating and started crying all the time. She clung to us and kissed our heads as if we were all she had left. Her desire to stay was more than a fondness for Weston. She'd always had an amazing sixth sense. It wasn't uncommon for her to tell one of us to get the phone before it rang or to dream about things that would come to pass. She was sure that some terrible storm was brewing and that we were sailing right into it. My dad didn't want to hear about it; he just started packing.

∞

MY DAD, Jim, was eighteen years old when he was stabbed, right in the heart. He was a student at the University of Southern California and used to drive around in a red Corvette Stingray.

He'd been walking to Van De Camp's drive-in with some friends when they got jumped by a Mexican gang. My dad was walking in front and got the worst of it. The gang leader's wife had been cheating on him with some gringos; my dad and his friends were in the wrong place at the wrong time when the leader went looking for blood. When my dad reached the hospital, he became one of the first recipients of open-heart surgery. Back then they hadn't invented the small, vertical chest incision, so they cut him in half and left him with a long scar that looked like a magician's trick gone wrong.

The surgeons saved his life twice that day. The first time with the heart surgery—he appreciated that—but he was bitter about the second. Since he was laid up in the hospital, he couldn't ship out to the Korean War with his buddies. None of them came back. Dad had been sent to military school from the age of five, and there was an expectation that he would follow in the footsteps of his father, Charlie, who'd received a Purple Heart and the French Croix De Guerre in World War I. He was hit by shrapnel in the left lung while leading a French-American force in the Meuse-Argonne offensive.

Charlie was a second-generation Irish immigrant, born in Boston to a well-to-do family. He was a real-estate tycoon, a respected surgeon, an all-round society type with one large skeleton in the closet.

He'd bought a large parcel of desert land in Palm Springs and fitted it out with a trailer. There were no neighbors, no passersby, no one to come between Grandpa Charlie and the trunkload of whiskey that he would use to drink himself into oblivion. When he was done with his binge he'd dry out for a few days, head back home, and go on with life as usual until the trailer, like the nesting ground of a migratory bird, would irresistibly draw him back.

My mom, Hildegard, was, and still is, a stunningly beautiful woman. Born in Germany, she lived through World War II being evacuated from one small village to the next. She was five years old when Hitler passed through town in one of his flamboyant, goose-stepping parades. Pushing through the crowd to see what all the fuss was about, she found herself face-to-face with the man himself, who passed her a little swastika flag. She turned to run home and show her mother, but as she did she fell and the sharp end of the flag cut her chin open. She decided it was a bad omen and that Hitler was not to be trusted. To this day she still has what she calls her "Hitler scar."

And, of course, she was right about Hitler. He led Germany to ruin as well as her family. They lost everything when the Nazis evacuated them and took over their home as a base camp.

As a little girl my mom sometimes had to steal cabbages so they had enough to eat, and most evenings found her walking the streets searching for her papa until she found him asleep in a bar or singing with his drinking buddies. Both wartime poverty and her father's drinking were deeply humiliating for her.

When she was older, she was sponsored by a fiancé to come to America and work as a dental hygienist. That relationship fell through, and she ended up living with the owners of the Brown Derby, the famous Hollywood restaurant. She worked on Mae West's teeth and dated William Frawley, who played Fred Mertz in *I Love Lucy*. She never sought out celebrities, but she was classy and extremely attractive and so naturally found herself moving in circles that attracted them.

Even in middle age, when a future governor of California tried to hit on her in their shared Germanic tongue, she gave him short shrift. It was at my birthday party, and she came over to ask me who he was.

7

"Mom, that's the Terminator."

"I don't care who he is, he's a very rude man. You should have heard him. He's been living in America too long."

When my mom's friends tried to set her up with my father, she wasn't interested and tried to push him onto another friend. But my dad can be determined when he sets his mind to something, and eventually he won her over with his Gregory Peck–style good looks and a ride in his Corvette Stingray.

My mom gave me the desire to improve my lot in life with style. She's an incredibly hard worker and fast learner. She took an unfinished education and ended up the manager of Giorgio's, one of the swankiest stores in Beverly Hills.

But back then, when my parents first got married, they were poor. My dad started at the bottom, working at a gas station, and slowly worked his way up the ladder at Shell one rung at a time.

I get my determination from my dad, my need to prove myself, to show the world that I can make it on my own without any handouts. But I've always been mindful of the toll that success took on both him and our family. He was always away, and when he was at home he was tense, high-strung, and not easy to be around. As a parent I guess you fall back on what you know, and he had been raised in a brutal military school and expected us to fall in line like those little Von Trapp kids in *The Sound of Music*. The problem was that we all had his stubborn streak, so conflict was inevitable.

When I say that my dad was stubborn and determined, I mean it. He had a hangover one morning when he was in his early forties, after a New Year's party with his work buddies, and swore he'd never drink again. Alcohol was his father's demon and he didn't plan on making it his. To this day he still hasn't touched a drop of the stuff.

BACK IN Houston it was still dark in the mornings when we'd jump on the bus that would take us to our new schools. We'd start sweating at nine in the morning and finish at sunset. The only place to swim was the bayou, which was teeming with venomous water moccasins. Swatting at mosquitoes, I used to watch the crawdads swarm all over the gutters. We used to jokingly call Houston "Satan's shack."

It was October 22, 1973, and two of my brothers had gotten into a fight with my dad about homework. Patrick was a rebellious fourteen and Jimmy was a year younger. My dad was always tightly wound at the end of the day and had no patience for kids who didn't follow the rules in his house. A futile, frustrating argument broke out.

"We're outa here!" Patrick said, slamming open the screen door and storming out of the house. From the table I watched him tie his blue bandana around his head and grab his bike from the lawn, Jimmy right on his heels.

"Where do you think you're going?" our dad yelled.

Over his shoulder, Patrick shouted, "7-Eleven!"

My brothers raced off down the street. Jimmy pulled ahead, laughing, with Patrick rushing to catch up. They were neck-and-neck for a block or two, and then Jimmy took the lead again, younger by a year, but faster. At the intersection, he slowed for a split second, waiting for the light to turn green, then leaned down over his handlebars and barreled through.

Patrick pedaled hard to catch him and had nearly made up the lost ground as he raced across the intersection. Jimmy saw a glint of metal out of the corner of his eye and skidded to a stop, turning back in time to see the driver who had run the red light hit Patrick at full speed. Patrick rolled all the way over the car and slammed down hard on the pavement. By the time Jimmy got to his side, Pat lay crumpled on the ground.

Jimmy tried to get Pat to move off the road but he was unconscious, blood seeping out of his head. In Boy Scouts, Jimmy had learned that you're not supposed to move someone who's got a head injury, so he left him lying in the road and tried waving down another car to get help.

It was a quiet street in a residential neighborhood. Fading in and out of consciousness, Patrick was lying in the intersection next to two fallen bikes. He must've been easy to see.

At dinner that night, we'd all been doing Monty Python and Rich Little impersonations, when out of the blue Patrick said, "You know, if I ever get hit by a car, I won't get hurt. I'm going to jump up quickly, then roll over the hood and down the back."

We didn't think much of it at the time; it's the kind of thing boys say all the time. But when the bumper hit his bike, that's exactly what he did. Patrick leapt up and rolled over the hood and down the back of the car. It left him with a broken leg and a head injury, but he was going to be alright.

Jumping up and rolling was a good plan. It would've worked, except the driver of the second car was drunk. He ran right over Patrick, killing him instantly.

EVERY DETAIL of that day is burnt into my memory. The neighbors had volunteered to watch us when my parents were called to the scene. I was sitting in their hallway with Vince when these two kids came to the door. They didn't realize that we were the siblings of the boy who was hit.

"Hey, we just saw an accident! A kid's head got fuckin' squashed like a melon!"

We were speechless, and the kids just kept going on and on like that until the adult nearest the door told them to get the hell out of there. Vince was the youngest brother, and I was the youngest child, so we used to fight all the time, but right then we found ourselves holding each other's trembling hands. Then the door of the neighbors' house opened again and my mom came stumbling toward us, clutching the bloody blue bandana left behind when the paramedics lifted Patrick's body from the street. I saw in her face that what the kids said was true—Patrick was dead.

She took us back to our house. A few minutes later I saw my dad walking toward us, having just identified his dead son. He was halfway across the front lawn when he suddenly fell down on all fours and started throwing up in the grass. He stayed there, alternately retching and weeping. I don't think he could get up. It was the first time in my life I'd seen him cry.

And then there was Jimmy. The memory of that day would come to cost him dearly. In the months that followed, Jimmy would wake up screaming every night. There are a thousand ways to blame yourself when something like that happens and he probably tried them all on for size. When he grew older he sought solace in drugs. Intensive psychotherapy and rehab brought him back from the edge. He's been sober for many years, but Patrick's death continues to haunt him to this day.

In the aftermath of Pat's death, my parents couldn't look at one another. We moved around the flat, alien wasteland of Houston in a daze. We'd only been there a few months, and we had no friends to comfort us, only the well-meaning strangers at church.

Our family never recovered.

It was the first time alcohol abuse had taken something beloved from me. It wouldn't be the last.

ON THE Sunday after the funeral, my mother got us ready for church, but when we filed out into the living room, my dad was reading the paper, still in his bathrobe.

"God is a bastard," he said. "I'll never set foot in a church again."

I completely agreed. Patrick's death had taught me that when fate swings against you, the only person you can rely on is yourself.

After less than half a year in Houston, we packed our bags and prepared to move home to Connecticut, minus our brother. But before we left there was something I had to take care of.

Unlike my father, I had taken Holy Communion. As I understood it, I was married to Christ, so things were a bit more complicated for me; I was going to need a divorce. I went out into the woods alone, to a place my mom had shown me on one of our family walks through the Houston countryside. In the shade of a weeping willow there grew a rare lady's slipper orchid. My mom had explained that I should always treat them gently, because they were endangered, to which my brothers had kindly added, "You could also be fined five hundred bucks or have your hand chopped off if they catch you messing with them!"

It was the closest thing I knew to a sacred place.

I took the tiny rosary I'd been given for my first communion and wrapped it in one of my favorite hankies—a little German number from my grandmother with "Edelweiss" embroidered on it—and buried it beside the orchid. Then I solemnly said the Lord's Prayer and called the whole thing off with Jesus.

Maybe that explains why, years later, when I took up praying in earnest, God took a while to return my call. He was probably wary of being dumped again.

2

ONE IN FIVE*

*Y*EARS PASSED, AND just when it looked like things might be returning to normal I received the news that would turn our lives upside down again. It was a couple of months away from my fourteenth birthday, and I was home alone in Connecticut when the phone rang. It was my dad calling from the other side of the country.

"Guess what? We're moving to California."

I burst into tears. I was so upset because I finally had my own friends and something that resembled a regular life. I'd even started theater classes, and now we were moving. Again. He must have felt bad about my dramatic reaction, because at the end of the conversation he told me for the first time that he

---

* "Nearly one-fifth of women (18 percent) reported experiencing a completed or attempted rape at some time in their lives." (National Institute of Justice and Centers for Disease Control and Prevention, "Prevalence, Incidence, and Consequences of Violence Against Women: Findings from the National Violence Against Women Survey," November 1998.)

loved me. He wasn't an emotionally demonstrative man, and the impact of that rare admission only made me cry more. I was settled in Connecticut. We had moved before and it hadn't gone well. Now the very idea of leaving behind everything that I knew and loved felt both strange and overwhelming, like taking an unexpected voyage to another planet.

The bad news was offset by my big dream that I would one day become a working actress. I imagined that our house would be near the San Gabriel Mountains with a view of the Hollywood sign, that my mom would take me to auditions, and that I'd be an overnight success.

Also, there was one bad memory of Connecticut I wanted to escape. When I was in the eighth grade, my boyfriend Frank and some of his friends raided a liquor cabinet and drank Jack Daniels and vodka until they passed out. When the other boys woke up, they found Frank dead. He had choked on his own vomit and died during the night.

So I'd learned, even at that young age, to stay well clear of hard liquor. My mother wasn't a big drinker, and my father had quit drinking, so there weren't bad role models around the house, but it seemed that with Patrick's death at the hands of a drunk driver and my boyfriend's death from overconsumption, the negative effects of alcohol abuse were beginning to haunt my life.

Looking back, I can see that those ghosts weren't done with me, not by a long shot. They would follow me across the country to my new life.

We flew out to L.A., and by this time my dad must have been feeling really bad, because he felt he needed to butter us up with a trip to Disneyland. I had my fourteenth birthday in the Disneyland Hotel. We decided to celebrate by taking a tour of our new house at Nellie Gail Ranch. With a name like that I expected something similar to what we were used to in Connecticut: beautiful period homes, acres of woods, and little creeks and ponds.

Nellie Gail Ranch turned out to be a cookie-cutter housing estate, a tract home development. Our house was in a little cul-de-sac. There was no lawn, it was the middle of summer and stinking hot, and only about 40 percent of the houses were inhabited. It was all new and sterile.

The houses were demarcated by a kind of alphabetic apart-heid. If you had a Plan C house you had more wealth and prestige than someone with a Plan B or Plan A. There was this ridiculous competitive element in the neighborhood.

My disappointment grew when I figured out that Nellie Gail Ranch was in Orange County, a good hour on the 405 freeway from Hollywood, which meant that it might as well have been the moon.

My mom was so sad there. Divorce was in the air. It didn't manifest itself until I was eighteen and already long gone from the house but you could tell that my mom would never forgive my father for moving to Texas; their eventual breakup was a slow-moving, unavoidable avalanche. I used to try to cheer her up—I'd stick all these little frozen Tex-Mex delicacies in the microwave and then bring them out and serve them up like I was a robot, which always made her laugh.

Not long after we moved my mom got a job, and then I pretty much became a latchkey kid. She was working at Saks Fifth Avenue in the swanky "designer salon," which was great, because she was able to bring home beautiful clothes. But it meant that every day I'd come home from school to an empty house. Dad worked late, Jimmy had moved out of the house by the time I was twelve, and Vincent and I weren't particularly chummy; our age difference of four years meant we didn't have much in common. He was out studying all the time and worrying about what college he'd go to. I'd read or roller-skate around our little cul-de-sac wearing shorts and a tube top. I wasn't a rambunctious child who needed lots of attention; I was a loner, which made it hard to work out how to fit into my new life.

School only complicated the process. I attended Laguna Hills High for my freshman year. I felt completely out of place because I was from Connecticut and very tomboyish, and all the other girls dressed like hookers in tight jeans, high heels, and makeup. I quickly adapted and copied them. I could see that my parents were surprised; they wanted to know what had happened to their little girl in top-siders and polo shirts. I was in the midst of transforming from the awkward-looking fourth son with short hair and braces into a young woman.

I went on my first proper date around that time with a young guy who picked me up in an old Dodge Dart. My brother Vince had a ball making fun of me because I wore a purple and red neon disco dress with Minnie Mouse high heels. I even had the Farrah Fawcett hairdo with the sausage curls down the sides and more eyeliner than Tammy Faye Bakker; it was just awful.

The only other people who lived in our cul-de-sac lived right next door: an airline pilot, his Asian wife, and their three-year-old daughter. He used to come over and be buddy-buddy with my father, and I guess that in an innocent, adolescent way, I thought he was handsome.

One day we were in our Jacuzzi with my father and he stuck his foot on my leg and started rubbing it up and down. It all happened under the bubbling water so you couldn't see it. I thought that was really weird so I got out of the Jacuzzi and went inside.

Not long after that I was walking home from school and he drew up beside me in his van and offered to drive me home. He was my neighbor, and anything was better than walking, so

I jumped in. The van had a plaid interior, with horrible brown fabric on the seats and two little round bubble windows at the back. They were thick and opaque; you couldn't see in or out of them. The second I closed the door I could tell he was drunk. He said he had to stop somewhere on the way home, and I didn't argue. He pulled up outside a liquor store, and when he came back he handed me a can of Coke that had been spiked with booze.

I felt pretty grown up, so I took a few sips and not long after started feeling really woozy. Maybe it was because I wasn't used to drinking, or maybe he'd put something else in the can besides liquor. He drove to an empty parking lot, and the next thing I knew he stopped the car and made a move on me. I panicked and tried to push him away, but he was a big guy, 200 pounds and at least 6'1". He just grabbed me and threw me into the back of the van. I tried fighting him off but he pinned me down and sat on my arms and told me how much I wanted it.

I knew how babies were made and I'd walked in once on my parents having sex, but there's nothing that prepares you for a grown man crushing you with his weight, grunting, his face turning red, and realizing that you're not strong enough to stop him.

I caught sight of those bubble windows set into the back of the van and that's when it occurred to me that no one could see me and that I might actually die. Another part of my brain was trying to rationalize things—this is my neighbor, he knows my parents, he can't kill me, but if my parents find out they'll kill him and probably me as well. That's when I went limp, because I thought, "Oh boy, I don't want to die in this van, I'd better get this over with."

He took my virginity. There was a little blood and a lot of pain. Then he drove back to Nellie Gail Ranch and dumped me outside the front of my house. He knew that neither of my parents would be home.

It was the first time in my life I was confronted with the fact that I wasn't invincible. I called a friend who picked me up in her mom's station wagon and took me to a free clinic. The doctor sewed me up and nodded unquestioningly when I told him I was eighteen years old, had forgotten to bring my driver's license, and had been on the bad end of a jungle gym accident. At that point, I began to fear that I'd be blamed for what had happened. My friend took me home, and I went inside, bruised and defeated, and showered off. If my parents asked why I was limping and shaken, I intended to say I'd gotten into a fight at school. They never asked.

Forget my virginity. What that man took was my trust in other people and myself. Before that, I'd had real confidence, instilled by an encouraging mother and a tough, intelligent father. After that I had doubts. I withdrew from school activities. My grades got bad. I retreated to my room and never went outside. I certainly never roller-skated again. I guess my parents blamed the change in me on adolescence and hormones.

I wonder now how he rationalized the rape to himself. I wonder why he got drunk in the first place before doing what he did.

Alcohol abuse is a demon that comes in many forms. I'd already felt the impact of the one that makes us so stupid that we can't operate a vehicle safely and the one that kills through overconsumption, but here was a new creature, the demon that excuses evil behavior. I'm sure that if he'd been hauled before a judge the first words out of his mouth would have been, "I was drunk, I don't know what I was thinking. And so was she. We'd both been drinking. It was consensual."

I changed in the weeks after the rape. I could feel myself withdrawing from life and I realized that I needed to do something.

I couldn't let him win. I still couldn't bring myself to talk to my parents about it, because Patrick's death had delivered a nearly fatal wound to their marriage and in my fourteen-year-old mind, I guess I was worried that my news might deliver the killing blow. And I was scared. There was the constant threat that it would happen again. He lived right next door, and we'd just moved in. I would have to see him again, see his house and that van every day that I lived in Nellie Gail Ranch. I needed to get away, so I talked my parents into letting me get out of Laguna Hills for the summer and headed up north to visit my cousin Caroline, who was about my age. I made a decision that I wasn't going to let the rapist ruin my life or take my virginity, even though he had, so I promised myself that while I was away I would choose a boy and have sex, and I'd pretend that it was my first time.

So I went to the state fair with my cousin and I met this guy who was about twenty. He was really tall with long blond hair, a country boy, very nice and sweet. After a couple of days of going back to the fair and flirting we went out on a date, while my cousin covered for me by staying at the fair. I told him what had happened to me. I told him I'd been raped and that I didn't want that to be my first experience and I asked him to help me. He was the sweetest guy. He made the softest, most gentle love to me and he kissed me and he held me. I needed to do that to try and get the effects of the rape out of my system. I needed to convince myself that not all men were assholes, and psychologically I needed to reclaim my virginity and some of my inner strength.

When summer was over I headed back to Laguna Hills. I knew that the rapist would still be there but I'd learned one thing about myself that allowed me to keep it all together. I had learned that I was a survivor.

3

BAIT AND SWITCH

RATHER THAN DYING down, things got much worse with the rapist next door. He started throwing pebbles at my window every night, trying to get me to come outside. I would lie in my bed petrified, praying that my parents would hear him. I guess after a few weeks he figured out that the pedophile Romeo approach wasn't going to win me over, so he gave up and started stalking me at school. He'd sit in his van and wait for me to walk home. I told my girlfriend, the one who'd taken me to the clinic after the rape, and she agreed to help. I'd hide in her car while she drove right past him. When I got home I'd lock myself in my room and wait for my hands to stop shaking.

Things didn't stay that way forever. It cost my parents almost every penny that they'd saved, but they found this great house in Laguna Beach and announced that we were moving.

Laguna Beach was only twenty minutes away by car, but it was one of the most exclusive beach communities in the United

States—a completely different world. It was a self-contained city bordered on all sides by ocean, hills, and woods. The closeness of nature reminded me of Connecticut, and that made it feel like home in a way that Laguna Hills never could. There was a thriving arts community, I was at a better school, and, best of all, the rapist didn't follow me. I hadn't realized until we moved to Laguna Beach that I'd been carrying this oppressive weight around, as if that guy in the back of the van was still on top of me. Now that weight began to evaporate.

The boys there walked around in surf shorts, the girls were naturally beautiful, and no one wore makeup or heels, so I had to change again to fit in.

My new school had a strong arts program; our most distinguished alumnus was Richard Chamberlain, and our football team was even called the Artists. I got onto the junior varsity cheerleading team, and we had little painting palettes on our cheerleading sweaters. We had have to come up with cheers to fit the theme: "Paint them into a corner! Pour turpentine on them!" It was all good fun and I felt my self-confidence returning.

∞

SOON AFTER we moved I was approached by a contemporary artist who wanted to photograph me for his exhibition in the Laguna Beach Festival of the Arts. He wanted to take a series of images of me in a bathing suit, posing up against a wall. I was nervous, but my parents looked into it and heard that he was a legitimate artist, and it seemed like a good opportunity to get some professional photos for a portfolio as well as some public exposure to help my acting career get going. Before the festival I got my own set of prints—I was over the moon with the result.

The photos were beautiful, and to this day I count them as some of the best ever taken of me.

I proudly met my family and friends outside the exhibition on the opening day. The photos were to be printed in large format and hung in a series along a wall. I struggled to see the pictures through the crowd of people that had gathered around them. It seemed as though I was a hit. I nudged my way forward and then stood, frozen in stunned silence. My excitement vanished, and black clouds of humiliation rolled in. The series was titled "Beauty Deconstructed," and the artist had splattered the life-size photographs of me with his own blood and feces.

Some of the people in the crowd looked at me and then back at the pictures and then back at me. I turned and ran. My parents followed me back to their car and I cried all the way home.

It was a horribly disappointing experience, but despite the embarrassment those photos led to a strange and interesting series of events.

A few days after the exhibition I was approached by a photographer named Pam Bouchard. She loved the images and sent them on to Eileen Ford in New York, who agreed to see me.

The Ford Agency has represented some of the world's top models, including Cheryl Tiegs, Christy Turlington, Christie Brinkley, and Jerry Hall. Some have even gone on to be successful actresses, like Elle MacPherson, Sharon Stone, and Courteney Cox. I figured that if I were lucky I could start out as a model and bridge into acting. I was already skinny, but I wanted to give it my best shot, so I stepped up my diet regime to political-prisoner-on-hunger- strike level.

Pam was openly gay and despite my parents being fairly straight-laced, she somehow convinced them that she would be a suitable chaperone, and off we went to the Big Apple. The hotel was cheap and nasty, but Pam had lined up a bunch of meetings, and once we started doing the rounds I found myself getting invited out to the coolest parties. And Pam was great. She really believed in me and helped me to believe in myself, and best of all she let me go wherever I wanted. I met Scott Webster, who was one of the first male supermodels and was, unsurprisingly, fucking gorgeous, and I found my way to Studio 54, where I saw things that fifteen-year-old girls are not supposed to see. With an intake of only 1,000 calories per day, I was lightheaded and literally dazzled by the bright lights and activity of New York City.

At one of the agency meetings I met a young model from Kentucky who was my age. We got along great, and she asked me if I'd go out with her, because she needed a partner for a double date that night.

"Sure, who are we going out with?"

"Matt Dillon and Billy Idol."

Billy had just come out with his single "White Wedding," which was all over MTV, and Matt was working his way through the film adaptations of the S. E. Hinton novels *Tex*, *The Outsiders*, and *Rumble Fish*.

Was that how it was every night in New York? You agree to a date and next thing you know you're hanging out with famous actors and rock stars? I was dazzled.

We met them at Billy's apartment, which was a total mess. Everything was on the floor, and it looked like the aftermath of a burglary. The only things in the fridge were water and champagne.

On a glass coffee table were some really tacky earrings, and Billy wanted me to wear them.

"Put those on, darlin'. Put 'em on, put 'em on. They suit you."

No, they fucking don't. Imagine earrings with three fluffy snowballs hanging on a gold chain. I wore them all night and only found out later that they belonged to Billy's insanely jealous live-in girlfriend and that if she'd seen me wearing them my odds of surviving the night would have been slim at best. I think Billy was hoping that she'd run into us and he'd get to watch a catfight.

But thankfully that didn't happen, and instead Matt and Billy decided that they'd show us their favorite New York haunts. We ended up at the Limelight, which was this huge Gothic Revival church that had been a rehab center before it was converted into a nightclub. That night Jimmy Page and Robert Plant surprised the audience by playing an impromptu set. I was a huge Led Zeppelin fan, and there I was in the front row just a few feet from my idols. Matt Dillon and Billy Idol faded into the background; I forgot they were even there until Billy tapped me on the shoulder. Matt was taking my girlfriend from Kentucky off to the bathroom for some recreational activities, and he thought that we should follow suit. And from memory he didn't put it that delicately.

By then my girlfriend had told me the story about the earrings, and to be honest, as much of an Anglophile as I am, I just didn't find Billy very attractive or interesting. Add that to the fact that Led Zeppelin were playing, and without giving it a second thought I brushed off my first celebrity paramour. He should have known he had no chance when stacked up against Jimmy Page working the fret boards of his double-necked Gibson.

The next day I was back at the modeling agency.

"Claudia, darling, you're the perfect height and you've got a nice face but please, we have to weigh you before we can go any further. Do you mind stepping on the scales? Thank you, darling."

I climbed onto the scales. I was 5'9" and 120 pounds. Zero body fat.

"Look, darling, we like you. You've got an interesting look but if you want to be a model you've got to commit to losing another five to ten pounds."

"Ten more pounds?"

It was ridiculous. How much more could I starve myself? I wasn't carrying any weight. We left the meeting, and I told Pam that I didn't know how to become the person they were looking for. I was upset, anxious, worried that I might be passing up my one big shot. And then Pam stepped up to the plate.

"You know what? You're fine as you are, I'm not gonna let you do this. Let's go home."

Thank God she said that; it was just what I needed to hear. I was a thin, pretty teenager and they wanted me to be anorexic. I went out and bought a bagel with cream cheese and felt a huge sense of relief. My friends at school couldn't believe that I'd turned down the chance to be a model, and I'll admit that the lifestyle had certainly been dazzling, but at fifteen I wasn't ready psychologically, and I sure wasn't going to kill myself for it. I refocused on my real goal—becoming an actress—which *was* a dream worth killing myself for.

IN LAGUNA Beach my best friend at school was Kara. She was this beautiful, tall brunette. She was carefree and her own person, and that resonated strongly with me. When I was with her I felt that it just might be possible to move to Hollywood and realize my dream.

My mom had this very cool 1959 Mercedes 190SL, which looked like it belonged in a James Bond movie. We'd drive it down to the beach and buy chocolate chip croissants and lattes. That was our little pleasure. Sometimes Kara and I would go to the gay bars, the Boom Boom Room or the Little Shrimp, and drink—in our cheerleading outfits, no less! We'd watch drag queens sing on top of pianos while we sipped Tanqueray and tonics. The drag queens loved us, all the gay boys loved us, because we were a couple of cute girls who wanted to have fun. I *loved* gay men, and I still do.

Kara and I had a friend who lived in Emerald Bay, which was our way of getting into the parties there. And they were the best parties. Our high school girlfriends were so jealous; if you had a house there, you were golden. They were doubly impressed when my newly acquired boyfriend picked me up from school in his Porsche.

Arthur Ash Wilder, III, Esq. (a.k.a. Tre) was only 5'11", but he had blond hair, beautiful blue-green eyes, and was he built. A six-pack, perfect body weight; you could crack an egg on his butt.

Kara and I had sneaked into this Newport Beach party. We were fifteen years old, but we were all dressed up and could have passed for twenty. I'd recently jumped up in size and filled out a bit, and now grown men wanted to meet me. It was a totally weird experience. I had been a fourth son, a tomboy. Three brothers had treated me like a fellow member of the Lost Boys from the minute I was born, and then one of them died and the others were so messed up by that that they didn't pay me any attention. Add to that the fact that my dad was gone all the time and that when he was home he was too busy fighting with my mom to pay his daughter a compliment. And Tre picked up on that. He was a real sweet talker, and I fell for him hook, line, and sinker. I thought, "This guy is serious." He was a lawyer, he was in tip-top shape, and he said that he wanted to see the world and conquer it at the same time, which was all very intriguing to me. It didn't occur to me that a thirty-year-old lawyer should know better than to sleep with a fifteen-year-old high school student. We'd go out and I'd drink Dom Perignon and Cristal; he'd drink single malt scotch whiskey with his friends. I'd always thought of myself as an older person trapped in a younger person's body, and here I was, hanging out with grown-ups. Cocaine was everywhere; it was the older person's drug. The first time I saw it was in a bathroom, thousands of dollars worth of powder laid out on a mirror. I tried it once and it was okay, but I didn't feel that I needed it. I was happy with champagne; I was having a good time. And besides, I'd learned a little something about drugs since moving to Laguna Beach.

BEFORE I met Tre I'd dated a football player named Ricky. His parents went on vacations all the time, and since nature abhors a vacuum, the empty house was instantly filled with partying teenagers. I went into the kitchen and saw a blender with a vanilla milkshake in it. I thought the brown specks in it were vanilla bean; it tasted great. One of the guys on the football team came into the kitchen.

"Hey! Who drank the shake?"

"I did. Sorry, I didn't know it was yours."

"You drank the whole thing?"

"Yeah, I'm sorry."

"You are so fucked! Ricky! Check this out!"

It turned out the brown specks were mushrooms, the hallucinogenic type. Suddenly I didn't feel so good. The walls were moving like waves, and the floor was falling out from under my feet. I ran to the living room so I could stand on the sofa. I looked around, and all of the lamps and lights in the house had gargoyles coming out of them. It was like that evil carnival in Ray Bradbury's book *Something Wicked This Way Comes*.

This "high" lasted the entire day and night, and my boyfriend babysat me through the whole thing. The one time he left me by myself, to go to the bathroom, I stripped off my clothes and climbed up onto the roof. He didn't leave my side after that. It was the pits, and after that hellish experience I decided to stick to champagne.

∽

SOMETIMES TRE would pick me up at lunchtime, take me home for a quickie, then drop me back at school. He'd tell his secretary he was out playing golf. To say that the Tre situation didn't go down well with my parents is an understatement of monumental proportion, though not in the way you might expect. True to form, they took opposing sides and dug in for protracted trench warfare. My dad was against the relationship. In his eyes, Tre was a deadbeat preying on an underage girl, and he'd be damned if I was going to see him while I lived under his roof. My mother supported my seeing Tre, because he was rich, handsome, and an attorney. She'd grown up without a lot of material comforts after the war, and she was old-world European in the way she thought about things. The age difference was less important than the opportunity to haul in a good-sized catch.

The fracture in my parents' marriage that ran right back to Patrick's death widened into a fissure, and I found myself with a foot on either side, struggling not to fall in. Things came to a head when my mom let me go away with Tre for a weekend in Palm Springs. My dad was pissed off and went for broke. He saw the whole thing in the light of my plan to pursue an acting career. He proclaimed that being an actress was little better than being a whore and that the Tre situation was already one step too many down the path of damnation. He told me to get out of his house if I wanted to play at working in Hollywood, and I didn't argue.

It turned out he was right about Tre, though. Tre was a walking façade. His blond hair was parted a little bit too far to the right because he was balding, and he'd inherited those beautiful blue eyes from his mean, low-class father. If I sound bitter it's because I was. Tre lived his life for his father, and when he died Tre took on his role and became desperate and chubby, an aging party boy. Before he crashed, though, he made sure, like any good kamikaze pilot, to take as many people with him as possible.

But in hindsight we all have 20/20 vision. I thought I knew what I wanted. I turned sixteen, kept on seeing Tre, and set myself seriously to the task of becoming an actress. I had a few months to get out, so I started working three jobs to save money and was lucky enough to have the world's coolest guidance counselor, a woman named Jan Fritzen, who convinced my parents to let me work toward finishing high school a year early.

I've found in life that if you're single-minded and tenacious enough, if you keep on putting one foot in front of the other, eventually the universe meets you halfway. In this case it happened at a coffee shop I was working at on the Pacific Coast Highway.

It was the first real cappuccino place in town, and the South African owner was a complete pervert. Every time he would pinch my butt, I would steal money out of the cash register. Eventually he wised up and installed a camera, but the pinching didn't stop, so I quit—but not before I got my big break.

The actor Barry Newman was a regular at the shop. He'd starred in the legal drama *Petrocelli* in the '70s. He hit on me a little, but when I told him I was sixteen, he backed right off, which I appreciated. We started chatting when he came in, and I shared my dream of becoming an actress. Barry introduced me to his friend Charlie Peck, a veteran Hollywood writer who'd been blacklisted during the McCarthy era. Charlie was a small, older guy who drove this huge Cadillac and had to sit on two telephone books to see over the top of the wheel. He took a liking to me because of my name; he'd been married to the Italian sex symbol Claudia Cardinale. We got on well, and he promised that he'd set up a meeting with Joan Green, an L.A. talent manager who represented Heather Locklear. I was blown away. At the time Locklear was the only actress to have appeared on two TV series simultaneously: *Dynasty* and *T.J. Hooker*. This was an amazing opportunity, and I remember trying to play it cool even though I had butterflies slam dancing in my stomach.

"Next Wednesday? Three o'clock? Sure I can get up to L.A."

Of course, I couldn't get up to L.A. on a bus or in a taxi, so I stole my mother's car. Up until that point I'd been allowed to borrow it to drive down the hill to school and back, and occasionally to the beach. So on the appointed Wednesday I skipped school and drove to Los Angeles. Halfway there I hit something on the freeway and it ripped up the entire underside of the car and totally wrecked it. I had no money to get the car towed. The police ended up taking me to a pay phone so I could call my mom. She took the fall for me, telling my dad that she was behind the wheel. But my luck held out; I was able to set up another meeting with Joan Green.

The next time I played it smarter and convinced my brother Vincent, who already lived in L.A., to take me up there, and I crashed on his couch.

Joan was totally professional but high-strung and slightly neurotic. She weighed me on a scale in her office, decided she liked the way I looked, and asked if I would come back and do a scene for her. "No problem," I replied and then walked out of her office wondering where on earth I was going to find a scene. I didn't know there was an actor's bookstore called Samuel French; I didn't know anything. I'd done plays like *Oliver* and *Annie,* but I sure as hell wasn't going to do a scene from either of those oldies, so I wrote a monologue about an eighteenth-century female musician who wasn't allowed to play the violin because she was expected to get married and just shut up. I brought my violin along and played a few notes and then launched into this monologue about a girl whose father didn't understand her passion for music and who was forcing her to marry against her will, and I cried and beat the violin and did the whole bit. Joan must have seen something in me because she signed me on for a three-year management contract right there. I went back to Laguna Beach and started packing.

With the extra credits I received from working at Cappuccino and two other jobs, which involved selling surf wear and shots of tequila on the beach, my guidance counselor managed to cobble together enough credits for me to graduate from high school at the age of sixteen and a half. I wasn't cut out for school, and I knew it.

I'd arranged to split a little apartment in L.A. with my gay friend Michael, who was moving up there to be a makeup artist for Christian Dior. I'd saved enough to allow me to pay rent and bills for three months. It was time to stand on my own two feet.

By then Tre had already commenced his kamikaze dive and I knew it was time to move on. For a grown man, he didn't take rejection well. "If you try to leave me I'll take from you the person that you love the most." I believed him. I didn't count on him being quite so calculatingly vindictive, but I believed him. We both knew he was talking about my mom. She and I had the same sense of humor, the same practical way of looking at the world. My dad had been absent for a lot of my childhood. My mom was my rock; I relied on her for support and encouragement. Tre's cheap threat didn't stop me from leaving him. I was done with men trying to pin me down. I went to my mother and warned her that Tre would come knocking on her door. She laughed it off. I felt better about the whole thing. I knew Tre was a smooth talker and that he was determined, but I trusted my mom. Problem solved. But that wasn't the end of Tre's run.

Shortly after that, my parents moved into separate places and started divorce proceedings. I was sad about the split and put it down to Patrick's death finally taking its toll. One day I drove out to Santa Monica, to my mom's new house. It was early in the morning; I was planning to surprise her. Parked out in front of her house was Tre's Porsche. There was no mistaking it for anyone else's car; the corny vanity plate read AAWILDERIII.

Was my mom having an affair with Tre? Was Tre the reason for the divorce? She knew I was trying to get him out of my life, and she'd still chosen him. I imagined him wining and dining her, helping her through the split from my dad. I was livid. My mom was the most important thing in the world to me. I'd assumed that the feeling was reciprocal, and yet there was the Porsche, proof that I didn't matter as much as I thought I did.

It was the latest model, a 911 Carrera that he'd bought just before I left him. It was his baby. I walked over to it and without a second thought keyed the shit out of it. I scarred it right across one side, both panels, in long, unbroken lines, like a bad Matisse painting. If art is an expression of emotion then this was the ugliest fucking piece of art you've ever seen—but, by that definition, art it was. Then I took out the notebook from my purse, wrote a note to my mom, and stuck it to her door.

How could you? Don't call me. I don't want to ever speak to you again.

∽

I RAN into Tre about ten years after we'd broken up. He came up to me at the pool of a swanky hotel.

"Claudia. I'm so sorry about what happened. Can you ever forgive me?"

"Are you out of your fucking mind?" I replied. "I will *never* forgive you."

The way I saw it, he stole my mother away from me and engineered my parents' divorce, and he did it deliberately and with malicious intent, just because seventeen-year-old Claudia didn't want to see him anymore. My family fell apart, and I wouldn't talk to my parents for another seven years; they didn't even attend my wedding. It was the event that would close the door on my old life, on my childhood world, and there was no going back.

If I had stayed at home and dumped Tre when my dad told me to, who knows what would have happened? I ran into my friend Kara years later. We were so alike at school; we'd both dreamed of becoming actresses, encouraged each other to go for it, but there she was, wearing a hippie dress, gorgeous as ever, and pushing a baby stroller, a swarm of kids buzzing around her. She'd married a mountain man and moved to a small town in Colorado, so I guess it's true, we are shaped by our choices.

∽

LOOKING BACK on those traumas, they stand out as fairly grim landmarks in that formative part of my life, but there was something positive that grew out of them. Patrick's death, my rape, and my troubled relationships taught me that no matter how tough the world gets, you can't give up on yourself; you just have to keep taking that next step. That lesson manifested itself as a voice in my head, driving me forward, and it was stronger than self-doubt or fear or the pain of betrayal. At the worst times in my life I would cling to it like a piece of driftwood after a shipwreck. But back then, at the start of my new life in L.A., I felt as if I'd left all the difficulties of the past behind me. I was buoyed with enthusiasm. I'd trusted that inner voice, had faith that I could be an actress, and it had paid off. Now, as it carried me up to L.A., I felt unstoppable, unsinkable. But then, they said the same thing about the Titanic.

My school photo, 1970

With my mom in Glendale, California, 1967

With Jimmy and Vincent at Monarch Bay, California, 1967

With my playhouse in Westport, Connecticut, 1968

38

My family minus one. Westport, Connecticut, 1973, after Patrick's death.

Fifteen years old, before prom, in Laguna Beach

LEFT: One of the photos displayed at the Festival of the Arts, 1980
BELOW: Clutching my modeling portfolio on the streets of NYC, 1981

39

TWO

WHEEL OF FORTUNE

BASTARDS AND
BILLIONAIRES

I ARRIVED IN L.A. in 1982 ready to share my talent with the world. Start the drum roll, get that red carpet rolling, polish those award statues until they gleam; Claudia's in town.

But then Joan told me that she couldn't get me paid work with the Screen Actors Guild until I turned eighteen. (I looked too old for the kids' roles that suited my age.) In the short term, that meant no income for almost three months. In the longer term, I'd be out of contention for the coming year's Oscars and Emmys. You think that way when you're seventeen. Still, I was upbeat. This was a small hitch. I could wait it out.

THE NEW apartment was another unwelcome surprise. My bedroom window was right next to the building's cluster of garbage cans. In summer it stank like hell. To add to the ambiance,

Michael was a chain-smoker extraordinaire, using the last ember on one cigarette to start up the next. He'd have a cigarette going in the shower, on the toilet, in bed, and sometimes there was so much smoke in the apartment that I considered camping out by the 405 freeway because there would have been less pollution.

I knew Michael was gay before I moved in with him, but I didn't know he had a bondage fetish. Our couches were wrapped in thick black leather belts, and a creepy studded leather mask was the central feature of the coffee table. It was like the S&M Mona Lisa; its hollow eyes followed you wherever you sat.

My room was like a different dimension. You opened the door from the smoke-filled bondage universe and stepped through the portal into Teen Girl World. I couldn't afford new things, so I'd decorated with various odds and ends brought from home: a frilly pink duvet with '70s rainbow sheets, a boom box, an oversize Led Zeppelin poster with the hermit from the tarot deck on it, and a small shelf with my favorite books. The only things I had that were definitely adult were the clothes that my mom had bought me—classy, expensive items—and the beginnings of an edged-weapon collection that my dad had encouraged.

Michael was a young, handsome guy, so he developed a thriving social life in no time at all, but I didn't know anyone in L.A. I'd sit in my room trying to ignore the smell of garbage and the sound of the guys in the next room slapping the crap out of each other in the throes of passion and wonder what on earth I'd gotten myself into. Then I started getting sick in the mornings. When I took a home pregnancy test, the strip turned blue.

∞

THE PREGNANCY came as a shock. I'd been on the pill. My mom always insisted that every time she'd been knocked up, three boys and one girl, she'd been using birth control. My mom is given to hyperbole, so I'd taken that with a pinch of salt. Now I knew better. I also knew I had to get an abortion. I was far too young to have a child, and at that time I felt as though Charles Manson would have been a better candidate for fatherhood than Tre. I went to a clinic in downtown L.A. and found myself sitting silently with a half-dozen miserable women, waiting for a bed. It was like a production line. They put me under for six minutes, scraped me out, and gave me a glass of orange juice when I woke up. A nurse took the empty glass from my hand and tapped her clipboard impatiently.

"You're all done. We need the bed for the next girl."

I walked out of there feeling miserable and alone, but I was determined to hold it all together. I went back to the apartment, sat down, and worked out my expenses. The abortion had eaten into my already meager savings; I couldn't make next month's rent. What if I lost my room? Where the hell do you go when you can't afford to live in a smoke-filled bondage den? If they'd given me an Academy Award right then and there, I'd have hocked it for fifty bucks.

I needed to stave off homelessness long enough to keep my dream alive, so I went down to a Mexican restaurant on La Cienega Boulevard and told the manager that I was a twenty-one-year-old Canadian (to explain why I didn't have any ID). I don't know if he believed me, but I got a job as a cocktail waitress. I had to wear this black leotard with fishnet stockings, high heels, and a little black bow tie. At the end of the shift I collected my tips—a grand total of twelve dollars. I went back to the apartment, locked myself in my room, and burst into tears. *Stop the fucking world, I want to get off.*

I was down to two choices: endure that shitty job or run back home with my tail between my legs. I convinced myself that something was going to happen. It just had to, because those two options were no options at all.

The next day I got a call. Joan had booked me for a five-line-or-under job on *Dallas*, which was enough to get me my union card. The clouds parted, and within a week I went from failed cocktail waitress to working actress on one of the most popular TV series of all time. It totally blew my mind to see Victoria Principal and Linda Grey walking around in person. It was only a small part, but it meant the world to me. I was an actress—a proper, working, Hollywood actress—and that little taste was all I needed to whet my appetite for success and dispel all doubt.

The episode was called "Some Do . . . Some Don't," and I was performing with Christopher Atkins (of *The Blue Lagoon* fame) in a storyline in which he was having an affair with Linda Grey's character. Larry Hagman was directing, and he showed up on set wearing lederhosen and a Tyrolean hat with a feather. He was a very nice, very funny guy. I learned later that he was drinking up to four bottles of champagne a day while working on *Dallas*. That didn't surprise me. It was a crazy successful show, and everything was laid on for the cast and crew. They put on steak and lobster for lunch. Everyone had his or her own private trailer. It felt very sexy.

Before I knew it I had another job, this time on *Falcon Crest*. Jane Wyman was a hard-ass pro, so all my scenes with her were very short and to the point. She was an old-school actress who commanded respect. Cliff Robertson was also in that series, and he was a complete asshole. I was running lines with Cliff when one of the assistant directors asked me if I could see my mark. I turned away for a second and told the assistant director that yes, thank you, I could see the mark just fine. Next thing I knew Robertson grabbed me by the throat and pushed me up against a wall.

"If you ever turn away from me when we're running lines, I will fucking destroy you!"

I thought he was out of his mind. It was my first experience working with someone who was so volatile, and no one came to help me out or put a leash on Cliff.

Next I worked on *T.J. Hooker* with Heather Locklear and William Shatner. Shatner was hitting on anything with two legs. He invited me into his dressing room at lunch to run lines and started turning on the charm while finishing up a plate of Thai food. I wasn't interested, but that didn't seem to faze him. He moved in for a kiss, and a wave of garlic breath hit me in the face. He couldn't have repelled a vampire any more effectively.

I began to wonder if this was how women were treated in the industry, if Robertson and Shatner were only the tip of a great, misogynistic iceberg.

I thank God to this day that I booked *Dallas* first, because that job bolstered my confidence just enough to allow me to shrug off those negative experiences. If I'd worked on those other shows first, faced with the idea of enduring a whole career of men like that, I might have considered donning the black leotard and heading back to the Mexican joint.

That year I went on to appear in *The Calendar Girl Murders* with Sharon Stone and Tom Skerrit and the action series *Riptide*. Joan got me so much work that by the end of 1983 my tax return showed $200,000 in income. I sent it home to my parents. I like to think of it as my "fuck you W2."

I went on to book my first regular role on a series in *Berrenger's*, playing Melody Hughes. *Berrenger's* was exciting, because we were on a big stage, the Lorimar NBC set, and we had a lot of stars in the show, including Cesar Romero, Jack Scalia, and Yvette Mimieux. And for the first time in my career, I was cast in a role that was much older than my actual age (in this case thirty at eighteen). This would become a recurring event.

When I knew we'd been picked up for thirteen episodes I fled my room in the S&M den and moved into a beautiful, spacious apartment on Hayworth Avenue where the Golden Age gossip columnist Sheilah Graham had once lived with her lover, F. Scott Fitzgerald. The great novelist had been in poor health, in part due to alcoholism. After he suffered a heart attack, his doctor advised him to avoid exertion, so he moved in with Graham to avoid climbing the two flights of stairs at his Laurel Avenue apartment. Fitzgerald died in Graham's apartment soon after.

Jeff Conaway, who I'd later star with in *Babylon 5*, played my lover on *Berrenger's*, and Anita Morris, who was a big-name Broadway star, played my southern mother. She was a very sexy redhead with an incredible body, and in the show we were both having a relationship with Jeff's character. For the first time in my life, if someone asked me what I did for work, I could honestly proclaim, "I'm an actress. I'm on NBC every Wednesday night at nine." I started buying beautiful things to furnish my apartment. No more leather straps and masks! I was living alone, I had a career, I was making money. It was heaven. Now I felt that I'd arrived in Hollywood. I was living the life I'd always dreamed of.

I'd hang out at Spago and Nipper's in Beverly Hills and Helena's in Silver Lake. One night I went out to a club called Tramp at the Beverly Center and found myself at a table drinking with Rod Stewart and nightclub entrepreneur Victor Drai, who would come in and out of my life. I met his wife when I was coming out of the bathroom that night. I recognized her immediately as Kelly LeBrock, one of the most beautiful women in the world. She was on the cover of *Vogue*, had starred in *The Woman in Red* with Gene Wilder, and was about to start shooting *Weird Science*. She pushed me back into the bathroom stall as I was exiting, locked the door, pinned me up against the wall, and kissed me on the mouth. It was the first time I'd been kissed by a woman, and it was one of the sexiest moments of my life. We went back and sat with Victor and Rod and carried on as if nothing had happened. It was our little secret. My heart was pounding as Kelly smiled seductively at me across the table.

Kelly and I are still friends to this day. I made pot brownies for her brother when he was dying of lung cancer and went to his memorial service at her home. Kelly is a strong, beautiful woman and a survivor.

We've both had the misfortune to star in a movie with her ex-husband, Steven Seagal. I played the part of a federal agent in *Half Past Dead* and discovered firsthand why Kelly had filed for divorce.

It turned out that my teenage fears of an industry filled with misogynistic bastards were unfounded. I've worked with only a few assholes over the course of my career, and Steven Seagal was one of them. He was convinced I was a lesbian, because I wouldn't sleep with him. Instead of reading his line, "Let's get in the helicopter and kick some ass!" he'd say to me, "Do you like it up the ass?" His other inspired reinterpretations of the script involved wanting to know if I liked pussy, if I fucked my brother, and if I was into threesomes. The definitive action star, Seagal would sit in his trailer, chowing down on pizza and fried chicken. He refused to jog or do stunts or even be around a running fan for the helicopter scenes. His close-ups had to be tightly framed to crop out his double chin and the "hairline" of his obvious toupée.

IT WAS 1984 and I was nearing my nineteenth birthday when *Berrenger's* came to an end, and I had the idea that I would do some classical theater in between television jobs. I won the role of Lady Percy in *Henry IV* at the adorable little Globe Playhouse in West Hollywood, but the instant I went into rehearsals my agent called to tell me I'd been cast as the ingénue in a Bob Hope movie that also starred Don Ameche, Frank Gorshin, and Yvonne De Carlo. I was conflicted. I wanted to do the movie, but I'd already agreed to do the Shakespeare, and I didn't want to break my word. To my relief, the director of the play, Louis Fantasia, told me, "Take the bloody film. The stage will always be here for you."

The original title for the movie was *A Nice, Quiet, Deadly Weekend in Palm Springs*, even though it was entirely shot in Vancouver. Thank God, they changed the title to *Masterpiece of Murder*. It was Bob Hope's last movie, and I guess he didn't want a ridiculous title at the top of his list of screen credits.

I ended up becoming friends with the location manager, Christine, because we were about the same age, and I was the only actor on the set who was under forty. After the movie was finished we decided to use the money we'd made to go to Europe over the summer. People in L.A. were telling us, "You've got to call Roman when you get to Paris, you've got to call Roman."

We could only afford to stay in a dumpy little hotel in Neuilly, a suburb just outside the most expensive part of Paris, but we did make the call. On our second day we sat for four hours with Roman Polanski at a fancy restaurant on the Champs-Élysées while he ate pricey shellfish and sipped fine champagne. He finished the bottle, announced that he had to go back to editing, and then hurried out the front door. When the restaurant manager presented us with the bill I told him what Polanski had told me, to put the meal on his tab.

"Mr. Polanski does not have an account here," the manager replied.

You've gotta be fucking kidding me!

Roman Polanski stiffed us for the bill and wiped out our entire summer budget in one fell swoop.

When I got back from Paris, I booked the TV series *Black's Magic*, with Hal Linden and Henry Morgan. Still nineteen, I was cast as a character in her late twenties with two stepchildren. Around the same time I started dating John Davis. John's dad, Marvin Davis, had owned 20th Century Fox before he sold the studio to Rupert Murdoch.

One time I was at a lunch at the Davis mansion. It was the day after Barbara Davis's annual Carousel Ball. John sat on my left, Henry Kissinger on my right. Opposite Kissinger was Gerald Ford. Kissinger was a funny guy. We were joking around in German, and he was very gracious, considering my German wasn't really up to scratch. After the meal, Barbara gave the signal for all of the women to adjourn to the other room so that the men could talk about important things that apparently could only be comprehended if you owned a penis. Barbara stood in the doorway and looked my way expectantly. I turned to John and whispered, "Forget it, I'm not leaving." I mean, when was I ever going to be in a room with Kissinger and Gerald Ford again? It was a once-in-a-lifetime moment. I wanted to stay and listen, and I'm glad I did. They discussed the Greek-Turkish crisis—Greece had reported that one of their warships had been fired on by five Turkish destroyers in the Aegean Sea. Greece had responded by placing its armed forces on alert. Although at nineteen I didn't have my finger on the pulse of global politics, I did appreciate that these were people who had real power and that the conversation that was taking place in my boyfriend's dining room could very well have a direct effect on the world events they discussed. It was exhilarating.

Not long after that I suggested to John that we go to Paris for a romantic weekend.

"I don't wanna go to France. I don't like the food."

"You're kidding, right? Tell me you're kidding." I couldn't believe him.

"It all tastes like stew. How many types of cheese do you need, anyway?"

When I'd go to John's parents' house in Palm Springs, I'd sit down to dinner and the servants would lift the lids of giant silver chafing dishes to reveal miniature hamburgers and French fries; that was their idea of fine cuisine. I was beginning to feel a little culturally starved.

One night we went to *Playboy* model and former Hugh Hefner girlfriend Barbi Benton's birthday party at Spago. Sitting across from me was a sweet Egyptian billionaire named Dodi Fayed. He was twenty-nine, ten years older than I, though we were both relatively new to Hollywood. He'd just finished working as a producer on *Chariots of Fire*, which had won four Oscars including best picture, as well as winning awards at Cannes and the British Academy of Film and Television Arts.

Dodi was suave, spoke several languages, and loved travel and fine dining. Before the night was over I gave him my number. He called the next day—from Monte Carlo.

"It's for tax reasons. I can't spend more than thirty days in any country."

"Oh, okay. Well, I enjoyed meeting you at the party. Give me a call next time you're in L.A."

"Actually, I was going to ask if you wanted to join me aboard Nabila. I'm going to sail her to the South of France. I've already booked your plane ticket."

How do you say no to a private cruise on the world's largest luxury yacht? The whole thing sounded so exciting—a life of international jet-setting. This was just the kind of guy I wanted to be with.

Dodi insisted that I bring some girlfriends, so I'd feel safe, and I invited Tracy Smith, who'd starred in *Bachelor Pad* and *Hot Dog*, and arranged to meet a second friend, Lana Clarkson, in the South of France. Lana later starred in Roger Corman's *Barbarian Queen* films and was shot dead by record producer Phil Spector in 2003.

53

Monte Carlo was exciting, an absolute blast. Then we went to Saint-Tropez where Lana and I were to shoot a promo for a movie called *Starlets* with John Hurt and Tony Curtis. Tony was a friend of Dodi's, and he joined us aboard the yacht with *Highlander* star Christopher Lambert. *Nabila* had been built for Dodi's uncle, Saudi arms dealer Adnan Khashoggi, who was at the time one of the world's richest men, at a cost of $100 million. It was named for his daughter. The ship was 281 feet long, as tall as a three-story building, and carried crew and staff of fifty-two, including armed security. It had a helipad, a Jacuzzi, three elevators, a movie theater, two saunas, a pool, a disco, a billiard room, and eleven suites with hand-carved onyx fixtures and gold-plated doorknobs. The suite I shared with Dodi had a solid gold sink. When you spat out your toothpaste, you knew you were doing it in style.

I met the girl the yacht was named for at a birthday party that Dodi threw for me in conjunction with an *Elle* magazine event. They gave away a white Rolls Royce, and I got to wine and dine with movie stars. There were even fireworks. Definitely my best birthday ever.

You can see *Nabila* the yacht any time you want. She starred as Maximilian Largo's mobile headquarters in the James Bond movie *Never Say Never Again*, along with Sean Connery. She was well cast. The sun deck was surrounded by bulletproof glass. She contained secret passageways, push-button doors and windows, two luxury speedboats in case a fast getaway were required, and even a three-room hospital. I suppose arms dealers and Bond villains have a lot in common.

I came to love Dodi, but I never felt the kind of attraction that makes you want to stop traffic and do it in the street. As a lover he was courteous, polite, and even a little shy. That uncertainty and hesitation surprised me when I was nineteen, but in the years to come I'd find that quality in a lot of rich men with powerful fathers. The super-rich, luxurious lifestyle Dodi lived took the edge off, too. In certain ways his was an exceptionally passive lifestyle. Everything was done for him. There were men to drive his cars, fly his plane, cook his meals, and fold his clothes. It might have been enviable for most people, but I found it oddly unappealing.

Aboard *Nabila* I was exposed to the European way of drinking. We'd have long lunches with exquisite wine and food and then go on to restaurants and parties until dawn. The champagne was always flowing, and Dodi paid for everything: the flights, boat trips, clothes, meals. I realized that this was par for the course for Dodi. He would romance beautiful women, shower them with gifts, and fly them around the world. It was dazzling and exciting, but something made me pull back. I insisted that I buy my own clothes and ticket home. No matter how spectacular Dodi's lifestyle was, I wasn't ready to swap my newly won independence for it. I wanted to have my own career, my own money, and my own home. Before she had her own career my mother was always looking to the man who controlled the checkbook, and she never wanted me to be a housewife. She wanted me to be powerful, so that no man could control me, and that's now ingrained in my character. I saw other women around Dodi desperately clinging to his wealth and decided that they were the antithesis of the person I wanted to be.

Around the time that I discovered my need for independence,

things started going wrong with *Starlets*. Tony Curtis was fighting a cocaine habit, and John Hurt was battling alcoholism. It was the first time I'd ever seen anyone struggle with alcohol abuse. He was a far cry from the composed, charismatic actor I'd admired on screen. He looked haggard and run down, like a knight on the wrong side of a dragon fight.

Starlets was supposed to be a French farce taking place during the Cannes Film Festival. They got a bunch of beautiful girls from all over the world and put us up in a gorgeous mansion, and they'd drive us down to the festival to shoot scenes. The problem was that there was no script and they had no permits to shoot at Cannes, so when they ran out of money we had to go in and steal shots.

They told me to put on a beautiful, red-carpet-worthy gown and sent me onto the central stage where Clint Eastwood was receiving an award. I sneaked up behind Clint and pretended that I was there with him while one of the crew hid in the audience and filmed with a camera hidden between someone's legs. That was the final straw for me. I was having fun on the Riviera, and there are few things cooler than hanging out on the yacht of a James Bond supervillain, but I had to get back to L.A. and get some real work. I had a career to build and I couldn't afford to lose momentum.

Dodi didn't quite know what to make of my wish to leave or my insistence on buying my own fare back to America. He was a jealous man, very insecure, but something in him touched me. Dodi had a childlike quality and I was very maternal in those days. I attracted men who wanted to be looked after. We talked intimately after we made love, and we decided that we would stay in touch and stay friends, but for now I needed to be my own person.

It was the last time I'd sail aboard *Nabila*. By the time I saw

Dodi again she had been sold to Donald Trump and renamed the *Trump Princess.*

I'll always be grateful to Dodi. He got me out of L.A. and took me around the world, which was just what I needed at that time. He gave me confidence in my ability to speak foreign languages, saying, "Your French is beautiful," or "Come on, speak Italian, you can do it." He never put me down, and he always told me I was smart and beautiful. He treated me as a princess and, because I refused to take anything from him, he also treated me as an equal. I didn't know it then, but we would remain friends and occasional lovers until his death, more than fourteen years later, beside Princess Diana in the Pont de l'Alma tunnel in Paris.

5

COCAINE BLUES

IN THE '80s the white line that ran down the middle of the Hollywood fast lane was painted on with happy dust. Everyone was doing blow, and I was no exception. I was nineteen and enjoying the attentions of a charming thirty-six-year-old Frenchman named Patrick Wachsberger, whose company produced the recent *Twilight* movies. I was 5'9" and a slender size six, but Patrick (pronounced Pat-REEK) was stick-thin; I could barely fit into his jeans.

In New York, they'd taught me that the skinnier you are, the closer you are to ideal beauty. Although I'd accepted the fact that I was incapable of building a career around being a human skeleton, the voices of Eileen Ford and her cronies still echoed in my head. French men like skinny women—I'd convinced myself of that, along with the notion that I had to lose more weight.

Luckily, I discovered that if you snorted cocaine you didn't need to eat. I was a size two in no time at all. I lived on one meal a day—breakfast. The only downside was swallowing. My throat was raw from a combination of cocaine and ocean saltwater spray, the discerning user's choice for flushing out encrusted sinuses. Add cigarettes to that and a little red wine to come down and *voila*, you have a gullet that struggles to swallow anything solid. I basically lived on yogurt and smoothies.

Some people take cocaine to feel powerful and confident. It had the opposite effect on me. It made me paranoid. I would become terribly self-conscious. All I wanted to do was lock myself in the bathroom and clean it from top to bottom with a toothbrush or sit down and do my taxes. So I never took cocaine for recreation. I used it as a weight-loss drug. Looking back, I suppose that spending $350 a week on a weight-loss medication might seem a little extravagant (not to mention just plain stupid), but hey, those were the days, my friend. Blow was everywhere, and that white line seemed to never end.

BEFORE THINGS got serious with Patrick I dated a handsome one-legged guy who worked in a shoe shop at the Beverly Center mall, and after him the hunky soap star Hank Cheyne. We went to Tortola in the British Virgin Islands and had a really fun, sexy time. Hank was plagued by the curse that comes from playing a bad guy on TV—he'd walk down the street in New York and random strangers would swear and spit at him.

I had a brief engagement to an Italian prince that didn't work out. We had a big engagement party at the Ritz hotel in London with Michael Feinstein playing. The prince was a Six Million Dollar Man, which is not to say that he could last forever in bed, but that he'd carry three stamps in his pocket worth $6 million—talk about portable wealth. The relationship had already been in trouble because his family wanted me to give up my career, move to Italy, and churn out babies. But things came to a head when I found out that the Ferrari Testarossa that he'd given me to drive around Switzerland actually belonged to his aristocratic lover, a woman in her midforties. That and he had a fetish for girls in high heels, corsets, and garter belts—the exact outfit worn by the prostitute on his first sexual encounter. It was fun for the first few times, but he insisted that I put on the same getup every time, which wore thin quickly. At that point in my life, it was just a little too weird.

Then I had a one-night stand with George Clooney. We first met on *Riptide* and then later on *Babytalk*, a TV series that tried to capitalize on the success of the talking-baby movie *Look Who's Talking*. I played the voice of one of the babies, and George played a guy who was sweet on the single mom. They still haven't sent me my Emmy for that performance, but I live in hope. George and I hooked up after our first meeting. After shooting our scenes we went back to my place, I did some blow, we had a good time, and then he rode off into the sunset on his bright yellow Harley, mullet cut whipping in the wind. He wasn't the George Clooney that you see now. Like a good red wine, he seems to have improved with age.

AFTER SIX months of dating, Patrick and I decided to get serious, and I gave up my apartment and moved into his designer home on Sunset Plaza Drive. It was my first grown-up relationship, and there was an aspect of it that made me more than a little uneasy. Patrick had a two-year-old daughter named Justine. He told me that the child's mother, Beatrice, lived in Paris and had a boyfriend and that he had been awarded sole custody. Patrick was always busy with movie-related business, and I could tell from the get-go that he was a hands-off parent. My worry was that he was looking for a replacement mom for Justine and had settled on me. It was an unfounded fear. Patrick had hired a nanny to help with Justine. The problem was that I was going through a period in my life in which I was more than a little baby crazy, and Justine was totally adorable. I unofficially adopted her and set my mind to raising her.

Of course, the cocaine had to stop. Two things helped me with that.

The first was that not many people knew I was taking it. I'd kept my habit to myself and never used it in public, unlike *Mike Hammer* star Stacy Keach. I'd starred on that show right before Keach got busted at Heathrow airport trying to smuggle ten grams of cocaine in his assistant's shaving-cream jar. I'd worked with actors who were so coked up that my lips went numb when I kissed them. I figured I didn't want to get that kind of reputation.

My second and much more effective aid to stopping coke was fear. I'd had a scare one night when I flushed out my sinuses. I blew my nose and a chunk of flesh and cartilage came out. I found a flashlight and hand mirror, looked up my nose, and I swear that I could see a hole. I shoved a blob of Neosporin up there in the hope of plugging it, popped a couple of Tylenol PMs, and tried to sleep. In the morning I opened the fridge and discovered a slice of the lemon tart I'd made for dinner the previous night. My guests had said it was divine and especially zingy. I took a bite, chewed, and moved it around in my mouth for a full half minute before I realized I'd lost my sense of taste. Another test, conducted with the help of some freshly cut flowers, confirmed that my sense of smell had departed as well. Cooking has always been an important part of my life, so losing my primary culinary senses was truly terrifying.

I stopped my coke habit like Superman stops a runaway train: instantaneously. I crushed it like a tin can. I was young and strong, and my ability to give it up so suddenly without any serious damage to my health gave me a false sense of invulnerability. That unfortunate misconception would catch up with me later in life. Some bad habits you can walk away from scot-free but others are like ivy: they wind their way around you tightly, mixing their tendrils with yours until you don't know where they end and you begin.

Luckily, about two weeks later my senses returned to normal working order, but after a warning like that I didn't need to be told twice. For the time being snow season was over.

ON THE home front, I was doing everything I could to provide a normal, happy environment for Justine. I was young, but I think I did a good job as a makeshift mom. We did craft projects together, dug our fingers into cookie dough, and I stuffed her tiny shoes with little surprises for St. Nicholas Day. I tried to fill her life with fun new experiences. I gave Justine her first party dress, her first Christmas, and her first Easter. I tried to make her life as special as my mother had made mine when I was a little girl. And I loved it. I had a perfect, beautiful little girl who even looked like me, so everyone naturally assumed that she was my daughter. I didn't contradict them.

Patrick and I threw dinner parties all the time. It was a glamorous life, but the coke parties made it stressful given that I was raising a small child. We would hire an Italian chef named Tono who cooked amazing dinners. It was a gastronomic tragedy, because no one but me ate the food. But, man, was the bartender busy! And you've never seen nostrils vacuum up blow so fast. Everyone was doing it. O.J. Simpson would bring his wife Nicole and spend the night flirting with every other woman at the party. Patrick and I had a guest bathroom, and I was constantly rushing in after guests, wiping neat little lines of white coke off the back of the black toilet and matching sink for fear that Justine's nanny would see them.

ONE DAY I got a call from my agent. New Line Cinema had just produced the original *A Nightmare on Elm Street,* and they were now planning to make a movie called *The Hidden.*

"They're recasting the role of the alien-possessed stripper. It's the only female role in the movie. It's light on dialogue, but you get to shoot machine guns."

I went along to audition but knew I was in trouble when I read that one of Brenda Lee Van Buren's essential character attributes was that she be "big busted." At 120 pounds and 5'9", I didn't have much going on in the chest department, but, never one to give in, I prepared for the audition by stuffing my bra with socks and tissues. I got an immediate callback, although this time they wanted me to come in wearing a bikini. I began to panic, worrying that my chest's secret identity would be revealed. I rose to the challenge and concocted an ingenious device made of shoulder pads and electrical tape.

I knew that wouldn't be quite enough, so I set about devising measures to draw attention away from my faux boobs. The next day I strutted into the production offices wearing a khaki dress with snaps down the front. When they asked to see my body I ripped the dress open in one dramatic movement, did a quick spin, thanked them, and left. An hour later I had the job.

I love acting. Aside from being Vladimir Putin's girlfriend, where else can you start your workday at a police academy shooting Steyrs and AK-47s and end it learning how to pole dance from Janet Jackson's choreographer? The guns I was good at, but the pole dancing—I had no natural ability in that department. The choreographer did her best, and then threw her hands up in frustration and sent me to some men's clubs to see experts in action. I took my best friend to the Aladdin, a strip joint on Sunset Boulevard, and came to appreciate just how athletic some of those girls are. I met the dancers after their shift. One of them was a former Olympic skier. Some were clearly drugged up and working to support their habits, but most of them were hardened pros earning serious money and seemed as sharp-minded as any executive I'd encountered in the entertainment industry.

Now it's bad enough when you have to put on a convincing strip show in front of cameras for the first time, but when I learned that I'd have to do it in a g-string made out of dollar bills my anxiety scaled previously unconquered heights; it's every actress's worst nightmare to see her butt fifty feet tall in a movie theater.

I decided that I needed to lose more weight for the role and visited a place called the Lindora clinic where they put me on a 500-calorie-a-day diet and shot me full of a combination of vitamins and a substance that I would later discover to be pregnant-horse urine.

My first day on set I was scheduled to perform the strip scene. The director, Jack Sholder, was not a happy man when he discovered that I'd duped them in regard to my physical attributes. Luckily, I'd already come clean to the wardrobe mistress, who'd set about designing a set of prosthetic breasts that I could wear under a cut-off T-shirt. It was a double win for me, because it meant that I also got to dodge the topless scene that Jack had planned on filming.

Working with Kyle MacLachlan was very exciting. By then he'd starred in the David Lynch movies *Blue Velvet* and *Dune*. Both he and Michael Nouri were total gentlemen, a real pleasure to work with, and the rest of the film went without a hitch. Well, mostly.

I was on the roof of a building shooting my final scene, and I mean that literally. I shoot Kyle with a machine gun, Michael Nouri shoots me in the head, and I shoot him back, knocking him over the side of a building. Kyle comes to rescue him, shooting me nine times in the process, rescues his friend, loads a fresh clip in his gun, and shoots me another seven times, and then I escape by jumping through a twenty-foot-high neon sign and fall three stories to my death. Simple, right?

In the movie business they attach little explosives called squibs to your clothes to make it look like you're being riddled with bullets. One of the squibs exploded close to my face, and a piece of the metallic jacket I was wearing shot into my eye. It burned like a son of a bitch but I kept on until we got the take. But after that, I lost the ability to shoot a gun without blinking. Back then I had the Bruce Willis open-eye stare down perfectly, and now I have this blinking reflex, and I look like a total amateur. I recently found myself at a firing range shooting antique firearms for charity with Joe Pesci and Lou Ferrigno, the original Incredible Hulk. I was determined to show these guys that I knew what I was doing, but the instant my blunderbuss went off, my eyes slammed shut, a reflexive protection against fashion shrapnel.

I attended the premiere of *The Hidden* and was pleased that my fake boobs looked convincing. Whether the horse piss worked I don't know, but when my butt had its premiere on the big screen, I breathed a sigh of relief; the nightmare had been averted—my alien-possessed ass looked pretty damn good.

BUT AS one nightmare ended, another began. I was a real movie actress now and, as I would learn the hard way, things change when you appear nearly naked on the big screen. Someone, somewhere out there, is looking at you and thinking that they'd like to get close to you—real close to you.

There was this guy who had seen *The Hidden* and decided that I was from Venus and had brought the AIDS virus to planet Earth. No kidding, this is what he actually thought. This guy would park outside my place and masturbate, and sometimes tail me in his car. I called the LAPD but their hands were tied, because this was before Rebecca Schaeffer was killed—the event that brought about the anti-stalker laws of the '90s. I went back and forth with the police until one cop took pity on me and said, "Look, we can't do anything about him masturbating, but I do think he could be dangerous. Do you own a gun? You're going to need one. So you wait until he's out front, put on something nice, and invite him in. Make sure he's inside the house and then shoot him. When we come over, you say that he broke in. But you make sure he's deep inside the house. Otherwise you're the one we're going to have to arrest." Really? No thanks. The guy creeped me out but I didn't want to shoot him.

I drove to a lunch meeting a few weeks after that and realized the stalker was following me in his car. He was really freaking me out, and as I tried to get away from him I accidentally ran a red light and got hit by a van. My engine blew up, my car was totaled, but all I could think about was my number one fan, who'd climbed out of his car and was now heading toward me.

I was convinced he was going to try to kill me. A crowd started to gather, so my stalker vanished, but in the meantime someone saw me trying to start my engine to try and get away. When the police arrived, I was arrested for trying to leave the scene of an accident. I explained about the stalker and why I was trying to leave, but they didn't believe my story. I ended up having to perform six months of community service at the old Globe Playhouse. I was back, not to perform Shakespeare, but to make cookies for the audience. I lasted three weeks in baking hell (all the while wishing I'd invested in a handgun and a lace teddy like that cop had advised) before I offered to pay to have the theater's roof repaired in exchange for their filling out my community service book.

The stalker vanished after that. He was the first but he wouldn't be my last. There would be a dozen other stalkers that would plague me to varying degrees over the years, including one guy who quit his job, sold his house, and tried to move into mine, thinking we were married.

The movie-star world isn't all champagne and caviar.

TIME PASSED, and I thought that things were going well with Patrick until I learned from a friend that he was cheating on me. Before I had a chance to confront him I had to travel to shoot my next movie. *Never on Tuesday* was the story of a pretty young lesbian who finds herself stuck in the middle of the desert with two horny young men played by Peter Berg (*Chicago Hope*) and Andrew Lauer (*Caroline in the City*). It's better than it sounds. We shot the movie in Borrego Springs in the California desert. The director was a young guy named Adam Rifkin, who was making his directorial debut. He always dressed in black Converse tennis shoes and a baseball hat. Little did I know that Adam was both talented and driven and that *Never on Tuesday* would be the first of many projects I would do with him over the course of my career. It was clear in the audition that they wanted a big-name actress for the female lead, but I tried my best to turn on the charm, and Adam fought hard to get me the part. I'd put a little weight back on since giving up cocaine, so when the studio offered me the role it was on the condition that I lose ten pounds and work out with a former Olympic gymnast, who had me running up and down the bleacher steps at UCLA on a diet of one bran muffin a day.

Charlie Sheen was flown in for a cameo role. He'd just come off *Wall Street* and *No Man's Land*, so his star was rapidly ascending. They didn't have a large budget, so my guess is the studio paid him with drugs and hookers so he'd feel like a total frickin' rock star from Mars.

Whatever they were paying him with, it worked, because A-list guys started coming out of the woodwork. Nic Cage wore a huge fake nose, playing a crazy man in a red Ferrari. Gilbert Gottfried played a lunatic salesman. Emilio Estevez and Cary Elwes (*The Princess Bride, Saw*) played hick brothers in a tow truck, gold teeth and all. There was a real party atmosphere, and we'd all hang out and play pool and drink tequila. It wasn't long before other members of the Brat Pack appeared.

I'd met Rob Lowe before, and, coincidentally, my makeup artist on that movie was Sheryl Berkoff, who would go on to marry Rob. (At the time, though, I think she was seeing Emilio Estevez.) This was just before Rob got into trouble with the first ever celebrity sex-tape scandal.

One night after partying, Rob and I went to a hotel on Sunset Boulevard that is now called the Standard, got drunk, did an eight ball, and ended up in bed together. We were so coked up that the sex was numb and not anyone's definition of fantastic, but the conversation was great. We bitched about our families and personal problems late into the night. I thought of Patrick and concluded that if you're going to have revenge sex, you might as well have it with the world's most beautiful man.

∽

I RETURNED to Patrick feeling much better. I learned from my friend that he'd given up his mistress, so I decided to put the whole business behind me, for Justine's sake.

It was bumpy at first, but after a while things settled down, and the three of us started to feel like a real family. Patrick and I traveled to Aspen for Thanksgiving and stayed at the Little Nell hotel. One night while we were making love I saw a huge starburst explosion in my head, a great flash of light.

"I think we just made a baby," I said.

Patrick turned away from me without saying anything, and that was the end of the discussion. An abyss had suddenly opened up between us. I wanted to keep the baby, I wanted to keep us together as a family, but when your partner isn't even slightly enthusiastic and you're twenty years old, it's hard to know what to say. If I pushed the issue and he demanded an abortion, then I'd be faced with a worse dilemma, so I kept quiet. On the way back to L.A. we carried on pretending nothing had happened, but you can't fool Mother Nature. She keeps the wheels of biology turning, and eventually things have to come to a head.

∽

THE MORNING I had to go for an audition for the sci-fi film *Arena*, Justine decided to throw the greatest tantrum spectacular of all time. Justine's nanny was off that day, and Patrick went to work as usual, so I had to take her along with me. She refused to sit in the waiting room, so I went into the audition with her clinging to my leg like a monkey. During the reading I had to get angry and cry and Justine turned her face up to me and said, "Don't cry Mommy, don't be sad." It was adorable but there was no chance I was going to get the part. I bought some pregnancy books on the way home and started taking prenatal vitamins. Then my agent called. The producers thought the scene with Justine was touching and had offered me the part. It meant spending the next two months in Italy.

I went home and sat down with Patrick. It was time to get serious about the pregnancy. I told him about Italy, told him that I wasn't going to leave America until we worked this out. My doctors were here, and I didn't want to fly with a baby on the way. He was very nonchalant about the whole thing.

"Don't worry about it. I have to go to Europe for a film festival anyway, so we'll both go to Rome. I know a guy there. We'll find you a doctor and get an abortion."

So there it was. With one careless comment, he had shattered my illusions about our happy family life. He expected me to fly to Rome and squeeze in an abortion before the film shoot just as if you might say, "Oh, you're going to the store? Can you take the trash out on your way?" I'd already endured one abortion with Tre's baby, and I wasn't interested in repeating the experience, but here I was with a man who clearly did not want a baby or the responsibility that went with one. Given the difference in our ages, I thought that I had to be tough, to put on a brave face, to show Patrick that he couldn't hurt me, but inside I was cut deeply. We were living together, and I'd proven I was a wonderful mother. He never considered my feelings. There was no discussion about it, no holding me when I was crying. It was a massive rejection.

Before heading to Rome we met up with some of Patrick's friends in France. Megève is one of the most beautiful ski resorts in the world, the place where Audrey Hepburn meets Cary Grant in *Charade*. I hated being there. I felt totally alienated. All of Patrick's friends knew his ex-wife Beatrice, and they didn't take to me at all. They spoke French too fast for me to keep up, and the ones who spoke English didn't bother to make the effort. I left the dinner party and walked out into the winter night. The air was crisp. A full moon overhead made the surrounding mountains stand out against the sky. The atmosphere was mystical. I was wearing a long fur coat, and I found a private place, out of sight of the house, and lay down in the snow. I looked up at the moon and asked it if I should have the baby. Since I was pumped up on pregnancy hormones and walking alone in the French Alps, it seemed like a perfectly sensible thing to do. I'm sure that Patrick was inside wondering why I was taking so long in the bathroom. I didn't care; I'd gone outside with another Patrick on my mind—my brother. I still felt his presence, I thought of him all the time, and I knew with absolute certainty that the baby I was carrying was a boy. Not long after I became pregnant it occurred to me that this baby should be called Patrick, after my brother, and that this might help change the other Patrick's mind. He was an egotist, so a son named after him might stir his interest, but it hadn't. Another thought had arisen, one that I hadn't been able to get out of my mind, that the child I was carrying had my brother's soul. Pat was trying to come back into the world. As I lay there I had a very clear sense of the child's life. I saw it like a series of snapshots. I could see his face—he had my brother's soulful, big blue eyes.

In the morning we'd catch a plane to Italy. This was my last chance to change my mind, to keep the baby and tell Patrick to go to hell. I asked for a sign, something clear and incontrovertible that would leave no doubt as to the course of action I had to take. It was a completely clear night and out of nowhere a huge bank of clouds appeared and covered the moon for a full minute. I began to weep. I'd been trying to act as if Patrick's indifference didn't matter, as if things would somehow work out in the end. Lying there in the darkness I knew that there would be no fairy-tale ending. I wasn't ready to raise a child on my own. My chest felt tight, my heart felt like water-laden cloth, clinging and heavy. I'd made my decision. I would be losing a whole person's existence, I'd be denying my brother the chance to come back into the world, and I cried and cried because I didn't know if there would ever be another chance after that, if his soul would ever want to come back to me again.

When I ran out of tears and my whole body was numb from the cold, I got up, wiped away the smeared mascara, and went back inside. I put on a smile for Patrick and his friends. He was laughing and drinking. He hadn't missed me at all.

In the morning we traveled on to Rome. We were shooting *Arena* at the Dino De Laurentiis Cinematografica studio near Rome, and I was staying in the city in a beautiful apartment near the Piazza di Spagna. The movie was about an intergalactic fighting competition between the champions of different planets, and they'd created incredible alien suits that the special effects guys would sit inside and operate. It starred soap actor Paul Satterfield and Armin Shimerman, who would go on to be a regular in the various *Star Trek* TV revivals.

I couldn't confide in anybody because I didn't want to appear unprofessional and no one was supposed to know I was pregnant. I was very self-conscious, because all my clothes were tight fighting—think gold lamé jumpsuits—and I was starting to show. It didn't help that I was sharing wardrobe space with Shari Shattuck, who had a gorgeous figure. Shari and I starred

together in the 1990 film *Mad About You* and the TV series
Riptide. She would also appear in *Babylon 5*, although she's best
known for her long run on *The Young and the Restless* and her
successful career as a mystery writer.

Patrick found me a doctor who looked older than the
Coliseum. This was Italy in the '80s, a conservative, Roman
Catholic country where abortion was illegal. You had to have
connections to find a doctor who would perform the procedure.
That day I learned firsthand how important it is to have both
a surgeon and an anesthetist. The guy put me under for what
was supposed to be eight minutes, and I regained consciousness
after eight hours. He'd over-anesthetized me. It was all a big
secret, so the next day I had to don my gold lamé jumpsuit and
go back to work, having nearly died and minus one child.

That experience changed me. I started building an emotional
wall to protect myself. Watching my parents as I grew up, I knew
what I wanted, and it wasn't what they had. I wanted to have a
nice house and perfect little children, one boy and one girl, and
a relationship with a smart, handsome guy who respected my
need for independence. That was my dream. After the abortion,
I knew I couldn't take that for granted, that in opening yourself
up to a partner you were just as likely to be run through with
a knife as embraced. Patrick made me wary of love, and after
being forced to give up my baby I never wanted to go through
something like that again.

Unsurprisingly, after we returned to L.A. things started to
unravel with Patrick. The abortion wasn't the death knell of our
relationship though, because I wanted to be there for Justine.
That little girl needed me. Out of nowhere Patrick told me he
was sending her back to Paris to live with her mother. I was hurt
and outraged. I'd lost one baby to this relationship already and
now I felt as if I was losing another. Of course I had no legal

rights, and no real way to protest what he was doing. By that time I had raised Justine for almost two years, and he didn't even give me the chance to talk things over. It was done, decision made.

He told Justine to say goodbye to me before he took her to the airport. She cried and clung to me and wouldn't let go.

"I don't want to go away. What did I do, Mommy? Why are you making me go?"

She kept on asking that again and again until Patrick pulled her away. I've been through a lot of shit in my life, a lot of physical and emotional pain, but that moment was truly heartbreaking. I've never experienced anything else like it.

Once Justine was gone I couldn't eat or sleep because I was so worried for her. I wasn't given her phone number in Paris, so I sent her letters and presents, little reminders of our life together. I never received a reply.

I'm not sure why he did it. Perhaps he was jealous of the bond I was forming with her, perhaps he thought that Justine was coming between us. If he really thought that, he was stupid, because after he sent her away I left him.

⌒

I WAS due to move out while Patrick was away at another festival in Europe. In the meantime I'd been cast in the Adam Rifkin film *Tale of Two Sisters* with Valerie Breiman. It was a very low-budget, experimental, fly-by-the-seat-of-your-pants kind of production. Adam needed a location to shoot the movie and asked if he could use Patrick's place.

"Absolutely. Mi casa es su casa."

The crew rolled in. Lawrence Bender of *Pulp Fiction* fame was the producer, and I was co-starring with Jeff Conaway again. We had a comedic sex scene in the back of a taxi.

It turned out that when Adam said "experimental" he really meant it. I can't remember there being a script at all, and Charlie Sheen was credited as the writer. He narrated parts of the story in a voiceover and contributed some of his own original poetry to the project. Even then he was developing his unique talent for self-expression. Here's an example of some of his freeform poetry from the movie:

> *They used to call me Wheezy*
> *Now they call me Moe*
> *Busted liver, three-pronged freebase device*
> *My chin, she is on fire!*
> *The erosion was fast, the lectures were not*
> *He pondered high atop the mountain of fig newtons . . .*

This literary gem is another example:

> *Black and blue skid mark lunchbox drools pasta prima*
> *Frozen bacon pie suffering from the heat cries out in salted pork.*
> *FREEZE FRAME!*
> *Mom and Dad are trying to think, we hope . . .*

Since there was no script, Valerie and I improvised our scenes. I would rant about my asshole husband who'd cheated on me, and Adam would cut to a picture of Patrick and me that was still up on the mantelpiece.

It was amusing enough at the time, but the icing on the cake came a year later when I ran into Patrick at Cannes. He'd just seen a screening of the movie and was totally perplexed.

"How did my house get into a movie? Why was there a picture of us? When did it all happen?"

I just shrugged, smiled, and walked on. In hindsight, it was the act of a twenty-one-year-old striking back at the older man who'd hurt her, but I don't mind telling you that at the time it was beyond satisfying.

I RAN into Patrick again in 2007 at Bill Panzer's wake. Bill was the producer and creator of the *Highlander* franchise, and I'd starred in one of the episodes of the TV series. The first thing Patrick said to me after twenty years of estrangement: "Why did you take the mirror?"

I'd had a gorgeous outdoor mirror that my mother bought me for my very first apartment. It wasn't expensive, but it was tall and beautiful with carved corners, and it looked perfect next to Patrick's swimming pool. Twenty years and that was the first thing he could think to say? Perhaps losing that piece of pretty glass was a reminder that he'd also lost the girl that went with it.

Some good came out of that meeting, though. Patrick told me that Justine was in town, now in her early twenties, and pursuing a career as an actress. That made me smile. Patrick passed my card on to Justine and she agreed to meet me for lunch.

She'd grown up and turned into a beautiful young woman, but the resemblance between us was gone. As we sat down together I was struck by the realization that Justine was older now than I was when I'd played my part in raising her. As we chatted and swapped pleasantries I realized that she didn't remember a thing, not a single thing.

"Don't you remember when you had the meltdown at Bloomingdale's and I bought you the party dresses?"

"Ah, no. Sorry."

"Don't you remember the Christmas when we made snow angels?"

"No."

"But what about the letters I sent, and the gifts?"

She asked me what I was talking about, which confirmed what I'd already suspected. Her mother hadn't passed on a thing I'd sent her. She'd actively worked to erase my memory from Justine's mind. Jealousy is a green-eyed monster, and I guess she'd gotten her claws into Beatrice. It was like being trapped in a sci-fi show where someone you love has all their memories wiped out. Memory gains so much of its power in being shared. Justine and I had a bond based on shared experience, but for her those moments were gone. It was devastating.

"So you don't really remember me at all?"

"Oh, no. I remember the feeling of you, and that you were a good person in my life and that I was happy when we were all together."

Later I did some reading on child psychology and consoled myself with the thought that, although the memories we shared in her early years were gone, the influence I had on her would have been formative and profound. I gave her love and attention and all the good things I had in me, and today, somewhere in her heart, that love burns on as part of the complex mixture that is grown-up Justine.

BLOOD, DEATH, AND TAXES

T WAS 1988, I was twenty-three years old, and I'd just landed a role starring in *Clean and Sober* with Michael Keaton, a movie about a real estate agent with a cocaine addiction. It was my first respectable big-studio movie. The director was Glenn Gordon Caron, the creator of *Moonlighting*, and I also got to work with Morgan Freeman and Tate Donovan, who later starred in *The O.C.* We shot the movie in a real rehab clinic in downtown Pennsylvania. It was gritty and smoke-filled, just what you'd expect a rehab clinic to look like.

Michael Keaton's performance was particularly good. He took a gutsy departure from his usual comedy roles and proved that he had the chops to cut it as a dramatic actor. The academy totally snubbed him for an Oscar that year.

I played the role of Iris, one of the patients in the rehab center. Iris is in for cocaine addiction as well, and she has an affair with Tate Donovan's character. Morgan Freeman, who plays the center's director, accuses Iris of being stoned and kicks her out of rehab.

When my brother Jimmy was in rehab, they made him watch *Clean and Sober* over and over. In one scene I have to wear a dorky leotard, and when Jimmy's friends found out that I was his sister they used to give him no end of grief.

Years later I ran into Morgan Freeman at a Cirque du Soleil show in Santa Monica. We talked about *Clean and Sober*, and he said to me, "You know, I always thought you'd make it because you've got those eyes that tell the story."

I thought that that was the kindest thing for him to say. It was nice that he'd remembered me and doubly nice that he'd been kind enough to compliment me at the height of his career.

Over the course of my own career I've played an addict of every kind of substance except for the one that finally beat me—alcohol. Later in life I would find myself in rehab, having graduated from playing the part of an addict to actually being one.

∽

BY THE time *Clean and Sober* was released I was twenty-three years old and playing the love interest in *The Heat*, a *CBS Summer Playhouse* movie with Billy Campbell, who would go on to star in *The Rocketeer*. Gary Devore, the writer, was a confident, charismatic man in his late forties who'd walk around the set in jeans and cowboy boots.

Gary was the best man at Tommy Lee Jones's wedding and was godfather to Peter Strauss's son. He was buddies with Kurt Russell and had written movies starring Arnold Schwarzenegger, Christopher Walken, and Billy Crystal.

We started up a full-blown Hollywood set romance. The sex

was exciting, so much so that I couldn't even really tell you what the show was about.

After filming *The Heat* we said our goodbyes and I went back to Montgomery Clift's old house, which I was renting in the Hollywood Hills. Monty had been a pain-pill addict and, like F. Scott Fitzgerald, an alcoholic. I didn't seek out the old haunts of alcoholic actors; that's just Hollywood. Close your eyes, throw a dart at a map of available rentals, and odds are you'll find yourself living in the house of a former movie star with a substance abuse problem.

Speaking of which, by that time Lana Clarkson was living with me. The house didn't have a second bedroom, but it did have a spare bathroom that the owners had at some point turned into makeshift accommodation for their kid. You haven't seen anything until you've seen an Amazonian blonde sleeping on a single bed balanced precariously on top of a tiny closet.

Gary called me up one night, and I mentioned that I was going to Canada to visit my friend Christine.

"Great! I'll come with you and we can get hitched."

"Are you serious?"

"Sure."

Six weeks later we were married. We hadn't even been on a date.

IT WAS an insane idea but it was charged with spontaneity, and something about that appealed to me. After the difficulties of my painful, drawn-out relationship with Patrick I figured that this would have just as much chance of working out as something that I overthought and overplanned.

At the time, Christine was a location manager, so she threw together a spectacular wedding for me. The only decision I had to make was whether I wanted a yacht or a helicopter. I took the yacht.

My friend Lana and I traveled to Vancouver together. She seemed more excited about the wedding than I was. Gary and I met up and did tequila shots in the limo on the way. Everybody was so fucked up on coke and booze that it was more like a frat party than a wedding. Aboard the yacht Lana swept into my bachelorette party, tears streaming down her face, wailing about how no one would ever want to marry her. I tried to get her to join in the fun but she preferred to make a dramatic exit. She couldn't handle so much attention being directed toward me on my special day and set about putting the spotlight back where she thought it belonged. Ten minutes later Christine confronted me, outraged that I'd made Lana the maid of honor after all the work she'd done. It turned out that Lana had gone up to the yacht's captain and signed herself up for the job on the marriage certificate without telling anyone, including me.

It wasn't what you'd call a traditional wedding. I still wasn't talking to my parents, so in place of my mother there was a skinny Japanese guy in drag wearing a fluffy hat. I don't know who he was or where he materialized from, but we were smashed and the wedding seemed to be coming together in its own weird way, so I went along for the ride. Gary had never met his best man, Donnelly Rhodes, who would play my father in an episode of *Murder, She Wrote*. Sci-fi fans will recognize Donnelly as Doc Cottle on the most recent *Battlestar Galactica* series. The piano player had missed the boat so someone's brother took on that job, and we sailed out to this "sacred" island for the ceremony where everyone's shoes got muddy. I was wearing a white dress

BLOOD, DEATH, AND TAXES

I'd bought in a secondhand store in L.A. and a
coat that kept getting ripped on branches and
spilled drinks. It probably wasn't the most auspici͏c
to a marriage, but it was lots of fun.

Instead of a reception we had a party at Donn͏ .͏ ͏ouse.
A cute friend of Christine's that I'd always had a crush on was
there. Caring for Justine had brought a level of restraint to my
drug and alcohol consumption, but now that she was gone the
party was back on. So when we ran out of blow, I went for a drive
with Christine's friend to find some more, still wearing my wedding dress. We ended up buying some from a pack of young
guys, did some lines with them and then drove back to the house
party. When we got back no one had noticed our absence, so we
snuck into the bathroom with the blow and started making out.

At the beginning of a marriage you're filled with hope and
optimism, and you can't see the cards fate will deal you. It turned
out that my cards were bad, but Gary got a worse hand. Within
ten years he would die in mysterious circumstances, sparking a
series of conspiracy theories and investigations that continues
to this day.

∞

I REMEMBER Gary saying to me, "Isn't it funny that we're married? You're not my type at all. I like leggy blondes with big tits."

Prior to me, Gary had had a long list of lovers including
Season Hubley (Kurt Russell's ex-wife), the producer and noto-
rious cocaine addict Julia Phillips, and Priscilla Barnes, who'd
played nurse Terri Alden in *Three's Company*.

Gary's writer's block started the same day a seven-figure IRS
bill arrived in the mail, courtesy of another ex-lover, Maria
Cole, Nat King Cole's widow. When Gary was married to her

he'd made the incredibly stupid decision to cosign some tax papers, which put him on the hook for millions of dollars of tax debt.

The only way for him to clear the debt was by writing more big-budget scripts, but the creativity needed to accomplish that was smothered by the depression that settled over him. He'd stare for hours at a blank monitor, type a few lines, and then delete them in frustration. I'd try to do nice things for him to cheer him up, but when he was in those moods he was an inconsolable asshole. After I got my head bitten off I stopped trying and would just leave him to stew until he came out of it on his own.

I pushed Gary to take antidepressants, but he gave up after a few weeks, claiming that he didn't want to be addicted to anything. I switched tactics and suggested that we try ecstasy. He got some from Julia Phillips, I think, and it was really high-grade stuff. We made love and talked and cried. It was wonderful. On Monday morning he was back to being an asshole. Unfortunately, you can't take ecstasy every day of your life.

DESPITE OUR money trouble and the stress that came with it, we did have our happy times, especially during our first year together. When the writing was going well and it looked like he might sell a script Gary would revert to the exciting, outgoing guy I'd married.

It was during one of these periods of relative marital calm that other turbulent relationships in my life would come to the fore.

One friend would betray my trust, while another bond that I thought was lost forever would be redeemed.

MY RELATIONSHIP with Lana had always been a problematic one. After her performance at my wedding, which had all but ended my relationship with my friend Christine, Lana set her sights on Gary. I don't know whether it was because she was still bitter about the wedding or whether she just wanted what I had, but when we'd attend the same parties she'd sidle on up to Gary and start flirting. Despite the fact that Lana was the leggy, blond, big-titted type, Gary was a faithful partner and when she didn't take the repeated hints that he wasn't interested, he told me.

For me, it was the last straw. I'd taken her to the South of France, let her live in my house rent-free, and loaned her thousands of dollars that she had never repaid. We'd starred in the same kinds of TV shows, we'd started out in our careers together, but Lana's optimism, her dreams that she would make it as a big-time actress, hadn't materialized to the point that she was self-sufficient. She was always relying on friends to prop her up. I told her to get lost. We stopped speaking.

The next time I saw Lana was at her funeral.

I'd heard that Lana was struggling. She'd broken both her wrists while entertaining at a children's party, had been fighting an addiction to booze and painkillers, and was struggling to keep her apartment in Venice Beach. Worst of all, she'd turned forty. As far as Hollywood is concerned, the day a woman turns forty, she is magically transformed into Methuselah and is suddenly unemployable.

On February 3, 2003, after working a shift as a hostess at the House of Blues, Lana went home with Phil Spector, the intense, weasely-looking guy who'd produced records for a host of famous artists and bands: from early R&B groups like the Ronettes, the Crystals, and the Righteous Brothers to the Beatles, John Lennon, Tina Turner, the Ramones, and Leonard Cohen. In addition to being a total fucking nutcase Spector had a history of drink and drug problems as well as a penchant for guns. He'd previously threatened five women at gunpoint—Lana was the sixth.

He shot Lana with an unregistered blue-steel .38-caliber Colt revolver. When the police carried Lana's body out of Pyrenees Castle (Spector's mansion in Alhambra, California), they took with them Spector's nine other guns, fragments of Lana's teeth and fingernails, her leopard-print purse, and her false eyelashes.

At the time of arrest Spector was on seven different prescription drugs.

It was a horrible way to go. Even worse, the fame that she had sought in life found her in death, though not in a form that she would have hoped for.

Her name, her clips, and her photos were screened on news and entertainment programs around the world. They referred to her as a B movie actress, and instead of vilifying Spector, they cheapened her. Leaked photos of her dead body appeared on the Internet. HBO began developing a film about Spector's prosecution that is being filmed at this writing, scripted and directed by David Mamet and starring Al Pacino as Spector and Helen Mirren as the prosecutor.

It's like *Faust*, a deal with the devil where you get what you've always wanted, your greatest desire, but it comes at a terrible price and in a cruel and twisted form. I wonder how much Spector will get for the movie. I don't suppose it matters—he won't have time to enjoy it. Phil Spector was sentenced on May 29, 2009 to nineteen years to life and was incarcerated in the California Substance Abuse Treatment Facility and State Prison in Corcoran.

NOW FOR the redemption story.

Not long after I had my falling out with Lana, I was following the Gulf War on TV with Gary when I had a sort of psychic
flash. I had an overwhelming urge to go to Hamlet Gardens, the
upmarket spinoff of the Hamburger Hamlet restaurant chain.

Gary tagged along with me, somewhat bemused. We stood in
the lobby for ten minutes.

"You still haven't told me what this is all about. Why are we
standing around like a couple of chumps? I should be home
working on my script."

"Just stand here with me. Wait with me."

I could feel that something was going to happen. Spiritual
currents run through my family; we're an intuitive bunch, especially the women on my mother's side.

After Patrick's death, my mom and I would sometimes see
him hovering above our beds. She'd see him as a little boy, I'd
see him at the age he was when he died.

And when I was seventeen and moving up to L.A. for the first
time, I had a bad accident, and the family gift reared its head
again. I was in the fast lane on the 101 when some Mexican
guys in a van pulled up beside me and started catcalling in a
mix of Spanish and English. My family had spent a little time at
my grandfather's house in Cuernavaca, Mexico after Patrick's
death, and my brothers and I would go and hang out with the
local kids. We learned how to sell iguanas on the roadside to
make pocket money, along with the most important words in
any language—the rude ones. I was driving this crappy Chevy
Citation that my dad had given me. It was about as maneuver-
able as a Sherman tank and ugly to boot. I was getting nervous,

not because they were being rude and offensive, but because I was a new driver and really needed to concentrate, so I flipped them off, hoping they would back off and leave me alone. And they did, but not before ramming me with the side of their van and pushing me into the center divider. I hit it at just the right angle to launch my car into the air. The Chevy flipped over and hit five other cars on its flight to the slow lane. By the time it came to a halt it was completely crumpled and I was trapped. My right leg had come out of its socket and my head was swimming. I looked up and saw a bridge over the freeway where people had gathered, hands over their mouths, horrified expressions on their faces. Luckily an ambulance had been traveling right behind me, and its crew saw the whole thing. They used the Jaws of Life to open up the Citation like the cheap tin can it was. A paramedic knelt down beside me as they cut away my seatbelt.

"What's your name?"

"I don't know."

I couldn't remember anything.

There's never a shortage of drama in my life. Sometimes it feels like I'm trapped in a soap opera. (Living in Hollywood can do that to you.) Well, here's the icing on the cake—I had amnesia. I had to go to memory therapy at UCLA after the accident.

They pulled me out of the car, and the ambulance took me to the Queen of Angels Hospital. As I was being rolled into the ER on a gurney I saw a pay phone and remembered that my mom was working at Saks Fifth Avenue in Costa Mesa, but I couldn't remember her name. I begged the nurse walking alongside the gurney to help me call her. I got through and I was yelling at her and crying.

"I've been in an accident. I'm in the hospital."

That was the only coherent information I managed to get out before the nurse pulled the phone out of my hand, informed me that the doctors were waiting, and hung it up.

I passed out and when I came around it was to the sound of chanting. I opened my eyes. My hospital bed was surrounded by chanting Koreans.

"Nam-myoho-renge-kyo. Nam-myoho-renge-kyo."

Then I saw a face I recognized: my aunt. Memories came flooding back. She was a Buddhist and had brought her friends along. I remembered that she chanted for money. She'd chanted for a new Volvo and got it. She'd chanted for a real-estate portfolio and it had been granted unto her. I remembered that she was eccentric and funny. Like all the women in our family she had a bent toward the spiritual, albeit tempered by a practical streak.

And then I saw my mom.

"How did you know I was here?"

"I just got in my car and it took me here."

It might sound strange, but despite the disagreements and feuds that have taken place between us over the years, despite the estrangement and family divides, my mom and I have always shared an invisible, unbreakable bond.

∞

I STOOD in the Hamlet Gardens lobby and wouldn't budge, just waiting for something to happen, and Gary was done standing around. He was heading back to the car when all of a sudden my mom came walking out of the dining room, arm in arm with Tre. It was an amazing thing. Somehow I'd been led to her, but if it was a minor miracle it was tarnished by the unavoidable truth that she was still hanging out with my asshole ex-boyfriend.

My mom and dad had split up years before, and I'd just assumed that Tre and my mom had run their course. Now I found myself in an extremely uncomfortable position. We swapped some forced pleasantries, I introduced my new husband, and then we went our separate ways. When I got home, though, I fell to pieces. I was an emotional wreck, and Gary had to hold me the whole night. In the back of my mind, I kept justifying her decision by thinking, "Well, he's giving her the attention my father never did, or else she needs a friend and I left home and I'm not around for her."

I don't know what force had led me to her, but I knew I'd been given a choice. I could either reach out and extend an olive branch to her or leave things as they were, a festering wound. I knew all about crossroads; I'd stood at one in the aftermath of my rape. You either let something ruin you or you take action.

I called up my mom, and we started talking again. She explained to me that I'd misinterpreted the incident with Tre's car—the event that had created a seven-year wall of silence between us. It had been out in front of her house because she'd borrowed it from him—her car was at the mechanic's—and after that they'd stayed in contact as friends. We talked things over. I put the past behind me. It was such a wonderful feeling to have her back in my life. We had missed each other immensely and had miles of ground to cover.

I called up my dad as well and started rebuilding bridges. I was married, I had a career, and now I was setting right the sins of the past. I was an adult, and finally my parents were actually listening to me. Now all I had to do was turn things around with Gary.

GARY, THOUGH, was heavily invested in misery. None of his writing opportunities had panned out, and the IRS bill was a monkey on his back, driving him into ever-longer bouts of depression.

I got a job working on Jon Turteltaub's first movie, *Think Big*, starring the "Barbarian Brothers" Peter and David Paul. They were these ridiculously over-steroided body builders who played two mentally impaired truckers transporting toxic waste across the country. The movie earned me enough money to take Gary to Hawaii in the hope that he could shake his writer's block. We were staying in a condo, and after a few days I ran out of things to read. The condo had a small shelf of bestsellers, all of them by John Grisham and Danielle Steel. I've never been a big reader of blockbuster novels, but I've always been a bookworm. I was desperate, so I picked a book at random, Steel's *Kaleidoscope*, read it from cover to cover, and thought that it would make a great movie.

Not long after we returned to L.A. I learned that the film *Kaleidoscope* was scheduled for production, and I was cast as Jaclyn Smith's little sister. Jaclyn arrived on set, right off the plane. She was exhausted, wore no makeup, and was still without a doubt one of the most beautiful women I've ever seen in real life.

My character was a gynecologist who couldn't get pregnant. And as with *Clean and Sober*, the role I'd play in *Kaleidoscope* would be a bitter foretelling of a personal tragedy.

∞

AFTER HAWAII I got pregnant, and that seemed to turn around my relationship with Gary. We were both really happy about the news. I felt that I was at a time in my life when I was ready for a family. I started buying pregnancy books. Gary and I started picking out names. We still loved each other, and I hoped, however naively, that the baby would help us forge a working relationship. These were the days before Dr. Phil or even Jerry Springer. We were not yet blessed with the universal talk-show wisdom that keeping a marriage together for the kids seldom works out.

I needn't have worried. I booked a job with a location shoot in Hoboken, New Jersey, working on *Maniac Cop 2*. It was the dead of winter. I was three months pregnant and not really showing. I didn't want to take the job, but we needed the money. We agreed that after the shoot I'd take the rest of the year off to have the baby.

Problems arose with my co-star Robert Davi, the James Bond baddie with the pockmarked face. He was always puffing cigars on set, and one day when I had really bad morning sickness I asked him not to smoke around me because I didn't want to throw up on his clothes. He told me to fuck off, flat out, just like that.

About two-thirds of the way through the shoot I was doing a stunt scene that involved being handcuffed to the steering wheel of a car. I was outside the car, and it was supposed to appear that I was running alongside it, unable to escape. The techs had built a little platform for me to stand on that I had to share with a camera so they could get some close-ups. It was too dangerous to have the car running on its own steam so they hooked it up to a truck that would pull it along.

On the third take the platform broke and I fell and hit the road at forty miles an hour, still handcuffed to the steering wheel. I hit hard and was dragged for what felt like a hundred feet before they realized what had happened and stopped the truck. The next morning, while I was shooting a scene with Robert Davi a huge gush of blood came running down my legs.

I asked them to stop shooting, apologized, and then ran to the bathroom. When one of the producers knocked on the bathroom door to see if I was okay I told him to get me to an emergency room. I was suffering a miscarriage.

I was resting up in the hospital when the producers called and asked me to come back to do some reshoots. They implied that I'd lied about being pregnant and threatened legal action if I didn't come back and finish the film within their scheduled time frame. So I went back to work, and they started shooting that same scene with Robert Davi. He made a point of lighting up his cigar in front of me.

"Now maybe you won't be such a hormonally imbalanced bitch."

What an ass. I couldn't wait to get done with that film.

The loss of the baby was painful for me, and it turned out to be the end of my marriage. I remember the exact moment the relationship had run its course and I decided to file for divorce.

I'd made Gary a really nice lunch, put it on a platter, put on some sexy new lingerie I'd bought just for the occasion, and went into his office. It was an attempt to recapture the excitement of our early days. Gary turned from his computer, his face flushed with anger.

"Get out! Don't you ever fucking come in here when I'm working."

He quickly turned off the monitor, but not before I noticed that the screen was filled with non-English characters. In the moment I'd seen them, the writing looked like Cyrillic. This was weird, because as far as I knew Gary didn't speak Russian, even though he had a Russian-Jewish background. I was offended and hurt. I dropped the tray and stormed out and that was that. I called a friend, got the name of a divorce attorney, and then closed the door to my heart once again.

With the benefit of hindsight I think my marriage to Gary was a big "fuck you" to my parents. I'd married a man who was exactly like my father. He wasn't very demonstrative, and he had a short fuse. It's the older-guy thing—if your relationship with your father doesn't work out, then you marry a guy just like him and try to make him love you.

⌘

WHILE I was filing for divorce with Gary I fell madly in love with graphic designer and restaurateur Rod Dyer.

I met Rod while dining at his restaurant Pane e Vino. We flirted from across the room, and after a while he came over to talk to me. I was wearing a 1930s-style suit, and Rod told me that he loved my tie, which was exactly the right thing to say. I put my hand on his knee, and he asked me to come back the following day and have lunch with him. When I did he presented me with a beautiful wooden box filled with antique ties and a deco-style card that he'd drawn himself. I was floored and immediately smitten. Short of a cheap ring with emerald shards that he bought for me when we got hitched, Gary had never given me anything. Gary loved women but he wasn't the romantic type.

I used to drive an '83 Harley-Davidson Sportster. When I wanted to see Rod, I'd tell Gary that I was going to the gym and then ride my bike across town from Mandeville Canyon to Beverly Hills. I'd see the sunrise above Sunset Boulevard as I raced along it, and then Rod and I would spend the morning making love. Rod was in the midst of a divorce as well and was living in the guesthouse of a famous producer friend. An hour or two later I'd get back on my Harley and race home. I guess Gary assumed the sweat was from my workout, and I suppose that, in a way, it was.

I divorced Gary, took my piano and my clothes, and moved into an apartment building on Doheny Drive. On my first day there I opened the paper and saw that my new movie, *Hexed*, had just been released in theaters.

We'd shot *Hexed* in Texas during a baking-hot summer. My co-star was Arye Gross, who has recently been a regular on *Castle* with Nathan Fillion. Arye played a hotel clerk who pretends he's someone else to go on a date with my character, a crazy super-model named Hexina. My character kills people and arranges the evidence to frame the hotel clerk. The director, Alan Spencer, fought hard for me to get the role and allowed me to try just about anything, which made it an incredibly fun shoot.

It was also the first time I'd been back to Texas since my brother died. We'd left him behind when we returned to Connecticut, buried in a Houston cemetery. I had a few margaritas and drove out to visit him. I got lost looking for the grave—my recollection was that it was under a tree next to a fence bordering a paddock with horses. But things had changed. Now a freeway ran along-side his remains, a thin wire fence separating him from the traf-fic that rushed by. I found the plaque hidden beneath weeds and after clearing the site wiped the dirt off it. I lay down on top of his grave and cried. My marriage was over, but my career was gathering steam. I think I was hoping I'd feel his presence or receive some kind of sign, but there was nothing—Patrick had moved on. If he was watching over me from the other side, then it wasn't from that place. I stood up and brushed the dust off of my clothes.

AS FOR Gary, he ended up marrying a girl named Wendy, whom I like a lot. She was a nurse at a plastic surgeon's office, and she had a lot of work done to her. She says to everyone that it made her look like Cher. I think she looks better.

Gary overcame his writer's block with the help of medication and managed to pay off all his tax debts. He took on a lot of script-doctor work, fixing problems with other writers' scripts, which pays well but doesn't earn you screen credits.

As for Gary's death, there are too many theories to cover them all here. It was reported in the media, private investigators were hired, conspiracy theories started up, and to this day it remains one of the most mysterious deaths in Hollywood history. I've been asked to do interviews about it at least a dozen times, and it still crops up in the news and in online reports from time to time. No one knows exactly what happened, but here's what I do know.

In June 1997 Gary spent a week working with actress Marsha Mason on a remake of the 1949 movie *The Big Steal*, which is about a man who fakes his own death. The movie was going to be his directorial debut. He was driving his Ford Explorer back to his home in Santa Monica when he vanished. His publicist believed he was acting out the life of *The Big Steal*'s main character. Wendy offered a $100,000 reward, and when the story hit the media all sorts of strange folk came out of the woodwork. There was a psychic on Leeza Gibbons's show who claimed Gary was working in an Alabama Kmart. There were stories of a CIA assassination. Apparently Gary had uncovered secrets about the US Army's conducting tests on live subjects in Panama using prohibited weapons. There were stories of black unregistered helicopters patrolling the California aqueduct near where he vanished. Wendy was even approached by men in black suits with mirrored sunglasses who advised her to drop her investigation into Gary's disappearance.

A year later his body was found in his Ford Explorer, submerged in the California aqueduct close to the town of Barstow.

That closed the official police investigation, but the autopsy and subsequent private investigation opened doors to more unanswered questions.

I'm normally one for accepting the simplest explanation for things, Occam's Razor and all that, but there were some odd facts that made it difficult for me to accept that Gary fell asleep at the wheel and drove his SUV off the road into a body of water.

First, it was unlikely that this was an accident at all, given that there was a lot of ground between the road and the aqueduct. Also, Gary was an experienced long-distance driver. He'd grown up in a trucking family, and when we were married he'd go for long drives just to clear his head and resolve script problems. And I mean long drives, thousands of miles. He'd be stuck on a script and then just up and say, "I'm off to Tennessee. I'll see you when I've got this story nailed."

Also, it was strange that Gary was found in the aqueduct at all, considering that I'd already looked. After his disappearance I'd enlisted the help of a friend who was an ex-marine. He assembled a team of divers and they went down into the aqueduct with infrared equipment and swept the area around Barstow from top to bottom. There was no sign of a car or a body. A year later, in the same area, after the police received a tip from an anonymous caller, the car and body miraculously appeared.

And then there was the Cyrillic I'd seen on his computer monitor. Wendy also reported seeing strange symbols on his computer screen, and when she asked him what they were, Gary had answered "encryption codes." I don't know what the ramifications of that are, but it's certainly added fuel to the stories about the CIA, and since those Russian sleeper agents were found in New Jersey in 2010, I'm sure it won't be long before someone is talking about Gary's death being connected to some foreign spy network. Who knows?

Last, Gary had a deformed pinky. It had been broken in a football accident, and he hadn't had it reset properly. Wendy put a photo of it in the reward notice she posted, as it was the simplest, surefire way of immediately identifying his body. When they pulled what was supposed to be Gary's body out of the aqueduct, the gun that he always carried with him was missing, along with both of his hands. After Wendy and his family pressed the police about the missing hands, another search of the car was conducted and some finger bones were found in the back seat. Wendy pushed to have them analyzed and the police coroner reported that no deformed pinky was found and that the bones were likely around 200 years old.

WHATEVER THE truth, whatever happened that night on the highway, Gary's death shook me and brought my own life into sharp focus.

After the funeral, I went to Gary's beach house and met Wendy in person for the first time. We got to know each other and ended up talking through the night. I had a headache, and Wendy told me to get some aspirin in her bathroom cabinet. It was filled with more pills than there are flakes in a snow globe. I asked Wendy about them and she explained:

"Well, I finally got Gary on antidepressants, and that really helped his mood. He was prone to depression."

I admired her persistence. I wish he'd taken pills with me, because it might have saved our marriage.

When I left the next morning, Wendy gave me a box of Gary's unproduced scripts. There was some great material in there, his best work. Schwarzenegger scripts sell, Kurt Russell action scripts sell, but sometimes they sell at the expense of scripts like

Come As You Are, a story about a female photojournalist. That script did the rounds in Hollywood for years, and came close to being made, first with Kathleen Turner and then Michelle Pfeiffer. But in the end it never got over the line.

Maybe if Gary had lived and made it as a director he would've had the influence to push it through. It was a great script, Academy Award material, and it's a tragedy that it's just sitting in a box in my attic gathering dust.

Up until Gary's death, I'd always believed that I would eventually find my Prince Charming to settle down with and raise a few talented, gorgeous children. But after his funeral, when I looked back on the life I'd led since leaving home, on the decisions I'd made, my path seemed clear. If there had been any ambiguity about the meaning of the sign the moon had given me that night in Megève, there wasn't now. I got it. Family life wasn't for me.

I had always known that I couldn't be the kind of dependent woman Dodi had wanted me to be. Losing Justine was unbearably difficult, and she wasn't even my biological child. After the accident when I'd lost Gary's baby, after Gary's death, all I could think about was what if I went and had a child of my own? What if I raised it and loved it and then that bitch fate swept in and things turned to shit again? I couldn't bear to think about that.

I'd been shaped by my early life. I was made to stand on my own two feet and I was at my weakest whenever I relied on another person for reassurance and validation. I was convinced that I had the answer. I was my own woman. I would enjoy men, but I didn't need them. This realization was like donning a suit of armor, a power that I'd accumulated through my own efforts, and I would set about making it stronger.

That inner voice continued to drive me forward. It told me that I could reach a larger audience and touch people's lives. I would be immune to criticism, self-doubt, and fear. I was going to be a film actress, the next Katharine Hepburn.

When I got a call from my agent telling me that I'd landed a role on a sci-fi show that Warner Brothers was producing, I said to her, "You know I'm working on my movie career. Are you sure I should be committing to a TV series and a five-year contract?"

My agent laughed.

"Honey, there's never been a sci-fi series that wasn't a *Star Trek* spin-off that ran more than a couple of years. Trust me, you'll be lucky to last for one."

It turned out that my agent couldn't have been more wrong. And it was lucky for me that she was.

The photo I used for my *Variety* ad announcing my role in *Berrenger's*

With Don Ameche and Bob Hope on the set of *A Master Piece of Murder* in Vancouver, Canada, 1984

At the Carousel Ball with John Davis, 1984

Lunch on the *Sakara* with Dodi, 1984

Pregnant with Patrick in Megeve

As the alien-possessed stripper Brenda Lee Van Buren in *The Hidden*, 1987

With Shari Shattuck on the set of the 1990 bomb *Mad About You*

With Gary when we first met on the set of *The Heat*, 1988

My wedding, 1988, Lana Clarkson on the right, Donnelly Rhodes in the background

With Jaclyn Smith and Patricia Kalember on the set of *Kaleidoscope*, 1990

With my big love, Rod Dyer, 1992

Hexed, Texas, 1993. I played a crazy model whose billboard gets defaced at the end of the movie.

THE RIGHT HAND OF VENGEANCE

T'S JANUARY 19, 1994, and a massive aftershock from the Northridge earthquake hits. Everyone on the set starts screaming and running out of the studio, and I'm left on my own, strapped into the cockpit of a Star Fury combat fighter, helpless to escape. I'm locked into a Michelin Man spacesuit, and the helmet I'm wearing is all fogged up, so I have to keep pressing this button in my hand to operate the fan. The plastic visor clears up for a few seconds. I wait. It's hot inside the suit, and the sound of the fan is getting on my nerves. Soon the aftershocks will subside, and then I'm going to give them a piece of my mind. They're going to see firsthand just how much Claudia and Lt. Commander Susan Ivanova have in common.

BABYLON 5 was something new to television—a science fiction novel in episodes. It wasn't a space Western like *Star Trek*. There were no cute kids or robots. Joe Straczynski set out to write a novel for television, an adult-oriented series. The result was a richly textured story fueled by politics, diplomacy, philosophy, religion, history, and science.

A five-mile-long diplomatic space station in a distant galaxy, *Babylon 5* had become "the last, best hope for peace" between intergalactic species. The characters schemed, clashed, struggled with their demons, betrayed one another and themselves, and sometimes fell in love. Conflicts weren't neatly resolved at the end of every episode. They were allowed to fester and build to a crescendo.

In the midst of it all, running the station and its crew as a well-oiled machine, was Lieutenant Commander Susan Ivanova.

A good cast and crew have a lot in common with a well-run space station. When you work on an established show like *Dallas* or *Columbo* everything runs smoothly, but *Babylon 5* was a new show being shot in an old warehouse in Sun Valley. It was Warner Brothers' first stab at sci-fi TV, and I couldn't help but wonder if they'd hidden the show away far from their Hollywood studio lot, just in case it turned out to be a massive embarrassment.

Babylonian Productions was a rabbit warren of corridors and offices. There were auditions taking place at the front of the building and actors walking around in alien prosthetics and Earth Force uniforms. Guys from the prop department would walk past carrying body armor and plasma rifles. John Copeland, the producer, would work as budget enforcer, railroad fob watch in hand, ensuring that the directors didn't run into overtime. In the office closest to the sets, keyboard eternally clacking away, was Joe Straczynski, the show's creator, executive producer, and lead writer.

I went in on my first day not knowing what to expect. I knew that I was replacing Tamlyn Tomita (*The Karate Kid Part II, The Joy Luck Club*). They'd decided she was too short and didn't have enough of a commanding presence to act beside the two male leads. The rest of the cast and crew, with the exception of Richard Biggs (Dr. Stephen Franklin), had already shot the pilot, so I was the new kid on the block. Michael O'Hare, the male lead, was all too happy to remind me of this. He wasn't what you would call a generous actor. When we'd enter the set together, he would intentionally broaden his shoulders to try to dominate the shot. The problem was that the *Babylon 5* doors would pull away from the bottom and up into the side of a plywood set, meaning that I'd catch the last part of it with my shoulder and make the whole wall shake. After several takes, I'd eventually have to follow a few inches behind him to avoid a clash, which I guess was his plan all along.

I think the role of male lead went to his head just a little. He propositioned some of the female cast members and was officious with the crew. In between takes he would unashamedly shuffle his junk, moving it around with his hand through the fabric of his uniform. When he caught me looking at him in disbelief he explained, "I have an average-sized penis but enormous testicles."

Great, thanks for sharing.

I ran into some familiar faces on set: Jeff Conaway (Security Officer Zack Allen), with whom I'd starred in *Berrenger's* and *Tale of Two Sisters*, and John Flinn, the director of photography, with whom I'd worked on *Jake and the Fatman*. I had a crush on John back then, but knew he was married, so I didn't make a move.

I hit it off right away with Jerry Doyle, who played Security Chief Michael Garibaldi. Jerry could do great Bugs Bunny and Elmer Fudd impersonations, which was especially funny since his character was also a Looney Tunes fan. We were always razzing each other, especially over the sci-fi technobabble, which doesn't easily roll off the tongue. Our dialogue was peppered with phrases like "Bolozian freighters, Minbari war cruisers, and tachyon emissions." The long speeches with tech-talk could be challenging but they also provided great fodder for the blooper reels.

There was a positive energy amongst the cast and crew. Everyone was really enjoying themselves, and any awkwardness with my male lead was forgotten by the time we wrapped my first episode, "Midnight on the Firing Line."

I was beginning to sense that not only was this going to be a fun job, but Susan Ivanova had the potential to be a rewarding, complex character.

Born in St. Petersburg, Russia in 2230, Ivanova had a passionate, fiercely loyal temperament, combined with a sardonic wit and cynicism that is as much a part of Russian life as vodka and borscht.

If nothing else I was glad to have a chance to wear less makeup, pull back my hair, and kick some ass. Finally, my height and authoritative demeanor were working for me. I've always been a tomboy at heart and this was the first time I hadn't been told to soften my style for a part:

> *Who am I? I am Susan Ivanova, Commander. Daughter of Andre and Sophie Ivanov. I am the right hand of vengeance and the boot that is going to kick your sorry ass all the way back to Earth, sweetheart. I am death incarnate, and the last living thing that you are ever going to see. God sent me.**

---

* *Babylon 5*, Season 4, Episode 19, "Between the Darkness and the Light."

WHEN THE second season started up we discovered that the studio had replaced Michael O'Hare. There'd been too many conflicts between our male lead and the cast and crew. Bruce Boxleitner was our new commander, and I couldn't have been happier. Bruce and I got on like the best of friends. He's a great guy, very genuine and caring, not unlike John Sheridan, the character he played. And I'd started settling into the character of Ivanova. In the first season she was extremely uptight, she had a pole up her butt, but by the second season there was more Claudia in her. She developed a sense of humor and started developing relationships. The steel was still there, but now it was wrapped in velvet.

And we do have a lot in common, Ivanova and I.

She had lost a brother and a mother (although I'd been fortunate enough to get my own mother back). I used to wear one earring in memory of my brother Patrick, and when I discussed this with Joe he was happy to allow Ivanova do the same. Like me, she'd built a wall to deal with the loss she'd endured, her family tragedies, and the conflict she faced between love and career. Those were strong themes in my own life, and that energy, those past personal experiences, seemed to shine through in Ivanova and I think the audience responded very strongly to that.

There are even similarities between our sex lives. One time, when I passed on some character notes to Joe, I inadvertently turned Ivanova bisexual.

Andrea Thompson played the ship's resident telepath, Talia Winters, my lesbian lover on the show. Andrea is one of the most amazing women I've ever met. Aside from starring in *Babylon 5* she's been a CNN reporter, the star of multiple TV series, a high-end real estate investor, and a jewel trader. And if that weren't enough she's beautiful, a gourmet chef, and a single mother with two kids. I should be insanely envious, but she's also absolutely lovely, and we have the same sense of humor.

Joe had written an episode in which a sleazy ex-boyfriend of Ivanova's visits the station, and that just didn't sit well with me. Having worked in television for over a decade, I suspected that if there was one ex-boyfriend then others would follow, and I couldn't see Ivanova banging her way across the galaxy while forging her military career. She was driven, and I didn't think that she had time for relationships. I objected, and in a throw-away line, told Joe that if it came down to it I'd rather be with an alien or a woman.

Andrea and I both thought it was funny when Joe started up the whole lesbian thing, but I didn't mind. Ivanova's sexual confusion—her love for Talia despite her hatred for the Psi Corps, the evil agency that Talia was bound to—added another layer of complexity to the character and also reflected my own sexual attitudes. I don't really differentiate between a man or a woman when it comes to love. Physically I tend to prefer men— that's what makes me heterosexual—but I've certainly had my flings with women. I've never thought of myself as gay or even bisexual; I prefer omnisexual. Love is part of life, and, man or woman, we're all stuck playing the same game.

∞

SO WHILE my character was having an affair with the station's resident telepath I was having one with the show's director of photography, John Flinn.

Things were starting to fade with Rod by then. We were head-ing in different directions, and I had almost no spare time out-side of filming the show. I still had a major crush on John, but he was very careful not to start anything until after his divorce. It was hard to wait. But we did. And once he was available we were free to do as we pleased. Sex with John gave me something to look forward to at the end of the day. When shooting was over and everybody went home we had fun in my trailer. I'd keep a six-pack handy, and sometimes we'd have a couple of beers. Then I'd have to get home and start learning lines for the next day.

Dating a man I'd had a crush on for so long was exciting in itself. Dating the director of photography when you're the female lead comes with certain perks. After all, the director of photography is the one who makes you look good, and a man in love is certain to take care of his lady. John was a complete professional to all of the actors on the set, but looking back at old episodes I do notice that I'm particularly well lit.

∞

DESPITE THE occasional near-death experience, like the afore-mentioned earthquake incident, *Babylon 5* was a career highlight.

Every day it was fun to go to work, because everybody was always in a good mood. I think it had a lot to do with John and his crew. The director of photography and the director set the tone of the set and we had very nice, very competent directors the majority of the time. Except for this one Italian guy who didn't have a clue what *Babylon 5* was about. He kept telling me, "You have to be more sexxxy. Be more sexxxy."

"Have you ever watched the show? Ivanova doesn't do sexxxy."

Years later, at conventions, I'd hear from actors on other sci-fi shows about personality differences between cast members. That didn't happen on *Babylon 5*. We didn't want anyone to spoil our fun. Joe Straczynski would listen to the cast and crew and keep his finger on the pulse of the production. If you were a prima donna, your character got reassigned or killed off, the preferred method being getting sucked out of an airlock. At the end of the day we had a group of people who meshed together extremely well, and I think that shows in the final result.

∽

EVERY ACTRESS hopes to be famous one day. If nothing else, you land better roles, and you don't have to worry about where your next paycheck is coming from. When *Babylon 5* came along I already had a certain level of recognition because of my eleven years in TV and movies, but being on *Babylon 5* took my career to a completely different level. For the first time, I had loyal fans who knew me by name. It wasn't stardom of the same wattage as Julia Roberts's or Tom Cruise's, but it was (and still is) a constant pleasure to be recognized and acknowledged for my work. Even when I went overseas to the UK, France, or Germany, people on the street would call out, "Ivanova!"

We all knew we were onto something good, but no one had any idea that *Babylon 5* would become such a phenomenon. It would last five seasons and spawn six films, countless novels, short stories, comic books, and a spin-off series. It won two Emmy Awards, Hugo Awards, and dozens of others. Today, eighteen years after we started, *Babylon 5* is still going strong, racking up more than $500 million in DVD sales and gaining fresh momentum on digital platforms. During my years on the show, from 1994 to 1997, *SFX* magazine voted me "the sexiest woman in sci-fi," and I was named one of "The 25 Women Who Shook Sci-Fi," as covered by the *Los Angeles Times*.

∽

WHEN THE show went on hiatus for a few months at the end of season two the producers flew me to London to do some television ads for *Babylon 5 Uncut*. So I called my old friend Dodi Fayed to let him know I was coming to town.

We'd kept in touch over the years. At one point I heard his mother had died suddenly of a heart attack, and I remembered how he used to call her every day. I found an antique silver cigar case with his initials on it and had it delivered with a note of condolence; even while he was in mourning he wrote back expressing his gratitude. He said that very few people had reached out to him after her passing, and that it meant a lot to him. He would later say to me, "If it meant giving up everything I have—cars, wealth, and women—I would do it to bring my mother back."

Dodi was glad to hear from me and invited me to stay with him in his Kensington apartment. Things were going well with John, but he was my on-set lover, a part of the show, and after two years of hard work I needed to get away from it all and let off some steam. As I flew into London I thought back to the pleasant times I'd had with Dodi when we last traveled around Europe and breathed a sigh of relief. This was just the thing I needed, a well-deserved break.

I had no idea he was going to ask me to have his baby.

8

DEATH BY IRONY

*D*ODI AND I laughed and loved our way across London. He'd just finished working as executive producer on *The Scarlet Letter* with Gary Oldman and Demi Moore. I told him about my adventures on *Babylon 5* and learned that he'd already enjoyed some episodes with European friends who were fans of the show. We always seemed to meet when things were going especially well for us.

Despite starring in a sci-fi series and having worked on two sci-fi movies I was woefully ignorant of the genre. Dodi set out to educate me and ran screening nights with movies like *Blade Runner* and *Alien*.

We had such a good time that he invited me to stay for a few months until *Babylon 5* started filming again.

WHEN DODI and I first started dating years before, he gave me a big gold ring with an amethyst set in it. The inner band was engraved with his name.

"They gave this to me after I completed my service in the Egyptian paratroopers."

It was a heartfelt gift, one that I'd cherished for more than a decade, but now it was time to return it. I was going through a period of returning keepsakes to old lovers. I'd sent one guy back his high school football ring and another his grandfather's wedding ring. It seemed like the right thing to do.

So one night while we were drinking champagne after making love I fished the ring out of my purse and pressed it into his palm.

"You should hang on to this. One day, when you settle down, you can give it to someone you really love."

He looked at the ring with a slightly confused expression. Then he looked back at me, then back to the ring, and then he burst out laughing. In that same instant I got the joke.

"You made these rings up, didn't you? There's a whole host of women out there with these things!"

He looked embarrassed for a moment and then it was my turn to laugh.

"And I schlepped it all the way back here so that you could give it to someone else!"

I HAVE to admit, in that environment even the air seemed better, more luxurious. When I remember Dodi, I always think of wonderful smells: the deep, musky tendrils of smoke from his Cuban cigars; the crisp, clean fragrance of his cologne; the sensual undertones from the exquisite leather seats in his private jets and cars. I loved the ambiance.

But there were downsides. An entourage of staff and armed security formed a protective perimeter around us 24/7. It always used to amaze me that Dodi could live like that. He told me that he'd been kidnapped as a child and that as a result he had grown up used to having a serious security presence. Having a battery of armed guards clear the way for him was second nature.

The idea of hiring men to lay their lives on the line for my safety made me a little uneasy. Even when I have security at sci-fi conventions I always go out of my way to make friends with them. Some of Dodi's guards were treated okay, but others would be swapped out and replaced like his girlfriends. For Dodi, they were so completely integrated into his life that they were invisible.

A billionaire lives in a rarefied world. Everywhere he goes the red carpet is (often literally) rolled out before him. Elegant cars with courteous, uniformed drivers picked us up at the door. When we ate out it was at the best tables in Michelin-starred restaurants. The chefs would come out to greet Dodi as an old friend, inquiring whether the food was satisfactory.

Dodi lived in another world that just happened to intersect with mine. You don't need to travel to an alien planet if you want to see another form of sentient life. You don't need an interdimensional transporter to visit a parallel reality. You just need a few billion dollars and the whole world changes around you.

⚯

WHEN I got back to L.A. I fell in love with a house in the Hollywood Hills but was $25,000 short of the amount needed to settle. I signed the contract anyway, not knowing where I'd find the money. The next day I opened the mail to find a residual check for a little over $25,000—my cut from the sales of Ivanova merchandising. Everything seemed to be going my way.

Back on set John was waiting for me with open arms. Neither of us asked any questions or offered any answers. We just started up where we'd left off.

Dodi and I talked on the phone as often as we could. Whenever I had a break from *Babylon 5* he flew me (first class, naturally) to meet him. During the production hiatus Dodi and I had been able to drink and dine with abandon, but while I was shooting the series I maintained a healthy diet and drank lightly or not at all. The one time I did drink too much, while at a friend's birthday dinner, John noticed it immediately the following morning when he was lighting me for a scene.

"What did you do last night, baby? Your eyes are all puffy."

I was so embarrassed I never did it again.

For all the fooling around we did, in the trailers and on the set, John and I always took the job seriously and maintained our professionalism. I didn't drink much at all in those years, even when I wanted to, because I had respect for the gift I'd been given. I was on a hit show, working with so many people I loved. The very thought that I could let my colleagues down and disappoint the fans by indulging myself with a drinking spree in my off hours was unthinkable. My drinking was still at the point where I could control it.

In 1995 I celebrated my thirtieth birthday with a party attended by the *Babylon 5* regulars. I noticed throughout the night that Jeff Conaway was acting a bit off. By the end of the party he was completely wasted and holed up in the bathroom doing lines. A mutual friend told me that Jeff was having a bad night—his wife was about to leave him because she couldn't handle his addictions anymore.

"Addictions? What addictions?"

"Cocaine, alcohol, painkillers, you name it."

I was stunned. I couldn't believe it. I hadn't seen any sign of that, because on set Jeff was a consummate professional. He was always on time, he'd have his dialogue down, and he was always friendly and sober. The only behavior that had ever stuck in my mind as being unusual was that he used to carry around supersized bottles of vitamins. I thought it was pretty cool that he had all of these pills, potions, and unguents in his trailer, so one day after an exhausting shooting schedule I asked him what I should take.

"Here, take a niacin tablet. That'll pick you up."

I brought it home and tried it. My skin turned bright red and started burning. I rushed into the shower and turned the cold tap on full force. That stopped the burning, but when I tried to get out of the shower I was hit by a dizzy spell and ended up lying on the floor feeling as if I'd just been through the spin cycle in a washing machine. The next day I went into work and tracked him down.

"What the hell were you thinking giving me that stuff?"

"Oh. You can't take the whole niacin pill. You have to build up a tolerance, so you should just take a little bit. I guess I should have told you that."

A few years ago I saw Jeff on TV. He was in a reality show called *Celebrity Rehab with Dr. Drew*. It broke my heart watching that. He looked like a frail old man, not the handsome, talented guy I knew.

He had a girlfriend who was bringing him drugs during the show, which ended up getting him kicked off, and then he'd come back and then get kicked off again. They were getting him to talk about his past, his tortured childhood, trying to get him to confront the fact that he was an addict, but it always puzzled me that no one did anything to treat his biological addiction. The more you drink or take drugs, the more the neuro-pathways of addiction and compulsion in the brain are strengthened. Why weren't the doctors on the show treating this instead of just the psychological component? Addicts attract other addicts, for comfort, for mutual justification, or, as in this case, just to help feed the addiction. I thought it was sad that there seemed to be no one there for Jeff. Maybe he'd burned through his friends and family, broken one promise too many. Most addicts do. I know I did.

Jeff, like many people I know, was an opiate addict. He had an accident early on in his career on the set of the movie *Grease*, while shooting the "Greased Lightning" scene, that left him with chronic neck and back pain. Most opiate addicts start their addiction after going to a doctor and complaining about back or neck pain; some of the painkillers that they're prescribed are derived from the same source as heroin.

Jeff had multiple surgeries to try to rid himself of the pain, but by then he was addicted to painkillers. One addiction led to another until they finally claimed his life at age sixty in May 2011. It was a tremendous tragedy that Jeff died so young, battling his demons to the end until his body wore out and couldn't take it anymore. In the aftermath I got the impression that the media were very blasé about his death. They even left him out of the Emmy memorial photo montage.

Jeff was fifteen years older than me. At the time, the news of his addiction was tragic, but I didn't see that it had any relevance to my own life. I had no inkling that before long the same monster that haunted Jeff would come knocking on my door, and I'd be designing my own detox-vitamin program. I was too busy living the life I'd always dreamed of.

THESE WERE the halcyon days. I was developing a strong fan base (and boy, are sci-fi fans loyal—I'd never seen anything like it). I was in constant demand at conventions, so I hired an assistant named Holly Evans to help manage the bookings. Holly is ex-military, loyal to the bone, and has stuck with me through all of the highs and lows. She's one of the best and brightest angels in my life.

When the *Los Angeles Times* ran an article asking people to choose the next host of the Oscars, Holly took up the challenge and contacted my fans, letting them know where to vote. From the *Los Angeles Times*, December 13, 2000:

The '01 Oscar Host: You Voted, We Counted

And you thought the presidential election results were confusing? In the wake of Billy Crystal taking himself out of consideration to host the next Academy Awards, we asked readers to nominate their candidates to replace him—and the wide range of responses made the margin of victory in Florida, whatever it might be and for whomever, look like a landslide. . . . The biggest draw, thanks to an apparent write-in campaign by her fans, was Claudia Christian of Babylon 5.

I got over 6,000 votes and left Jim Carrey and Steve Martin for dead. I've got my dress picked out in case the Academy decides to call. It doesn't matter if they don't—fifteen years after my last appearance on *Babylon 5*, I'm still in demand at conventions around the world, and Holly is still making the bookings. You can't beat loyalty like that.

Unfortunately, there is a point at which loyalty crosses the line and becomes obsession.

I'D BEEN receiving crazy-colored, hand-knitted items from a fan who claimed to be a postal worker. He would send me packages containing homemade tea cozies and doilies that he'd knitted himself, and I sent back thank-you notes. Then he wrote to say that he was finally going to meet me at a convention in upstate New York. He had a gift he wanted to give me.

I was sitting at my table signing things for folks and having a pleasant time when I saw something large and furry out of the corner of my eye. I looked up to see a giant tribble (a furry alien creature from *Star Trek*) waddling toward me. The tribble stopped at the table, identified itself as my postal worker fan, and held up an enormous black plastic garbage bag. From out of it, he drew a hot-pink, lime-green, and purple afghan large enough to cover a California-king-size bed. If it were the '60s and I were on acid and living in a commune, I'd have appreciated it. But since I hadn't eaten a trunkload of magic mushrooms that morning, I had to draw on decades of acting experience to conjure up convincing superlatives.

"It's . . . um . . . beautiful. Colorful. Handmade."

"I made it myself. For you."

"And I appreciate that. It must have taken some finesse to create such a work of art. Thank you, thank you so much."

I could tell the giant tribble was pleased. I could hear him purring inside the suit. He waddled off, but not before promising to deliver another gift later in the day.

I was expecting a Day-glo cloak the size of Rhode Island or a scarf long enough to span the English Channel, so was I in for a surprise when, about an hour later, another giant tribble came lumbering toward me. It was the same guy, but the costume had been modified. Wires stuck out of its head, and dozens of strong red lights flashed around its furry body. This was clearly a scary tribble, a tribble with unfinished business.

"I am a morphed tribble. Now you will be morphed, too."

And then a gun emerged from the mass of fur and he shot me. I felt the bullet hit me in the ribs, and I fell back, clutching my side. My life didn't flash before my eyes, but the next day's headline did—"Death by Irony! *Babylon 5* Star Shot by Sci-fi Alien." I was supposed to die a dignified death in bed in my Tuscan villa at ninety, clutching my Oscar in one hand and my Screen Actors Guild award in the other. Instead, I was lying on the ground clutching my ribs as my security guys wrestled a giant tribble to the ground.

I pulled up my shirt to reveal a reddening, nasty-looking bruise and a fat, rapidly rising welt. There was no blood. I wasn't going to die. The gun was real but the bullets were blanks— the same caliber that killed Jon-Erik Hexum and was involved in Brandon Lee's death. If the blank's paper seal had hit flesh instead of bone it could have damaged an internal organ or, on an unlucky day, killed me. I was pissed off. I got up and scanned the room for the guy—I wanted a piece of him. But he was already being dragged away by security, and my friends were gathering around, shepherding me back toward the green room. Later on in the day I received yet another black garbage bag. This one had two hand-knitted pillows in it, in the same headache-inducing neon color scheme. I tried to piece together his thought process in my mind. This was actually meant to be the second gift, but somehow he'd been taken over by the morphed tribble, decided to shoot me instead, and then came around without any memory of what had happened, threw the pillows into the bag, and had them sent to me from jail. Maybe one of the pillows was meant to be from the relatively harmless tribble and another from the totally fucking crazy tribble? Who can say?

The same guy approached me at a convention ten years later, I kid you not, and opened with, "I bet you don't remember me."

I looked at him, completely amazed.

"Oh, I remember you alright. You shot me."

On the previous occasion, after the security guards had ripped the head off his costume, I'd gotten a good look at him. That face was burned into my brain. He had unkempt hair and wore a pair of bedroom slippers. He looked stunned, scratched his head as if trying to recall what I was talking about, and then finally brightened up.

"Oh yeah! I shot you!"

Join me for a moment in trying to imagine a life so rich and varied that you cannot remember shooting an actress at a sci-fi convention while wearing a tribble costume and then being wrestled to the ground by a security team.

Then there was the guy at a Las Vegas convention in '97. He'd been sending flowers and love letters to my Hollywood P.O. box. He'd written of his plan to sell his house, quit his job, and move to L.A. so that we could be together. In the world he'd created in his mind we were already married. His sister wrote to me shortly after, stating that she was concerned about his mental health. Apparently he had indeed quit his job and sold his house, and his sister and family had no idea where he was. That worried me. I didn't even go to pick up my mail, because I was frightened that he'd be there, waiting. Then another letter arrived notifying me that he was coming to pick me up from my next convention in Las Vegas. In his fantasy world I'd left my wedding ring on the sink of our kitchen prior to flying to Vegas, and he was simply being a good husband in returning it to me.

All of this led to my sitting at the police station while a bunch of cops circulated the photo the stalker had conveniently sent me for my bedside table. I went to the convention accompanied by my friend Damon and a team of policemen who looked as if they'd just come out of the armory in *The Matrix*. They wore fancy-looking headgear, walkie-talkies, and guns. They set up checkpoints and started patrolling while I signed things and talked with the fans. A few hours passed, and then this nice Aussie girl who had been staying at Damon's came up and pointed to a guy who was circling the table.

"Hey mate, isn't that your stalker?"

She'd seen the photo two days ago at Damon's apartment and somehow memorized the face.

"Yes, it is the stalker, mate, and thank you so much."

Apparently he'd been circling the table for about an hour, and she had thought that the armed escorts had been hanging back with some grand plan in mind when in fact they just hadn't spotted him at all.

I urgently gesticulated in the direction of the stalker and finally my S.W.A.T. team rolled into action. Walkie-talkies screeched, bodies tumbled, and the cops ran in and handcuffed the guy before dragging him away. After Gary I've never married again, but whenever I contemplate the prospect, the image that instantly springs to mind is that stalker with a stack of policemen piling on top of him, desperately trying to fish a wedding band out of his pocket and yelling at me as if we were long lost lovers.

"Claudia! You left your ring back at the house! Quick, take it. People will think you're available!"

That always helps bring me to my senses.

But this definitely wasn't the last crazy person I would run into at a convention.

People have tattooed my signature on their bodies and legally changed their names to Susan Ivanova. I can list at least a dozen other stalkers through the years—both male and female—and I have the restraining orders to prove it. I wish I was making this stuff up.

I'm generally open and sharing with my fans, but there is a line, and if you stay on the right side of that—and don't stalk me or try to kill me—then we're all good.

∞

I HAD a break from *Babylon 5* at the end of the third season and headed off to spend time with Dodi again. I began to remember why I'd broken things off with him back when I was a teenager. Dodi was a good companion, well-versed in navigating his upper-class domain, but he had a jealous streak a mile wide.

Whenever I was visiting his world, Dodi liked to know where I was at all times. He gave me keys to his apartments in London and Paris but still insisted I sign in and out with security using a codename. Sometimes I was Black Swan, other times I was Red Hawk. It's very cool at first—you feel like you're in a James Bond movie. But the luster quickly wears off, and then it becomes just plain irritating.

"I'm Black Hawk."

"I'm sorry. I don't have a Black Hawk on the list."

"Um . . . Red Hawk?"

"Sorry. That was yesterday's code name."

"What about Black Eye and Bloody Nose if you don't let me into the building?"

I went to use his flat in Paris while he went away for business, inviting my cousin Kati to join me. She's ten years my junior and has always been like a little sister to me. We were excited at the prospect of hitting Les Bains Douches and some of the other hot nightclubs in town.

Always exceptionally generous, Dodi had a meal sent over from the Ritz and then called to tell me that we had a curfew. If we weren't home by 11 p.m. every night, the guard had orders not to let us back in. The whole situation was all the more ridiculous because I knew the guard. He was this gorgeous guy I used to work out with at a gym in West Hollywood. He'd worked as an actor and bodyguard, and now he was dressed in a butler suit telling me when I had to be home for bed. He was really embarrassed but explained that there were people watching him and that he'd be fired if he didn't toe the line.

My cousin rolled her eyes. That little disappointment was the beginning of the end for me. I enjoyed the luxurious lifestyle but never had much patience for the drama and control that went with it. The rich man's entourage—the housemen, security guards, and attendants at every turn—was starting to get on my nerves. I liked my privacy and the freedom to come and go as I pleased.

When Dodi returned we sat down and had a heart-to-heart. I expressed my doubts about his lifestyle, that it wasn't for me. I told him that I needed to get back to L.A. to prepare for the upcoming season. Instead, Dodi convinced me that we should cruise the Atlantic for a few days on his yacht *Jonikal*. The weather was welcoming, and my mood cleared as well. It had been more than a decade since Dodi and I had traveled at sea, and I was looking forward to reliving the experience.

At sea there was less interference from others. Dodi and I had enough privacy to enjoy each other and reconnect. As we relaxed together all the tensions and petty annoyances that had been building up between us drifted away.

After we made love on the gently rocking boat one night a sweet intimacy settled over us. We started talking about our lives. Dodi poignantly confessed his fear of dying without becoming a father. His father Mohamed was overbearing and had never spent much time with him as he was growing up. Dodi dreamed of having kids who could be "normal." Kids he could take to the park or the movies without having to mobilize a private army. The whole issue had been weighing on his mind. At the time, I assumed it was because he'd recently turned forty and was having a midlife crisis. Question: What does the man who has everything regret missing out on when he hits middle age? Answer: A normal life. In retrospect, though, I can't help but wonder if he had a premonition of his own death, much as my mother had of Patrick's.

While I lay with my head on his arm he asked if I'd consider having a child with him. I was totally caught off guard. Dodi and I had dated on and off for more than a decade, but I had always considered us to be ships passing in the night.

I was certainly touched. Dodi trusted me because I didn't want or need anything from him. I had my own money, my own home, and my own career—in contrast to the flock of hungry seagulls who usually hovered around him.

"I've known you for a long time now. We have a strong friendship. We would be good parents."

I was hit by a powerful wave of emotion. My heart lit up as I entertained the possibility that it might just work.

I told him I'd think about it, that I needed time.

We had voyaged southward and entered the Mediterranean. Now we anchored at Monte Carlo. He was going away for a few days on business, and I could sense he was going to press the issue when he got back. We held each other for a long time, and when we let go and looked into each other's tear-filled eyes, we kissed and hugged and said our goodbyes.

Back at his Kensington flat I sat surrounded by photos of Brooke Shields and other models and actresses he'd dated. I had promised Dodi that I'd think it over seriously, and I did. I knew one thing for certain—I didn't love him. I mean, I felt a kind of love, a tender, maternal affection, but it wasn't a mature, soulful love, the kind I'd felt with Rod and John Flinn, the kind you build a lifetime partnership on. And what kind of partnership would it be, anyway? He'd asked me to have his children, but he didn't ask me to marry him, and that didn't sit well with me. Wasn't I good enough? Would Dodi's other girlfriends keep coming around and competing with our children for his attention while I raised the kids? Screw that.

Then there was his family. Dodi treated me with respect, but his family existed in a different culture. I'd seen his father's relationship with the mother of his youngest children, so I knew that if I had Dodi's child—with or without marriage—I'd have to spend more time in that household. Women have to eat in a separate room, apart from the men. I was a young, successful, independent Western woman. I didn't tolerate that kind of thing when I was at the Davises' dinner with Kissinger, I didn't let Dodi get away with it, and I sure as hell wasn't going to sign up for a lifetime of it. And even if I somehow managed to avoid the family, I knew I would probably lose control of the child if anything ever happened to Dodi.

Still, I rang my mother and asked her for advice. It was a big decision, and I wanted to make sure I was being objective.

"Hi mom. Dodi asked me to have his baby. I was wondering . . . "

"Do it!"

Was that what she thought of me? That I needed to cash in and settle for a second-rate relationship? In hindsight, I'm sure she meant well. All parents want their kids to settle down, but right then and there my mother's enthusiasm to see me knocked up and "taken care of" was the deciding factor. I was and still am a very stubborn person. I got up early the next day, wrote Dodi a note, and caught the next flight back to L.A.

I love you Dodi, I always will, but even though you think I'm the most mature girl you know, I'm still a girl. I want my life and I want to see how it plays out. I'm sorry to leave without saying good-bye . . . but we had our beautiful goodbye in Monte Carlo after an incredible weekend. Please call me when you come to Los Angeles, I miss you already. CC

I knew it would make him angry, and later I heard from mutual friends that it had. Dodi had never spent much time around independent women, and he certainly was not used to being turned down. It felt like the coward's way out, but I also saw it as a way for him to save face. From Dodi's point of view, he had honored me with the ultimate request—to have his child— and I simply wasn't ready for it. It seemed kinder just to go.

My relationship with John Flinn was quickly approaching its end, too. We were coming up to the two-year mark, and I'd never had a relationship that lasted more than three. He was very understanding about the whole thing and very forgiving. I was still relatively young, and he could see that I was restless and in need of a change.

As fate would have it I met another man who would light a fire in me I'd never felt before. There was something combustible between us. We both felt it, a little foretaste of an earth-shaking encounter, and it wasn't long before we fell headlong into the flames of a tumultuous affair.

TOWARD THE end of season four Joe Straczynski started calling me into his office for private conversations. He didn't do that with many cast members, but I felt that it was a natural progression of the friendship that had been growing over the course of the series. It was common knowledge that I'd broken up with

John, but I hadn't advertised the fact that I had started seeing a new paramour. One day Joe asked me if I'd like to go and see a show with him. I agreed, and never gave it a second thought. We were all pretty buddy-buddy on the set and the cast and crew would often socialize after work, though Joe had never asked me to go anywhere with him before.

I suddenly knew I'd made a mistake in accepting his invitation when the next day a dozen red roses appeared at my front door.

Shit, this is a date!

But maybe it wasn't. Maybe Joe was just being nice. I went out to meet him, and when I saw the black stretch limo pull up any doubts I'd harbored were washed away.

Fuck, this is definitely a date!

I was more than a little freaked out. I'm not normally thrown off guard by men, but it does make a difference when your boss, the guy who puts the words in the mouth of your character, who can kill or dishonor your character, asks you out on a date. It's not entirely inappropriate; this was Hollywood after all, and things like that do happen. But that night it totally threw me for a loop. I wondered what people would think. Here I am, I've just come off a long relationship with the director of photography, and now I'm climbing into a limo with the show's creator. And then I started to worry about Joe's expectations. I'd said yes to seeing the show, I'd accepted the roses, and then I climbed into the limo with him. How do you give back roses without causing offense? In hindsight, I should have made a joke about the whole thing: *Roses? You know, I don't date writers, Joe. I married the last writer I dated, and they're still searching for his body.*

We went to the show, and I endured some awkward conversation. It was clearly an uncomfortable evening for both of us.

When he dropped me off back at home I quickly thanked him and closed the door to the limo before he had time to move in for anything physical.

It was a small thing, really, just a miscommunication between friends. But these things do change relationships. They change how people act toward one another. After that night I don't think we ever recaptured the trust and friendship that we'd previously enjoyed.

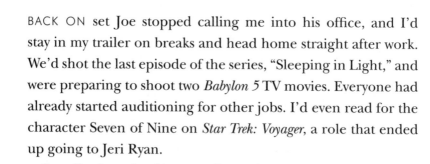

BACK ON set Joe stopped calling me into his office, and I'd stay in my trailer on breaks and head home straight after work. We'd shot the last episode of the series, "Sleeping in Light," and were preparing to shoot two *Babylon 5* TV movies. Everyone had already started auditioning for other jobs. I'd even read for the character Seven of Nine on *Star Trek: Voyager*, a role that ended up going to Jeri Ryan.

I really thought that any discomfort between Joe and me would vanish once the show was over. But sadly for both me and Susan Ivanova, that wouldn't happen.

JOE HAD originally intended *Babylon 5* to run five years. Every season our ratings got better. Internationally, our popularity was higher than ever. Under ordinary circumstances we would have been able to complete the five-year story arc without a hitch. But in the fourth season the network—Warner's Prime Time Entertainment Network—started having financial trouble, and it looked as if we weren't going to have the money to do a fifth. Just to be safe Joe shortened the story arc so that by the end of season four all the loose ends had been tied up. The story was over. We filmed what was supposed to be the last episode, and my manager signed me to star in a TV movie on the USA cable network called *A Wing and a Prayer*. It was the first time I was the star of a Movie of the Week. I'd been a co-star, guest star, and everything in between, but never "the star," and it was a big opportunity to take a leap forward in my career.

Then we learned that TNT and Warner Brothers had come through with the money for a fifth season.

That's when the problems started. I couldn't sign up for twenty-two episodes because I needed the first few episodes off to do the Movie of the Week. Joe promised that he would write me out for those episodes. He'd done the same thing for some of the other cast members. I was happy with that, but the cable network wasn't prepared to take me on if I was double booked, because it would affect their ability to get insurance. I pressed my manager, because I was committed to continuing with the show, and he got USA to agree that everything would be okay if I got a guarantee in writing from Babylonian Productions stating that I would be released for those episodes that would be shot while *A Wing and a Prayer* was shooting.

Joe told me that he was unable to do that. If he renegotiated in writing for me then it would open the door for the rest of the cast to do the same, and that would affect the budget and scheduling and jeopardize the entire fifth season. TNT wanted all the lead actors, which included me, committed to all twenty-two episodes.

They set a deadline for me to sign the contract. I was caught between a rock and a hard place and hoped that Joe and the producers could find some way to work around it.

Joe and the key cast members attended a sci-fi convention in the UK, and some of the studio guys were there, too. They plied

133

us with wine and good scotch, and we went to bed at the hotel completely bombed. At 3 a.m. someone knocked on my door. It was a producer with a contract in hand. He started blabbering, pressuring me to sign. I found out later that they tried the same thing on some other cast members who still hadn't signed on for the new season. I rang my manager in L.A. to ask him for advice.

"Claudia, no fucking way are you signing *anything* at 3 a.m. in a foreign country when I haven't even seen the contract. I've been asking these guys to fax me something all week, and they haven't sent me a goddamn thing!"

I packed my bags and left the UK. The deadline passed, and by the time I got home there was a fax waiting for me telling me that I was fired from the show. My manager contacted them to see if we could salvage the situation. The producer's reply was that we were a "a day late and a dollar short."

That's show business. They had to move on with their production schedule. Joe had scripts to write and he needed to know if the female lead was part of the story. I understand that. I was upset that I couldn't continue with the show, and I really felt that things could have been worked out. But at the end of the day it was something that often happens in the entertainment business—two parties who can't reconcile due to scheduling conflicts.

What I don't think any of us were expecting was the explosive reaction of the fans when they learned negotiations had broken down and I wouldn't be coming back. Joe had dumped a male lead and numerous other cast members, so I don't think he or the producers anticipated there would be much of an issue in replacing me. Instead, the blogs and forums started filling up with questions from fans demanding answers. Joe started receiving death threats. I got my share of hate mail as well. There were even fans asking questions about the technicalities of contractual agreements, show-business law, and what could be done to get me back. Sci-fi fans really are a loyal bunch.

Ultimately, losing Ivanova meant that Joe had to make substantial changes to the development of season five. An episode entitled "The Very Long Night of Susan Ivanova" was renamed "The Very Long Night of Londo Mollari" and given a completely different storyline. Even now, when I attend conventions fans often complain that my character should have had a better send-off, and I tend to agree. Writer Harlan Ellison wrote something into an episode implying that my character left for more money. I think it was a personal jab at me, and I think it was in poor taste. Ivanova and I have one more thing in common: neither of us is so career-oriented that we would choose wealth and advancement over personal loyalties.

Eventually things did die down. I shot my movie, the fifth season of *Babylon 5* went ahead, and I literally traded places with Tracy Scoggins. I appeared on the *Highlander* series as the immortal swordswoman Katherine, while Tracy left *Highlander* to play *Babylon 5*'s Captain Lochley.

Ironically (and maybe a little irritatingly), they were able to book her initially on an eight-episode contract.

I VALUED my friendship with Joe, and it was sad for me that things ended the way they did. I still think of him fondly and can't thank him enough for creating a character of such dignity and integrity that she would continue to resonate so strongly with our audience.

Below are some excerpts from a live AOL chat between Joe and me from happier times, when the series was just starting to gather a large following. It's moments like these that I enjoy remembering and talking over with fans:*

> QUESTION: *Claudia, what do you see in Ivanova's future?*
>
> CLAUDIAB5: *Lots of sex, drugs, and rock 'n roll and the Captaincy.*
>
> JMS AT B5: *(stunned silence)*
>
> CLAUDIAB5: *You told me to express my humor, Joe.*
>
> JMS AT B5: *(Current needs: glass rum, gun, two bullets.)*
>
> CLAUDIAB5: *On my way.*
>
> . . .
>
> JMS AT B5: *What most folks don't know, btw, is that Claudia (not kidding here) has a genius IQ, and reads a massive number of books per week.*
>
> CLAUDIAB5: *Here's your fifty bucks, Joe.*
>
> JMS AT B5: *I live to serve.*
>
> . . .
>
> QUESTION: *jms and cc: what is the general mood of the show taping? Is there a lot of joking, etc. or does everyone pretty much take things seriously?*
>
> CLAUDIAB5: *We have a ball making B5. At least I do.*
>
> JMS AT B5: *Simple answer to the question: as you walk down the halls of the B5 production office . . . the one sound you hear the most is laughter. And every day, everybody eats lunch together behind the stage, writers, actors, producers, directors, crew, everybody. People have fun, have birthdays, hang out after work . . . it's a great, fun environment . . . and a lot of practical jokes.*

And Joe was right. *Babylon 5* was great fun, a ball to work on, one of the highlights of my career, and I never tire of sharing the joy we had making it with the fans who continue to watch and support it.

---

* *EXTRA Online*'s live interview with J. Michael Straczynski, executive producer and creator of *Babylon 5,* and actress Claudia Christian, who plays Lt. Commander Susan Ivanova on the show. Copyright 1995 America Online, Inc., all rights reserved.

∞

DESPITE MY regrettable exit, after four years on a high-rating sci-fi series there was no shortage of work for me. Checks came in the mail every day, and life was good.

But, as we've all learned from the daytime soaps, when things are going well for too long disaster is bound to be lurking right around the corner, waiting for the perfect moment to strike.

This time, disaster had a name and a face.

Before I met him, if you'd told me that the devil had a Scottish accent I'd have thought you were pulling my chain.

Now I know better.

Standing in line with Andreas, Peter, and Mira. Season one of *Babylon 5*.

The dreaded "Michelin Man" suit on the set of *Babylon 5*

Fooling around with Jeff Conaway in the human makeup trailer

With John Flynn at a party

Sunbathing on one of Dodi's yachts

With Dodi. This was taken on the trip where he asked
me to have his baby.

One of the zillions of conventions I've attended!

With my buddy, practical joker Jerry Doyle, on the set of *Babylon 5*

Soaked in fake blood for "Between the Darkness and the Light," the episode where my character, Susan Ivanova, dies

With my sweet friend Pat Tallman. I'm grateful to have met her on *Babylon 5*.

THREE

BAD MEDICINE

HIGHLAND FLING

"THEY MAY TAKE our lives, but they'll never take OUR FREEDOM!"

It was 1996, and *Braveheart* was the movie of the year. It blazed through the Academy Awards, sweeping up five Oscars, including best picture, and five additional nominations. It was a tragic, historical romance with an epic scope—easily one of my favorite films of all time. I saw the movie with my mom, and when the reluctant hero Robert the Bruce appeared on-screen, I turned to her and said, "God, I wish I could meet a man like that!" Especially as he was played with such smoldering intensity by green-eyed Scottish actor Angus Macfadyen.

A few months later I was having an early lunch with girl-friends on Sunset Plaza Drive when I saw Angus with Justin, an old friend of mine. Angus had a glass of white wine in one hand and a cigarette in the other. It was noon. He caught me looking at him and started staring back. I was surprised by the intensity of his gaze. His eyes contained all the qualities that attracted me to his character in the film. I'd try to match him, to maintain eye contact, but then I'd get embarrassed and turn away. I rejoined my girlfriends' conversation, trying to ignore him, but eventually I'd turn and look and our eyes would lock again.

I plucked up my courage and walked over to his table on the pretense of talking to my friend. It was very exciting—a big, heart-pounding moment.

Once I started speaking, cool, confident Claudia resurfaced. This guy was just another actor. I'd left Dodi Fayed, for God's sake. This guy was small-fry by comparison. The three of us chatted. I flirted with Angus a little. Reassured that I was back in command of my senses, I said my goodbyes and headed back to my friends. Angus came up behind me and touched my arm. Everything else seemed to fade away.

"Claudia. Can I see you again?"

"Sure. Justin's got my number."

Cool. Calm. Collected. I walked away trying not to show the prickling of excitement that ran across my skin and made the hair on the back of my neck stand on end.

On the set of *Babylon 5*, I'd check my phone messages every half hour to see if he'd called. I went crazy waiting for him to call, and after a week I finally rang Justin.

"What's going on? Why isn't this guy calling me? I don't normally have this problem!"

Justin explained that that was just Angus. He'd been holed up in his apartment for the last week drinking like a fish while he completed a series of paintings.

"Paintings? What's he painting?"

"Oh, it's depressing stuff. Really macabre. You know, the devil and all that."

That should have set the warning bells ringing right then. A guy ignores you for a week because he's too busy getting loaded and painting the devil. But looking at it through eyes dazzled by animal attraction, the image of the tortured artist not only seemed romantic but also bound Angus more tightly in my mind to the character of Robert the Bruce. I'd never met a man like Angus before—dark and brooding—the archetypical Scotsman. This was new and forbidden fruit.

I finally got a call from Angus, probably prompted by Justin, and we went out to dinner. It turned out we had very similar taste in literature, which is worth more to me than a super yacht and a solid-gold sink. He told me that he'd once been engaged to Catherine Zeta-Jones, before she came to America and became famous. Apparently, in her biography she claims that he was the best sex she ever had. I don't know if I could make the same claim, but what he lacked in technique he made up for in enthusiasm. After making love we stayed up till four in the morning reciting poems from memory.

His favorite was Dylan Thomas's "A Grief Ago," which speaks of "hell wind and sea"—a wild, turbulent love.

I often recited Byron's "When We Two Parted."

In secret we met—
  In silence I grieve,
That thy heart could forget,
  Thy spirit deceive.
If I should meet thee
  After long years,
How should I greet thee?—
  With silence and tears.

Unfortunately, those poems would serve as the bookends of our entire relationship.

ANGUS STARTED writing poems for me. He'd leave them in his mailbox, and I'd pick them up on the way to the *Babylon 5* set. It was like a high school relationship, intense and disarming. I was utterly smitten.

He moved into my house a few months later, and by the time I'd finished working on *Babylon 5*, our relationship was in full swing. We'd smoke and drink wine, make love and read poetry. And we'd fight. We'd scream at each other, smash glasses, break furniture, and hurl insults. We had epic, alcohol-fueled battles that ran on into the night.

He'd just finished playing the wild, madly in love Richard Burton in *Liz: The Elizabeth Taylor Story*. Our love affair, he said, was as passionate, artistic, and crazy as theirs. It was a love that blinded me to the voices of concern from my friends, who'd started referring to us as Dick and Liz. They thought Angus wasn't brooding or romantic but just plain rude. My mother once asked him, out of politeness, what he felt about his native country's history.

"Fuck history. Where's my fucking chicken?"

And I got up and got him his chicken. My mother was appalled.

Soon, he'd have such a hold over me that my friends would give him another name—the devil.

Angus reveled in all the bad habits that I'd kept in check throughout my career. He was undisciplined, he didn't care about his body, he drank, he smoked, and he spewed his own inner darkness all over the horrible canvases that were now piling up in my pool house. The fights got worse, and I realized that he took a sadistic pleasure in them. He'd smile if he could make me cry.

I knew it was an unhealthy relationship, and, looking back, I suppose my friends hit the nail on the head. Angus might not have been the devil, but he was certainly *my* devil.

SNIDE AND Prejudice was a new Philippe Mora movie, and Angus and I were both cast in it. He played Adolf Hitler (I kid you not, this is how weird Hollywood can get), and I was cast as a character representing all the women in Hitler's life. The whole story was built around inmates in an insane asylum and, to be honest, the movie was a piece of shit, its only saving grace being the other talented cast members that I had the pleasure to meet—Mick Fleetwood from Fleetwood Mac (I'd been a fan since I first bought *Rumors* as a kid) and René Auberjonois from *Star Trek: Deep Space Nine.*

Things with Angus were as bad as ever, but I couldn't bring myself to leave him. I'd become emotionally dependent. And since I couldn't leave, I found myself drinking more and more to numb myself to the pain of our relationship. It was the first time in my life that I drank to escape. Before that, alcohol had only ever been a lubricant that made a night out more fun or a fine meal even more pleasurable. Now I was using it as an emotional painkiller.

IN THE summer of 1998 I went out to lunch with my friend Galen Johnson and Alejandro Jodorowsky, the French-Chilean avant-garde filmmaker, comic book writer, and spiritual guru. Jodorowsky was an interesting guy. He talked about how John Lennon had given him a million dollars to make his movie *The*

Holy Mountain, and he'd come close to making what would have been the most interesting and bizarre adaptation of Frank Herbert's novel *Dune,* to have starred Salvador Dalí and Orson Welles with music composed by Pink Floyd and production design by comic-book artist Jean "Moebius" Giraud and surrealist artist H. R. Giger. Galen told me that Jodorowsky was supposed to have psychic powers and had invented his own spiritual healing system called Psychomagic, which sounded more like a Hitchcock pisstake by Mel Brooks than a form of therapy. After lunch Jodorowsky went on his way and Galen told me to sit a while longer. When I'd gone to the bathroom Jodorowsky had given him a message to pass on to me.

"He said that you were going to have a drinking problem, that you'll struggle with alcohol and your weight when you get older and that you need to watch out now."

I laughed out loud and Galen joined in. Even with the emotional drinking Angus was driving me to, it seemed ridiculous. I couldn't see it. I hasten to add that Jodorowsky also predicted that I'd be married and fabulously successful within two years of that lunch, so if he had a psychic flash of me at age thirty-nine as a size fourteen with a glass of champagne in hand, then I must have also been holding an Oscar aloft in the other while I straddled Prince Charming. I should have taken the warning as it was meant. He had nothing to gain, and was just sharing an insight, but I wasn't able to hear him. My drinking problem was already underway, but it was operating in stealth mode, flying beneath the radar of my conscious mind.

∞

ANGUS WAS offered a job in China doing a crap action film, and I encouraged him to take it. I was hoping that while he was gone

I'd have time to get back on my feet. Also, I'd been keeping a secret from him. Marilyn Grabowski, *Playboy*'s West Coast editor, wanted me to pose for her magazine. I knew Angus would go apeshit if I said yes. In the fantasy world that he imagined he ruled (population two), I wasn't for sharing. I felt better the second he was out of the house. I found that I could make my own choices just fine without someone standing over me whispering disparaging comments in my ear. I agreed to do *Playboy* and started training with a former ballerina, who had me doing hundreds of lunges every day. By the time she was finished with me I was in the best shape of my life.

Angus invited me to join him in Shanghai, and, feeling empowered by my time alone, I agreed to go. I was myself again—outgoing, funny Claudia. I felt fantastic, I'd stopped drinking, and I'd never looked better. But I underestimated Angus and his need to re-establish a hold over me. He was a master of the devastating one-liner, and when I arrived in China he knocked my legs right out from under me with the first words out of his mouth: "Look at you. This is an improvement. When we first met I thought you looked a little chunky."

This from a guy with a belly like Winston Churchill's. When he was offered the role of Peter Lawford in the TV movie *The Rat Pack*, they only gave it to him with a proviso that he lose thirty pounds. I tried to help him exercise and eat healthy food, but eventually gave up. He was an unapologetic glutton.

In hindsight, I think there were two poisons in our relationship. The first was Angus's need to project his many inadequacies onto me. The second was that he would keep me bound to him by constantly tugging at the ropes of my own emotional weaknesses. By criticizing me, targeting my fears, and then switching back to false affection, he kept me weak.

IT'S HARD to enjoy your first visit to China when your travel partner makes it his mission to be rude to every Chinese person you meet. On the set of the movie he got off to not so good a start by insisting that he rewrite his part. He was perfectly correct in saying that they'd written him as a second-rate James Bond villain, but his attempts to inject Taoist philosophy into a character who battled kung-fu kangaroos were equally terrible, and you can imagine how the Chinese might love having a Westerner lecture them on his superior knowledge of their culture.

One night when we walked into the hotel restaurant the hostess asked, "Smoking or not smoking?"

Angus held up his cigarette. "What the fuck do you think?"

Angus wasn't racist, he was just universally rude. Most Scottish people I've met are funny and have a clever, wry wit, but not Angus. He could have held up the cigarette and said something like, "I'd continue this battle of wits with you, but you're obviously unarmed," but he lacked the imagination for humor.

I left dinner early and hit the gym. I needed to keep in shape for my upcoming photo shoot. I was watching the TV while running on the treadmill when it was announced that Dodi and Princess Diana had been killed in a car crash in the Pont de l'Alma tunnel in Paris. It hit me hard. I sat down in the gym and cried. Dodi had been my friend for nearly twenty years, and I deeply regretted not being able to talk to him one last time, especially after leaving him so abruptly.

Dodi's fears of dying childless had come to pass. He'd started seeing Diana not long after we parted ways, and I wondered, with our last conversation on my mind, if he'd asked her to have the child that I'd refused him.

I went back to my hotel room to learn that I'd booked *A Wing and a Prayer*. Fortune's wheel had turned in my favor, though the news was bittersweet. I had an excuse to get out of Shanghai, and I took it. I needed time to myself, time to process the news of Dodi's death.

Back in L.A. I got a call from producer Bill Panzer. Adrian Paul, the star of the TV show *Highlander*, had decided to move on, and they were looking for a woman to take over the series. He wanted me to play the part of Katherine in the *Highlander* episode "Two of Hearts." This was just the thing I needed to get Dodi off of my mind. *Highlander* was a dream job—the shoot was in Paris, I'd get to play an eleventh-century immortal and mess around with swords, and there was even the possibility that I'd end up as the star of my own series.

When Angus got home he was uncharacteristically kind to me; he had sensed that after Dodi's death I'd started to pull away from him. Always the optimist, I decided to invite him to Paris—it was our last, best hope for peace.

The *Highlander* set was heaven: horses, history, and mud. If I could just do historical dramas for the rest of my life, I'd die happy.

I'd started collecting knives and swords when I was a kid. My dad had been given some gifts when he opened a bank account, and one of them was a good-quality pocketknife. All of my brothers argued over who should get it, including Patrick, who wanted it for skinning, but when we drew straws I was the winner. There were cries of outrage, but my dad decreed that fair was fair and I got to keep it. When Patrick died I put it on his coffin as they lowered it into the ground, a parting gift. I loved that knife, at first because it was something my brothers wanted but couldn't have, and later because it became a symbol of the love I held for Patrick. That was where my love of knives started and an interest in swords naturally followed on, but my dad wouldn't let me start collecting until I turned seventeen.

Now I got to swing a medieval broadsword and be tutored by one of Hollywood's leading sword masters, F. Braun McAsh. He was a very friendly, barrel-chested guy with a deep voice—a walking encyclopedia of arms and armor.

I wanted to do all my own fight scenes, but I had to convince the producers that I knew what I was doing or they would use a stunt double. One little mistake with a sword and an actress can be left incapacitated for a week.

Things couldn't have worked out better on that front. After a minor accident on the set the producers had decided to institute a water-only policy, which was counter to the French crew's traditional three-hour drinking lunches. I don't think the American producers were aware of the French tendency to strike at the smallest infringements of their conditions, and disrupting the national pastime of eating and drinking was, to the crew's minds, a catastrophic violation of human rights.

While protracted negotiations took place I got to spend more time with F. Braun learning how to fight. He'd pledged to the producers that every *Highlander* episode would feature a sword technique that had never been seen on film or television before, so I had lots to learn. He was patient and encouraging and taught me some neat tricks from his theatrical fencing repertoire (how to look good dueling on camera) and knowledge of historical sword fighting (how they really killed people with ruthless efficiency in times of yore).

My character, Katherine, was one of the oldest immortals in the *Highlander* series. She had even posed for the illustrations in the *Kama Sutra*, so I had to create a complex character—confident but with enough vulnerability that she could fall in love with a mortal man, who was played by Steven O'Shea.

The crew liked me, and I thought I had a shot at being the new star of the show. But at the end of the day they went with Elizabeth Gracen, who'd been in the original series. Also, she had slept with Bill Clinton, so she was in the news a lot; when it comes to TV ratings any publicity is good publicity. She chopped off her hair, dyed it white, and the new series was a flop.

ANGUS AND I both had films at Cannes that year and decided to go together. It was 1998, I was thirty-three years old, and my biological clock was ticking like a time bomb.

I found out that I was pregnant in the bathroom of the Carlton Hotel. Clutching my pregnancy test, I told Angus the news through tear-stained eyes. We hugged, agreed it was the best thing in the world for both of us, and, right then and there, made a pact to raise the child together.

But because it was Angus, I expected the worst. I secretly hoped that things would work out, but I began to steel myself for the next fight. It never came, though, and by the four-month mark I was proudly sporting a baby bump. Things had changed. I felt secure in this relationship for the first time. I was finally going to be a mother. I just knew that I was going to have a boy with green eyes and dark hair. This was Patrick wanting to come back again.

And then Angus stopped having sex with me. I understood why—he had a Madonna-whore complex. God forbid you have sex with the mother of your child. What I couldn't deal with was his sudden obsession with virgins. Angus had worked on a film with a blond actress who claimed she was a virgin. He would go on about it all the time: she was angelic, she was a born-again Christian, and she was only eighteen years old. I don't know what the big deal is with virgins. Terrorists blow themselves up for a paradise filled with virgins. If I were a guy my idea of paradise would be a harem of sexually experienced bombshells, but then that's just me. Angus was certainly titillated by the idea of going where no man had gone before, and I guess I felt the same sense of injustice that a bald man or a guy with a small dick feels. How do you compete? She's a virgin, I'm not, and there's nothing I can do to change that.

Then one day, on his way out the door with a buddy, Angus casually turned back to me and said, as if it were an afterthought, "I've changed my mind. Get rid of it."

The emotional blow was so strong that he might as well have punched me in the belly. He left and I fell to the tile floor and cried so hard that a few hours later the baby spontaneously aborted.

After my failed relationship with Patrick Wachsberger, I had sworn that I'd never again become pregnant by a man who had no real interest in raising a child. Yet here I was, soaked in blood and frightened to death by what my body had just done. I didn't know if it was the botched abortion in Italy that ruined my chances of having children, but something had made the whole process precarious. I just couldn't seem to hold on to a child, and the fact that I'd lost one over an emotional outburst just didn't make sense to me. I was a strong, healthy young woman.

But the next morning, while getting a D&C at my gynecologist's office, I decided that God had saved me from a horrible future with the wrong man. I'd invested in love and I'd been burned again. The bricks I'd started laying after the losses of Justine and Patrick's baby had now become a wall, and I decided that I would make it stronger and stronger so that nothing could get in and hurt me like that again. It didn't occur to me that when you build defenses that strong you reach a point where even good things can't penetrate anymore.

⌒◯

I CAME home from the supermarket one morning to find my friend Christine sitting in our kitchen. Lately, Angus had decided that I was drinking too much and got into the habit of lecturing me while he was drinking whatever was his poison of the day. Now he'd taken things to the next level. Christine had flown in from Canada after Angus called her up and told her he thought I had a serious drinking problem. Seriously, the source of all my woes, the pathological, selfish pig who drank like a fish, thought that I was the one with the problem and had staged a half-assed intervention. I drank soda water while Angus sat there looking smug and self-righteous, sipping on tequila mixed with orange juice at ten in the morning. In addition to confronting me about my drinking, Christine admitted that she was attending AA meetings and battling her own demons.

Interventions can work, but a person has to be ready. She has to recognize the problem in herself, and in this case, a pissed Scotsman and a well-meaning friend in the same boat didn't have the right to preach to me.

It didn't stop me from drinking. If anything it made things worse. I took it as it was truly meant—yet another attempt by Angus to cut my legs out from under me and keep me weak.

⌒◯

ANGUS WAS slated to play Orson Welles in Tim Robbins's *Cradle Will Rock* in New York and he had to quit his comfort eating and binge drinking to play a young, svelte Welles.

After he flew to New York I dumped his things in the garage, called him at his hotel, and told him it was over. It was one of the most difficult things I've ever had to do. When someone has that sort of power over you, you're constantly pulled in two directions—one part of you is still chattering away, trying to convince you that it can still all work out, while deep inside, every cell is screaming out to end it.

I felt as if I were standing on a rock in the middle of the ocean, waves crashing all around me. I had to cling to the idea that I was going to leave, so that it wouldn't be suddenly ripped away from me and lost forever—I was living Dylan Thomas's hell wind and sea. When he came with his friends to pick up his things, I hid in my bedroom. That's how rattled I was. I watched him through a gap in the shutters. As soon as word got out that I'd broken up with Angus I was surrounded by family and friends who couldn't have been happier at the news. I felt as if I'd been handed a get-out-of-jail-free card. I had my health back. I quit the social smoking and the excess drinking. I was reborn.

Angus went on to shoot *Titus* in 1999 with Anthony Hopkins. The veteran actor was by then a recovering alcoholic, and I heard that he recognized that Angus had a problem. Hopkins tried to help him stop drinking but failed. Angus was too tormented to stay sober for long. I wish *I'd* had Tony Hopkins at hand. I'm sure he'd have noticed that I had a problem, too, though I couldn't see it at the time.

With Angus out of my life, I thought that things would get better. I didn't realize that I was only just now starting down the road to hell. By joining Angus in his own downward spiral I'd opened a Pandora's box. Angus had given a voice to my fears and insecurities that I'd previously kept under control. Hell, he'd even discovered new ones. His own inner monster had spoken to the darkness inside me, and now that sought to rear up and displace my previously confident inner voice, the voice that had always served as my guide.

I'd drunk with Angus nearly every night, but had never imbibed during the day. That would change.

I'VE NEVER seen Angus again, except for one occasion years later when I was sitting at a studio waiting to audition for a commercial.

He was chubby and dressed in an old suit and cowboy boots, a faded fedora perched on his head.

He walked right by me. Caught up in whatever shit was going on in his head, he didn't even notice I was there. I chose not to confront him, because I knew that if I did it would have been as Lord Byron predicted—with silence and tears.

10

THE MONSTER'S GAMBIT

*T*HE DAY OF the *Playboy* shoot arrived. I was slightly hesitant about being photographed naked, but there were two factors that helped drive me on.

In 1999 I did a film called *The Haunting of Hell House*, based on a Henry James story, with veteran British actor Michael York. During the shoot his wife Patricia McCallum, a photographer who specializes in nudes of celebrities, asked me if I'd take off my clothes and walk through the fields on Ireland's Connemara coast. Michael and Pat were a very cool couple, and I didn't want to seem like a prude, so I ended up standing knee high in grass, a script in hand, wearing nothing but a corset and a pair of boots. In another shot she had a topless wardrobe woman pretending to fit me for a dress. It was all very shocking for the local community, but Pat was a great persuader and managed to convince them not to run us out of town. Her exhibition went on tour, and my photos, along with a host of other celebrities', ended up on the walls of some of the world's best galleries. God only knows how many people saw my nether regions, but I figured I was in good company. I knew *Playboy* would be a different kind of experience but once you've taken your clothes off in public and the sky doesn't fall on your head, it makes it easier to entertain the idea again.

The second factor was much more practical—economic reality. My *Babylon 5* residuals were still coming in, but I had a sizable mortgage, had spent a lot of money on renovations, and had my assistant's wage to pay. The bills were mounting up, and *Playboy* was offering very decent money.

As a working actress you can't help but have body issues. It's not as bad as being a model, but it's a pitiless industry when it comes to weight.

A few weeks after yet another miscarriage with my then boyfriend (yes, I was on birth control and yes, I wanted to keep it), I got work as the guest lead on a TV series called *She Spies*. I went to wardrobe for fitting, hoping they could hide some of the pregnancy weight I was still carrying, only to discover that they wanted me to squeeze into a catsuit. I plodded through the mediocre dialogue, ignored the disparaging looks from the thin girls in the show, and went home satisfied that I'd done my best. I later found out that the casting director told my agent that he would never hire me again because I was "chunky." That's Hollywood. No one gives a shit about you or your feelings. You're a product, a storefront mannequin. Ordinarily I'd have been fine with that, but with the pregnancy hormones still raging through my system I was reduced to a sobbing lump.

I heard a whispered voice, coming to me from the darkness.

You're fat, you're disgusting, your career is over.

I recognized the voice and wasn't concerned by it. It was my monster, the little devil that sits on everybody's shoulder. It had always been there, throwing in its two cents' worth for as long as I could remember, but since my breakup with Angus it had gotten a little louder. Angus had made me particularly sensitive about my appearance, and the monster was keen to make hay while the sun shone.

I was going to appear nude in a glossy magazine that would be seen by millions of people around the world. I'd been anxious about my butt appearing on a fifty-foot screen in *The Hidden,* but that was nothing compared to a permanent, published record of my naked form.

What are you worried about? Seriously, you're prepared. You've trained hard, you're in the best shape of your adult life. Playboy *shoot? Bring it on.*

Ah, there was my angel, my armor, the strength and confidence that had carried me forward into a successful international acting career. And it was right. I'd done a million lunges, I had buns of steel, I was beautiful, and the next time a casting director called me "chunky," I'd roll up a copy of my issue of *Playboy* and use it to smack him upside the head.

The shoot ran over four days, and I can tell you right now that being a nude model isn't anywhere near as easy as it looks. I'd have to sit in one spot for hours and then climb a steel wall and hang there with the photographer yelling, "Stick your butt out a little more. Suck in your gut!" It's a surreal experience. In one pose they had my head on the floor and my ass up on a divan, which I suppose looks sexy in the photos but in reality nearly ripped all the muscles in my already-injured neck. The suffering paid off, though. When I saw the Polaroids, I was thrilled.

Wow. Good job, Claudia, you look fantastic. You worked so hard, all that exercise and dieting. You deserve a treat. It's time to party and let your hair down.

Sometimes the devil on your shoulder has the best ideas, and now I saw no danger in indulging. She was right; it was time to party.

I flew to the UK for work, gave up on sit-ups and lunges and hit the pubs and restaurants with abandon. Beer and chips, wine and desserts, I let myself go and loved every minute of it.

Then *Playboy* called. The photos weren't "edgy enough." They wanted a reshoot. I had to get back on the plane to L.A. and do the shoot within twenty-four hours of landing. I was a blob, completely bloated from flying and living it up. I drank nettle tea and prayed. The shoot they published was disappointing. To me, the original shoot was fresher and far more beautiful. Luckily, I was able to secure the rights to both sets of negatives, but what should have been a naked triumph after all the training I'd done failed to have the curative effect on my self-image that I'd hoped for.

See, I told you. You're fat. Your career is going down the gurgler. You'd better go on a starvation diet or something. Now that's going to be tough, so get yourself a good stiff drink.

I waited for those words to bounce off my armor, for my angel to knock the monster down a peg or two with some devastating comeback, but all was quiet on the angelic front. While I was waiting for her to show up, I opened a nice bottle of merlot and poured myself a glass. After the second glass, I'd forgotten that I was waiting for anything.

In the strange way that the mind works, when we're in a vulnerable place, the voice of our darkness, that little whispering monster, is never held accountable. When our confidence, our belief in ourselves is sufficiently silenced, the monster's voice is all that's left, and it masquerades as our true self, leads us to believe that its running commentary is true insight. It isn't, but I didn't know that at the time, and so I bought it. I didn't realize it, but I'd opened the door to the world's most persistent sales-man. The monster had planted a foot firmly inside the door and didn't plan on going anywhere.

∞

I SAID before that telling Angus to get out of my life was one of the strongest things I've ever done, and I wasn't exaggerating. I wasn't just rejecting a man, I was rejecting my own shadow, my weakness, and my self-doubt. It was as empowering as it was frightening, but that darkness, that monster is a bitch. Just when you try to reclaim some of the ground you've lost, that's when she digs her teeth in and won't let go. And she did. Literally.

One night, as I was holding my cocker spaniel Lucy on my lap and petting her, she had a brain seizure and attacked me, maul-ing my face. I fell backward, but after a struggle managed to get her off and lock her in the kitchen. But by then the damage was done. She'd ripped off part of my lip, the flesh underneath my left eye, and a bit of my cheek.

I was in a panic. I couldn't just go to an emergency room. What if I got some intern who tried to sew my face back on? Acting career over. I called my best friend Trish.

"My face is a wreck, I'm in big trouble. I need a good plastic surgeon."

I gently lifted the washcloth I was using to hold my face on and took another peek in the mirror. "Make that a great plastic surgeon."

Trish told me she knew of only one person who'd had really good plastic surgery, and in Hollywood that's saying something.

So I called up this actress at 11 p.m., and she referred me to Dr. Brent Moelleken, who had been featured in ABC's *Extreme Makeover* and Discovery Channel's *Plastic Surgery Before & After.*

I figured that a plastic surgeon wouldn't work at night, so I'd have to wait until the morning to see him. I barely slept, my hand welded to my face. Now and then I'd have to press the skin back on, trying to get it to stick in place.

When I finally got into Dr. Moelleken's office he took off the towel and frowned.

"I wish you'd have come to me last night. You shouldn't have waited. Now I've got to cut away a lot of dead skin. There's too much necrotic tissue."

So I underwent reconstructive surgery, fists clenched, totally fearful of the end result. Because I was missing so much flesh under my eye the doctor had to invent a new procedure to reconstruct my face, the internal cheek lift, so that the eye wouldn't droop. Then he sewed up the scars to make them look like the existing laugh lines around my eyes. When the surgery was over, he told me that he had high hopes.

"I've never really done this procedure on a dog bite, but you should be fine."

I left with a sore, swollen face and a mind filled with images of Frankenstein's monster, his face held together by stitches.

Recovering from the surgery meant that I couldn't work for the next couple of months. When I looked at myself in the mirror, I could see that my eye was hanging at a funny angle. I'd never been the depressive type but now I felt black clouds rolling in.

Dodi and Princess Di were still much in the news, and constantly hearing about my old lover's death wasn't particularly helpful. The coverage had died down after the accident, but now there was some blonde on TV claiming that she was engaged to Dodi during the time I was staying at his Kensington flat. I had no idea if she was telling the truth or not, but I never saw her at Saint-Tropez or Monaco or Paris. There wasn't even a photo of her in the flat. Perhaps Dodi had put my paratrooper ring to good use.

Lying on my couch, feeling totally adrift, I heard the voice of the monster clearly for the first time. It was a step up from the usual whispering and prodding. The petty compulsions that I'd given in to with Angus had gathered power. My little devil had grown up and was no longer content to sit on my shoulder and be brushed away. She was a fully formed monster and she wanted the starring role. Her voice was commanding, loud, and clear. And since it was the only one ringing inside my head at the time, I mistook it for my own.

You know that you're deformed.

That voice spoke to my deepest fears, but it seemed to make a lot of sense.

Don't worry. There are roles for people like you. You can put on prosthetics and play aliens for the rest of your life.

The voice was right. My career was over.

I still hadn't pulled myself together after Angus, and now with the dog attack and Lucy having to be put down (she tried to bite four other people), I uncorked a bottle of wine, lay down on the couch, and went to town. There were strong emotions brewing, and I needed to wrap myself in the numbness I'd sought when I was with Angus. I needed some emotional medicine.

My angel must have been kicking around in my brain somewhere, though, because as I was sobering up from that first big solo binge good news arrived like Noah's little white dove. And I thanked God, because it turned out that Dr. Moelleken was a genius after all. The stitches were removed, and when the swelling went down the scars faded and my face regained its former shape. If I looked really, really close in the mirror I could see some small scars in the lines at the corners of my eyes, but the face that looked back at me was my own. Big sigh of relief. My Frankenstein crisis was averted—no need to buy neck bolts.

That good news let some of the light back in. My self-image bounced back. I realized that I had drifted out to sea, that I'd gone far too far, and I reined in my drinking once more. The monster had underestimated the power of hope. It only takes a little light to drive away a lot of darkness, and once I gained some perspective I rushed back to dry land and a survivable lifestyle.

∞

I TOOK a new lover, a young southern guy named Taylor who I met on the set of the film *True Rights*. I was playing an obnoxious middle-aged reality-TV producer, and I had to wear a wig and a fat suit. Taylor started flirting with me when I was wearing the fat suit. He didn't know what I really looked like, and at the end of the day when I took it off, he got a pleasant surprise. He got an even bigger surprise when I took him back to my place. Taylor was kind and funny, just what I needed. He had a beautiful body, a great head of hair, and golden skin. Sexually we were a perfect fit.

Despite the bad memories of Angus and Lucy's attack, I loved the house I was living in. I wasn't even contemplating a move when my Realtor neighbor asked me if I wanted to double my money and sell up. I've always had a good head for business, so I agreed, and he took me to look at a 6,000-square-foot mansion in Los Feliz. It harked back to Hollywood's Golden Age, built in 1914 and perched on a hill next to a wacky-looking Frank Lloyd Wright house that looked like a Mayan temple with jaws. It was a two-story dwelling with classical revival architecture and a view of Los Angeles. It dripped movie-star quality. It was the kind of place you see in *Architectural Digest.* It had a large, beautiful foyer, two master suites, four additional bathrooms, four fireplaces, three offices, and a gorgeous designer pool. My Realtor friend advised me to buy it. He thought it was massively undervalued. He needn't have bothered with the sales pitch. I'd fallen in love with it at first sight, before I'd even set foot inside the front door.

This was the house of my dreams, and for the first time in my life I could afford it. I'd landed a job as the voice of Jaguar cars and was getting paid handsomely to go into a sound booth a few times a week and put on a phony British accent.

I sold my old house to David Boreanaz, the actor from *Buffy the Vampire Slayer* and *Bones,* and moved into my Hollywood dream home.

Los Feliz is a very artsy community, so I settled right in. So did my boyfriend Taylor, who moved in with me and immediately lost his job. Unable to pay anything toward his upkeep, he started doing jobs around the house. This was okay at first—he did his best—but somehow the situation seemed to drain the blood from our relationship. I didn't like the idea of supporting a man. He was turning out to be a bad influence on me when it came to drinking, as well. He was much younger than I, and when we'd go toe to toe at clubs and parties I'd always come off much worse the next morning.

When it became clear that Taylor wasn't making any effort to find work I decided that I wasn't going to keep on supporting his new career as a houseboy and drinking buddy, so I sent him on his way.

I didn't need a partner, my face was fixed, I had the house of my dreams, and I'd put my darkness behind me. The monster's power play had failed, and she had been kicked out of the driver's seat, demoted back to passenger status. What I didn't realize was that the monster was in it for the long haul. She hadn't disappeared, only retreated as a tactical gambit. She'd given up the battle with the idea of winning the war. The incident with Lucy had nearly sent me so far under that I hadn't been able to surface in time, but the good news about my facial reconstruction had been like a life preserver, allowing me to pull myself back up to the surface. But now, with every single sip, neurological pathways were beginning to form, and before long those pathways would become an eight-lane expressway. Alcohol addiction is a learned behavior, and the lesson I'd learned was to turn to the bottle when things got tough.

And so the monster sat, and she waited and watched. She waited for another dark wave, one that would wash over me and send me so far under that I'd never be able to get back up for air in time. She'd be waiting for me, down in the darkness, when my strength ran out.

The monster knew me better than I knew myself. She saw the extreme ebb and flow of my life, the pattern formed by my genetics and my circumstances and my personal choices. She knew she wouldn't have to wait long.

11

WHITE BUFFALO MEDICINE

THE WHITE BUFFALO was a script I'd written in 1996. My career was then on the rise with *Babylon 5*, and I was creatively charged. One night I'd read an article about Miracle, the first white buffalo to be born since 1933. When I went to bed, I had very vivid dreams and woke up at 2 a.m. with the whole story worked out in my mind. I'd never written a script before, but I'd worked on them from the other side of the fence for so long that I had some sense of storytelling and knew how to format the thing to make it look right. Inspired, I wrote the story out in under a week in short, intense bursts.

The Lakota have a legend about the White Buffalo Calf Woman. To them, she is a prophet or even a messiah. And they believe that when a white buffalo is born, it's strong medicine—a sign from Mother Earth and the universe that things will change, that powerful magic is in the air.

And by 2002, that's exactly what I needed. On some level I

could sense that I was walking a tightrope. Beneath me was my monster, constantly probing me for weaknesses and calling out for me to slip. I was wary but not frightened, because I was going to keep putting one foot in front of the other until I reached the other side. Waiting there for me was *The White Buffalo*. I'd spent seven years working on it, tinkering with the script, schlepping it around trying to drum up interest, and all of a sudden it started gathering momentum. I could see it, just in front of me, beyond my reach but clearly visible—the story closest to my heart completely produced and projected onto a forty-foot screen.

It's a sweet family movie about a young boy whose parents get divorced. His father goes off with a new partner. His mother travels to India to "find herself," and dumps the kid on a ranch with an uncle he's never met. A white buffalo is born, and Native Americans from around the area gather at the ranch. They dance and pray and hang medicine bundles on the fence. The bank is about to foreclose on the ranch, and a conflict arises between the uncle, who wants to sell the buffalo; the kid, who forms a bond with it; the Indians, who want to claim it as a sacred symbol; and some Hollywood investors who want to turn it into a circus attraction.

The project was my baby. I'd been growing it for seven years, and now I knew the time was right. I was going to bring this thing into the world and make it live. *The White Buffalo* was hope, and it kept me moving forward and positive.

I showed the script to my Hollywood friends, and everyone who read it loved it. I was convinced that it would get made. I just needed backing of some kind to get the ball rolling. You know what they say, ask and ye shall receive. Well I did ask and the money came, but it was in a most disgusting and unexpected way.

I WAS doing this piece-of-shit movie called *Nightmare Boulevard* (also released as *Quiet Kill*), and I'm telling you, it was aptly titled. I was starring with Corbin Bernsen and Ron "Hellboy" Perlman, and the whole thing was financed by this sleazy-looking Chicago car dealer with hair plugs who'd decided he was an actor. I played Corbin's wife, and the story was that I'd become bored with him and started having an affair with my tennis coach, who was played by (surprise, surprise) the Chicago car dealer.

The nightmare began with the bedroom scene I was in with Mr. *L.A. Law.* I was wearing pajamas, and he was wearing boxers. It wasn't a sex scene—the movie didn't have any. We were just sitting up in bed while the crew set up the lighting, the budget being too tiny for anything as glamorous as stand-ins. Then, right out of the blue and in front of everyone, Corbin leans over and grabs one of my breasts and says, "Oh, they're real." Then he reaches under the sheets, into his boxers, and pulls out a hand covered in sticky, white goo and holds it up in front of my face.

"Oh my god!" I reeled back. I was in total shock.

He grinned and said, "See what us stars can get away with?"

So the guy with one of the world's biggest snow globe collections (yes, you read that right) turns out to be a total, masturbating misogynist.

I jumped out of bed, yelled at Corbin, then at the producers, and then I quit. The producers came running after me as I was leaving the set, my bags in hand. I gritted my teeth, readying myself for a fight. Honestly, what was there to say? There were thirty people on the set when it happened—they didn't have a leg to stand on. But it turned out they didn't want a fight.

"What do you want? Just name it. We want to make this up to you. We want to keep you on this movie."

It turned out that they were almost as mortified as I was about what had happened. They didn't want word getting around

about what had happened on their set. I've never had a producer offer me carte blanche before or since, so I didn't miss a
beat in replying.

"You're going to have to option my next film. It's called *The
White Buffalo*."

So I walked out of *Nightmare Boulevard* with a movie deal and
some up-front cash, and if you ever wanted proof that there's
such a thing as instant karma, Corbin Bernsen walked off the set
at the end of that day only to discover that his brand-new BMW
had been totally vandalized. The windows were smashed in, the
hood and side panels dented beyond repair. I was pleasantly
surprised. I guess stars can't get away with as much as they'd like
to think they can.

NOT LONG after that, my friend Hilary Saltzman read the script
and decided to help produce the movie. I was set to direct it.
I'd written the male lead for Sam Elliott and then shown it to
Bruce Boxleitner, who's a big fan of Westerns. We'd done table
readings and castings, we'd gone to the Disney ranch to scout
locations, and we had a crew. I was still on good terms with John
Flinn, my lover during *Babylon 5*, and he was going to be the
director of photography. Treat Williams had read the script and
liked it; it was underway.

Hilary was doing a great job. She even found somebody who
knew the Native American keeper of the white buffaloes. By that
time two more had been born, and these were very special. They
neither shed their coats nor changed color as they got older.
They were the real deal, and they'd been shipped to a secret
location in Santa Ynez so they wouldn't be killed. While the
white buffalo is a sacred symbol of hope to the Lakota, people

are people, and for a very few the white buffalo seems a form of medicine so powerful that they'd kill the animal to possess it.

What I'm going to tell you next really happened, I bullshit you not. If I had been alone I'd have had doubts, but there were three of us—myself, Hilary, and Alan, who was one of the other producers.

We drove to Santa Ynez and pulled up at a fenced-in pen. There was a partly Native American guy waiting for us. He had blue eyes and looked a little like Andy Kaufman, but with a braid of dark-brown hair that hung all the way down to his butt. Another guy sat by the back of the pen, a handsome Native American fellow with chiseled features and long hair. He was bare-chested and had brown, weathered skin and looked as if he'd stepped out of an old Edward Curtis photo. The handsome guy didn't say a word, he just sat there staring at us while the first guy, whose name was Phillip, brought out a long pipe.

"You've got to smoke this before you can see the buffalo."

So we all joined in this ritual. We stood in a circle and Phillip sang a prayer. It turned out that he was a Lakota traditional singer, and he started drumming and singing a high-pitched, wailing song that sent chills up my spine. Then we sat down and smoked some tobacco and sage from the sacred pipe, and I'm telling you right now that was all that was in the pipe, no hallucinogens or anything like that. When the ritual was done, the hot-looking guy pointed to the pen, and when we turned to look, the previously empty pen now had two white buffaloes walking around in it.

There was only one entrance to the pen, right next to us, and it hadn't been opened. There was no way someone could have let the animals in while we were doing the ritual. We were right there. There weren't any flashes or smoke or magic curtains. Then Phillip said, "I put a medicine spell on them, to keep them hidden. You smoked the pipe. Your medicine is good. You can see them now."

We were totally blown away. It was one of the most bizarre, mystical things that's ever happened to me. We received permission to film and photograph the buffaloes as reference for the CGI* white buffalo calf we were going to create. It was a huge thing, a great privilege, and we drove out of there feeling really good about the movie's prospects. I could feel that white-buffalo medicine working its healing magic. I'd almost made it to the end of the tightrope.

That magic took on an additional dimension when I struck up a romance with Phillip, the half-Indian guy, and found out that he was of the elk medicine. I knew that the elk had something to do with sexual energy, but I didn't understand the significance of that until we went to bed, and then, holy shit, did I get the whole elk thing!

We embarked on a very odd relationship. He was completely broke, never had more than a dollar to his name, but he'd do cleansing rituals at my house and stay there when I traveled. Eventually we stopped seeing each other, but things ended amicably, and we stayed good friends.

Another happy relationship, one more step forward, but I still wasn't back to my former strength. There were still dents in the armor from my previous relationships that hadn't been hammered out. They were the places the monster pressed on, but things were looking up.

The White Buffalo movie was rolling along beautifully. It was one of those projects that *wants* to come into the world. We had investors. We were going to do the whole thing for a million

---

* Computer-generated imagery, the technique used by filmmakers to produce lifelike digital animation.

bucks. Things were all lined up. Only a few more steps and I'd be clear—my life, my career, my emotional healing would be complete, and my life would move forward into a new phase of growth and prosperity.

And then there was Kenny.

I'D MET Kenny only once, very briefly, before the night my friend Hilary brought him to my house. He was a wannabe producer, which is a nice way of saying he was unemployed, and he was very interested in the projects I was working on. There was a sci-fi time-travel show in development called *Hourglass* that I was going to star in with Alexandra Tydings, who played Aphrodite on the TV series *Xena: Warrior Princess*. We were to play two scientists in neoprene catsuits who get sent into the past by accident and have historical adventures. Then there was a reality TV show, *Wild Cooking*, where people would be given twenty dollars to buy their own ingredients. They'd hike to a remote location, cook a meal in twenty minutes on a camping stove, and be judged by a famous L.A. restaurateur. And of course there was *The White Buffalo*.

That night we were drinking, and as the night wore on my tendency to make stupid decisions increased proportionally to the amount of red wine I imbibed, and that was a lot.

"Claudia, Kenny was going to stay with me, but I've got the kids, and it's a long way to Agoura Hills. Can he stay here? It'll only be for a few days."

"Sure, why not? I've got three spare bedrooms."

I invited Kenny to stay for two nights, and that turned into a week. He started talking about my film and TV projects as if he owned them, and I started hinting, fairly bluntly, that he should go and find his own place. He promised he would, but instead he'd spend every night drinking and cooking. He'd encourage me to join him, and at that time I didn't need to be asked twice to do either.

The conscious checks I'd put in place, those little reminders to keep an eye on my tendency to overconsume, were banished. I could control myself when I was alone, but now I had an enabler, someone who was actively tempting me on a daily basis. Within a week I found myself in bed with Kenny, things turned romantic, and without asking he decided that his guest status had been upgraded to that of live-in partner.

Kenny had dark hair and brown eyes. Sometimes he looked handsome, and sometimes he looked dorky. He's the kind of guy who doesn't feel embarrassed about shuffling around the house in novelty slippers and pajamas covered in cartoon moose. But Kenny was insidious, like a creeping vine. He knew exactly how to find the gaps in my armor and the old wounds that lay below it—he just had to keep me eating and drinking. He was an emotional eater, and I got hooked into his trip. I'm usually a salad-and-grilled-fish gal, but with Kenny my intake of red wine increased along with my diet of fatty foods. I was chowing down pizza and going halves on big plates of lasagna, which was totally unlike me.

Kenny wasn't a dark soul like Angus, but he was a user. He saw a way to live off me and help his career at the same time, and so he moved in, stretched out, and made himself at home.

I'm not saying I was without fault. It takes two to tango. If I'd met a healthy, successful, straightforward guy who drank lightly or not at all, I probably could have held off the disease for a few more years. But I didn't meet that guy. I believe you attract people at certain points in your life, that you send out signals letting people know what you want, and sometimes what you're looking for isn't a good thing. My monster was whispering in my ear, and it wanted to drink bad medicine.

∞

KENNY AND I went on holiday to Havana and spent New Year's Eve in a musty room at the Hotel Nacional de Cuba drinking champagne and making love. If the heroines of *Hourglass* had appeared suddenly in modern-day Cuba, you'd have forgiven them for thinking they were in the 1950s. The cars were rusted classics, men wore suits and hats, and no one had built anything new in fifty years.

We ate and drank and then drank some more. People opened up their homes so you could go in and have dinner, which was pretty wonderful. An older woman sang soulful songs while we ate yet another variation on chicken and beans. We went to Hemingway's favorite Havana bar, El Floridita. The daiquiris were mediocre, so we gave up on them and started downing cubanitos, a concoction of rum and tomato juice, and man, did they have a kick! At other times, when I'd consumed too much wine and passed out, I'd wake up at 2 a.m., after the alcohol wore off and the sugar kicked in, but spirits, and those cubanitos in particular, knocked me right out.

Even at that early stage in our relationship Kenny didn't want to let me out of his sight or do anything on his own. At first I thought his need to be near me all the time was sweet, but by the end of that trip I felt slightly claustrophobic around him.

I came out of that holiday with love handles that had their own zip code and a roll of fat hanging over my jeans. I had Holly book me into a convention straight away. I had to get some distance from Kenny, not just personally but also professionally. He hadn't just elbowed his way into my life; by then he was also trying to take over any of my projects that looked like they might be going somewhere, especially *The White Buffalo.*

Kenny's producing background meant that he could calculate budgets and that seemed reasonable (when you're pitching a show it helps a lot if you've got budgets drawn up), but that benefit came with a much greater liability—Kenny himself.

This was in the day when cell phones had a walkie-talkie feature that could be used by two people in the same vicinity—someone could start talking to you without having to place a call. It got to the point where Kenny was buzzing me every five minutes. It was like having Jim Carrey's character from *The Cable Guy* in your life—it was driving me crazy. I'd be driving along and I'd hear his voice coming through the phone.

"Hey, it's me. Are you there? Are you there? Hello? Hey, it's me? Answer the phone. I know you're there. Hello?"

Even worse, Kenny did the same thing to Hilary and Alan and to the movie's investors, and they didn't like being badgered, not at all. They called me and asked that Kenny stop bothering them. Instead of backing off, Kenny read this as the signal to pounce. He'd get in their faces, chewing them out like Jack Warner, except that Kenny didn't actually have any power or innate confidence, so he just ended up offending and annoying people.

As for me, I was in a kind of fugue state. I knew this guy was a walking disaster but the relationship and the bad habits it fed were keeping me from seeing the seriousness of the situation. I'd lost my enthusiasm and energy, and that made it hard to act decisively. Then I discovered that Kenny had been accessing my computer and reading my files. The mild claustrophobia that had started in Cuba was now all but suffocating me. Added to that, my drinking was getting to the point at which other people were starting to recognize that I had a problem.

⚭

HILARY AND I went out one night and had a couple of glasses of champagne. I never drink and drive. Even the thought of getting a ticket terrifies me, let alone getting into an accident, which is why I did most of my drinking at home. But this night I'd had a few glasses on an empty stomach before Hilary arrived, so my judgment wasn't what it should have been. I was driving, it was getting dark, and I missed a red light on Sunset Plaza Drive as people were trying to cross the street. I had to slam on the brakes fast to stop from plowing into them. We were thrown forward, but luckily had our seatbelts on. I pulled over. Hilary was visibly upset.

"You almost killed those people! What's wrong with you?"

I thought she was overreacting at the time. I don't think that now.

I had some conventions lined up in Europe, and they couldn't have come at a better time. I desperately needed space to gain some perspective on what was going wrong in my life.

⚭

BEFORE I left for Europe I'd managed to strike a deal with the Angola prison in Louisiana related to filming *The White Buffalo*. The prison maintains a buffalo herd, and was not only going to let us work with the prisoners who managed the buffaloes but also let us film, lodge, and eat there. By this stage we'd done storyboards, casting, and other preproduction. I'd found my lead boy, which was no easy feat, and I had two men willing to play the uncle. While I was in London I took some time to revise the script. You only have to look at the story and themes in that script to see my whole life laid out. On a deep level we know ourselves, know what's coming, what our life story is, the lessons we have to learn and relearn. It's nearly impossible to consciously recognize these things ahead of time, and yet they're so clear when we look back.

In the story, the boy's parents were alcoholics. In the opening scene the mother has this flask that she's swigging from and is trying it keep hidden from the kid while she's speeding without a seatbelt down the highway.

Right there is my sense of abandonment following my parents' divorce, my looming drinking problem, and my life starting to run away from me at high speed as I head into the unknown.

In a sense, the little boy was Patrick, as well, with his love of Native American culture. The white buffalo calf, as the center of the conflict, being claimed by different parties for their own purposes, was my soul hanging in the balance between light and dark.

If that sounds a little melodramatic it's because our inner lives are. We experience sweeping emotions, devastating disappointments, and ecstatic highs, but as we mature we learn to regulate the power of those experiences, to keep the sound of them muffled under a layer of manners and self-censorship. Those learned strategies allow us to deal with the complex range of interactions that life throws at us, but in our inner world these forces are still at work, driving us to courses of action, many of which we only consciously rationalize after the fact. In dreams and in art, as we create, our emotions and experiences resurface, and as we express them they make the drama in the average soap opera look about as exciting as eating cardboard.

The climax of the movie comes when the buffalo's fate is put in the boy's hands. I think that in a sense I was asking Patrick to help me find a way through my own inner conflict.

One night in London I went out to dinner at Hush with Roger Moore's kids Geoffrey and Deborah, who I knew through Hilary. When I was alone with Deborah she told me that she was worried about me, that Hilary told her I was on drugs. I was livid. It was highly unprofessional of Hilary to be spreading gossip about me, especially in an industry where reputation is so closely linked to livelihood. As far as I was concerned, you could call me a drunk—the truth is the truth. But I wouldn't stand for being called a drug addict. I considered that an unforgivable offense. That night I wrote in my diary:

Hello!? Why do people think I do drugs? I think when I drink too much, my personality changes. That must be it because I don't do coke anymore and I hate pot and have never popped a pill in my life!

I knew what had made up Hilary's mind—it was the night back in L.A. when I'd almost had the accident. She saw the state I was in and couldn't believe I was that fucked up just from alcohol.

I was highly defensive, and in the heat of the moment I told Deborah about some personal things that Hilary had said about her. I regretted that almost instantly, but the damage was done, and that led to something of a falling out between Hilary and me.

On the European convention trail I drank far too much—it was hard to say no with fans offering to buy—and found myself laid up in bed with a terrible case of flu. It occurred to me that my immune system was weakening. I was getting sick a lot more often than usual, but I put it down to stress, getting older, and my busy schedule. I still hadn't made the connection that my drinking was affecting my health. I felt fat. My arms looked like legs of lamb. Lying in bed, sick as a dog, I began to perceive my need for alcohol as something more than a kind of little devil, an irritating prick of a thing that sat on my shoulder and whispered in my ear. It was more as if I had my own internal Kenny. I felt it as a serious, ominous presence, but I still underestimated it. I hadn't stepped into the arena yet. I didn't have any sense of the monster I was really up against, but there were signs that I recognized. I had concerns. I started praying, something I hadn't done since I was a little girl.

"God, drinking is a waste of time and money. It's a waste of the talent I've been given, not to mention that it's keeping me fat. Please, help me get rid of the desire to drink. I've had enough."

I recovered from the flu and felt much better. What's more, I didn't give alcohol a second thought. Not long after that I was dining alone at the restaurant at the Balmoral Hotel when the maître d' asked me if I wanted to sit in the bar and have a drink or go straight to my table. I replied without a thought, "I don't drink." I was very pleased with myself and hoped my newfound temperance would find some staying power.

Heading home I felt empowered. Without alcohol the whole Kenny problem came into sharp focus. Was this the best I could do? Kenny? The thought that I'd be stuck with him forever terrified me. This guy was like a tumor. I was still upset about the business with Hilary but determined to set things right, to take charge of my life. Kenny had to go, and if he wouldn't leave on his own, then, just like a tumor, he'd have to be cut out.

WITHIN THREE days of returning to L.A. I was drinking again. Kenny didn't accept my decision to stop drinking or my insistence that we needed to go our separate ways, starting with my telling him to get the hell out of my house.

"You're overreacting. There's nothing wrong. Please, give me a chance. Let's talk this out."

And as he was talking he'd top off my glass. My steely resolve melted. He was my enabler. It was as if my internal monster were feeding him his lines, saying just the right things to take the edge off my words, giving Kenny room to turn things around and keep clinging on. Kenny figured he had a winning card, and he just kept on playing it, but I'd been in that place before, with Angus. I hit the point where I realized that if things continued, this guy was going to suffocate me and somehow I'd end up dead.

It came down to a scene in the kitchen with me on my knees crying and begging for him to get out of my life. He saw I meant it, that I was desperate and right on the edge of taking drastic action of some kind. So what did he do? He stole money that had been put into a neighborhood driveway fund and took my LeRoy Neiman painting of the Piazza del Popolo. He used it to decorate his new apartment, which was, I kid you not, exactly fifty feet from my back door. You could throw a stone at his front door from my house.

It was like *Fatal Attraction* with the sexes switched around. He even took some of the leftover paint I'd used on the walls of my house and painted his apartment the same color. And he ramped up the flood of phone and answering-machine messages to the point that I was getting more than fifty a day.

I was worried enough that I felt I had to take out a restraining order to keep him away from me. When I requested the order, the official took one look at my cell phone record and signed off on it straightaway.

◌⃝

A FEW weeks later I was due to fly to Louisiana, to meet with a woman associated with the prison and work out the details for shooting *The White Buffalo.* I boarded the plane in Los Angeles and found Kenny sitting in a seat a few rows behind mine. That's when I thought, "Holy shit, this guy is really stalking me." I was done with playing nice. Fear motivated me to find my strength, and I turned to the flight attendant and said, "I need you to remove that man; I have a restraining order against him, and he's not to be within a hundred feet of me."

Federal marshals boarded the flight and dragged Kenny out of there, and all of a sudden he wasn't so pushy and aggressive. When I got back from Louisiana I was seriously worried about what his next move would be, but it seemed that being dragged off the plane and held in custody had flipped a switch in Kenny's brain. He got the message that it was over and that he'd gone way past what could be considered normal behavior.

And then I got the bad news about the movie. Everyone had been doing their best to ignore Kenny and move forward, but by then he'd already done too much damage. The investors had decided to pull their money and put it into another project. And he didn't just capsize *The White Buffalo.* *Wild Cooking* and *Hourglass* fell off the table as well, even though we'd pitched *Hourglass* to *Highlander* producer Bill Panzer and he'd loved it.

So, though I was finally free of Kenny he had dragged my dreams down with him. My movie had gone the way of the buffalo. And if you want to know exactly what it was that I lost, allow me to share the very last scene with you: They set the white buffalo free with the rest of the herd on protected land. We see an aerial shot of this little speck of white in the brown sea of the brown herd; she's free, no longer a circus attraction. The white buffalo was Hope—hope that I'd move forward with my life toward a bright and happy future, that my career would take the next step forward and flourish.

My mom saw that clearly. To this day she still asks me when I'm going to make *The White Buffalo*. She's convinced that everything in the universe will align for me if I can just make that movie. And I still haven't given up. The White Buffalo Calf Woman is powerful medicine, and I believe that if the movie is meant to be, then a miracle will appear at the right time, like the birth of a white buffalo.

MY RELATIONSHIPS with Angus and Kenny were bad medicine in the conventional sense of the word as well as the spiritual, Indian one. Relationships like that can kill you, literally, if you can't break away from them in time. I couldn't see it at the time; it seems as though you can only ever see these things with the benefit of hindsight. But I'd heard the monster whispering, and on some level I knew the role Kenny would play in my life. The moment I allowed Kenny to overstay his welcome, I didn't just fall off the tightrope—I took Kenny's hand and stepped off, dropping willingly into the darkness below.

SO NOW I was alone, a chubby mess, and my drinking hadn't let up at all. I was stressed and exhausted. I'd thrown everything into trying to patch up the holes Kenny had made and keep the movie afloat, all to no avail. I'd put on ten or fifteen pounds, and when the auditions for on-camera parts suddenly dried up, friends and colleagues would talk to me as if I were a contestant on *The Biggest Loser* who needed to go on a starvation diet before their bones and organs failed under the weight of their own body mass. I didn't care that I wasn't landing any on-camera acting jobs, because my voiceover career was in full swing. I did computer games, animated movies, commercials, you name it. *The White Buffalo* might have been dead, but the checks kept rolling in, and that allowed me to bankroll my new creative passion—remodeling my house.

I lost myself in building a relationship with my house. I figured that was one partnership I could count on.

12

THE FALL OF BABYLON

I'VE MOVED MANY times in my life because I was always looking for home, a place that was a reflection of the best parts of me, and now I knew that I'd found it. I poured my heart and soul and almost every penny of income I generated into making the house match the idealized picture in my mind. It was my baby. I spared no expense. The place was a hive of busy men in overalls. I've always loved redoing homes. My mother is one of the most talented interior designers in the country, and both my brother and stepfather build luxury homes; it's a family passion.

At the same time that I was throwing every spare dollar into beautifying my home I was investing just as heavily in another project—working at drinking myself to death. Creation and destruction, birth and death, they're all part of the same cycle.

Cooking and entertaining always come first for me, so the kitchen was the number-one priority. In the mornings I'd counteract my hangover by drinking enough tea to drown an Englishman and then hit the granite shops to pick out materials. By the time I finished, my kitchen was incredible: massive marble bench tops, French-style cupboards finished in seafoam green (a four-layer process that involved painting and aging the wood), and two Sub-Zero refrigerators. I had Wolf ranges that ran along an entire wall with a custom Ann Sacks tile backsplash depicting an idyllic Italian country scene. You could feed a small army out of that kitchen.

My next greatest love, after cooking, is books. I had a two-story library built with hand-carved oak bookshelves. A double-length rail ladder allowed me to slide along the shelves to browse my thousands of volumes. I had brass plates made with the names of the subject categories engraved on them: History, Cooking, Religion, Fiction.

I was pretty fucking pleased with myself. I owned my own mansion, and I'd decked it out just the way I wanted.

Yet something was missing, one more thing that I couldn't quite put my finger on.

A wine cellar. You need a really big wine cellar.

The monster was speaking again and once more, it was making what seemed like pretty good sense.

You deserve it. You've worked hard to get where you are. You deserve to celebrate in style, and for that you'll need to fuel the amazing parties you're throwing.

Something kept me from indulging in that particular fantasy right away. I knew I was drinking more than usual, and it certainly wasn't like me to drink alone. Maybe a wine cellar wasn't the best idea. Instead I went shopping for tapestries, created outdoor rooms, and converted one of the extra bedrooms into a huge walk-in closet.

It might have been my dream house, but they say that in

dreams a house is a reflection of yourself, your body. I think that putting my house in order was subconsciously an attempt to save myself from the disease that was slowly creeping up on me. I was perfecting my external world while my interior one was steadily crumbling away. Also, throwing myself so completely into my renovation kept me from having to acknowledge my emerging drinking problem. It kept it just below the surface of my awareness.

191

And then my friend Trish's husband, Martin "Mutt" Cohen, asked me if I wanted to invest in wine futures. Mutt was a big-name music attorney. He handled groups like Chicago and Boyz II Men, and he was a wine aficionado and head of the L.A. division of the Confrérie de la Chaîne des Rôtisseurs, the world's oldest and largest food and wine society.

"Two thousand is going to be an excellent year. Buy them up and in ten years you can either drink them or sell them. Either way you'll come out a winner."

I was flush—another check had just arrived—and I thought that idea sounded just peachy. Mutt wrote me a list of every single French wine that I should buy: Château La Freynelle, Christian Moreau, Château Ducru Beaucaillou Saint Julien, Château Lafite Rothschild, all the best stuff. My bill was just under fourteen grand. A year later they arrived all at once. By then I'd already completed construction of my ultimate wine cellar, a shrine to Bacchus where I could accord my drinking the status it deserved. Somewhere in the darkness my monster was smiling and sharpening her claws.

∞

MY 720-SQUARE-FOOT basement conversion merited an article in the *Los Angeles Times* entitled "Den of Festivity." I hired my friend Michael Weiss, a highly skilled carpenter who builds sets and props for movies and TV shows, to do the work. He was one of the McStaggers, a group of my friends named for their love of drinking and partying. We used to have medieval parties, dressed in period costume. Michael was known as Haggis McStagger. They called me, quite undeservedly, Trouble McStagger. Michael quickly got carried away and didn't have a hard time convincing me to transform the basement into something spectacular—a party room that looked like a castle dungeon. Michael's design even dedicated a wall for the display of the cutlery collection that I'd been building since my father gave me that jackknife—it now included knives, swords, and daggers, which added to the medieval ambience. The wine cellar had a sealed, self-closing door and storage capacity of 2,000 bottles.

When the journalist for the *Los Angeles Times* asked Michael why a house with a single resident needed the space of an average-sized house set aside for wine and its consumption, Michael replied, "Claudia entertains a lot. I'd come back with 20 to 30 cases [of wine], and a few weeks later it would be gone."

Sure, I partied a lot, just not always with other people. I was falling headfirst into alcoholism. On some level I knew that, but at least, as I consoled myself, I was doing it in style. And I reassured myself that I had it under control. If I had to, I could stay sober for up to six months, and then I'd make up for it by drinking solidly for two weeks.

The dungeon was furnished with benches and lamps of medieval style and a bed in a Moroccan motif that Michael built. The bed was eight feet by ten and stood in an alcove—a nice place for guests to enjoy a private *tête-à-tête* (or more).

Alexandra Tydings, a newly appointed McStagger, added the final touch—a sign that read, "Welcome to the Dungeon."

The dungeon was a hit, and I threw some of the best parties I've ever attended in my life. We could easily fit twenty people down there at a time, and keeping the wine cellar stocked required constant vigilance. I was drowning in wine, but no one touched my French futures. I had them tucked away, off limits. They were an investment, they were young, and they were the *crème de la crème* of my collection.

I spent considerable amounts of time and money constructing my own underground temple to addiction, a shrine to the disease that was eating away at me. What can I say? Like all the pleasures of the netherworld, it seemed like a good idea at the time. We even had a sex swing that a friend bought. I never used it. I didn't like the idea of the woman sitting there doing nothing while the guy spun her around or pushed her like a child at a playground, but I let it hang there. Somehow it seemed to fit the atmosphere.

AROUND THIS time, I landed the ultimate voiceover job—a character in a Disney movie. I played Helga, the sexy villainess in *Atlantis: The Lost Empire*, a film that also starred Michael J. Fox, James Garner, and Leonard Nimoy. It was a departure from the Disney musical movies that were popular at the time. It was darker, aimed at an older audience, and was more story-driven. They even got Mike Mignola, creator of the *Hellboy* comics, to consult on the production sketches.

I was so excited! I was going to be a Happy Meal toy. *Babylon 5* was great, but you know you've made it when you can buy an action figure of yourself with a hamburger, fries, and a Coke.

I recorded my part in the studio where they made *Snow White and the Seven Dwarfs* and shared a recording booth with Demi Moore, who was working on *The Hunchback of Notre Dame II.*

Atlantis was a blast. And because I had a great job, I was happy and the drinking stopped. I sobered up and began to feel like my old, confident self. I can say now, with the 20/20 vision that hindsight gives us all, that if I had been working on a regular series back then my alcohol addiction would have been postponed. I'm not saying it wouldn't have caught up with me eventually. You can't escape genetics, and my brother Jimmy and I share a bad gene, no doubt about it. But when I'm working fourteen hours a day, I come home happy and exhausted, go to bed, get up, and go back to work. There's no time to drink, no idle mind for the devil to work with.

But the problem with animated films is that there's a lot of time between studio sessions. Between movies I'd do my Jaguar spots, but they were only a few hours a week, if that.

When I walked out of the Disney studio at the end of *Atlantis* I cried all the way home. I'd loved working with the team at Disney. I wasn't used to all the positive feedback I received there. That rarely happens when you're working as a live-action actress. Occasionally, if you do something extraordinary, the crew responds with spontaneous applause, but those moments are few and far between. Directors rarely give you anything, but these Disney guys laughed and encouraged me. They wrote extra dialogue, asked me to do multiple takes simply to amuse them, and I ate it up. I felt needed and talented and funny and all of those things that fed my soul.

"Yeah, that's great! Go bigger, go broader! Sexier!"

That enthusiasm buoyed me up. It helped keep me afloat. *Atlantis* gave me a reason not to drink.

AND THEN my career—just like the mythical Atlantis—vanished overnight. One minute it was there, the next minute it had sunk to the bottom of the ocean. I lost the Jaguar account—they decided that the voice of Jaguar should be a man's. I'd done the one thing my parents had always told me not to: I'd spent my money, thinking that I'd always make more. I'd poured nearly every penny into my house. But of course the expenses don't go away. There was still the mortgage, the cost of keeping up a mansion, and I had responsibilities to the people who worked for me. I waited for the next job—it wouldn't be long coming— maybe my film career would pick up again or I'd land another juicy voiceover gig.

You're all washed up. Those Hollywood assholes don't want you anymore. But that's okay. I'm here for you. Say, I could slay a drink. Anything in the cupboard?

I was sick of waiting, so I took the monster's advice and relieved the mounting pressure with a Veuve Clicquot, a nice bottle I'd set aside for the party crowd. They'd stopped coming around, anyway. I felt less and less like partying with friends. I was doing fine on my own. I was short on money, short on friends, short on work, but at least I wasn't short of a good drink.

More time passed, and I began to get desperate. My fan base was still strong, so I started selling my underwear on eBay with a little three-by-five card with a lipstick kiss on it. As pathetic as I felt while shipping them out to their respective buyers, they did sell well—but not well enough to pay my mortgage. So I sold the copies of film and TV scripts I'd saved, memorabilia, artwork, and eventually jewelry and antiques. I sold everything I could sell, short of myself, to save my house. The whole situation was ridiculous, because I only owed half a million on a house worth more than four times that. I only needed one job to hang on to it. One paid job would lead to another, and the ball would start rolling again. I put out the word that I needed a gig, tried to call in old favors, sent out head shots to producers and directors I'd worked with before. The phone was as silent as the grave.

Staring at the phone, drink in hand, it dawned on me that

I now spent so much time drinking that it had pretty much become my new career. The realization that I'd gone pro hit home, hand-in-hand with the acceptance that I was an alcoholic.

Before that, I was aware that I'd go on binges, but I'd rationalized to myself, quite convincingly, that they were just reactions to emotional triggers. My mom had remarried, and both she and her new husband used to get on my case about my drinking. They knew that there was something going on. My mom's father had been a drinker, and she could smell a lie a mile off. She offered to pay for me to go to therapy. I think she was desperate to find a reason for my behavior. No one imagined that it could be a physical disease. Everyone just thought I was being indulgent and self-destructive. I figured that therapy was worth a shot. There was no doubt that I was carrying around a mountain of unresolved shit.

A dear friend recommended a good therapist, and I started seeing her three to four times a week at $200 a pop. I really wanted to fix myself; I was committed. And talking through that stuff with someone who can see the problem with fresh eyes and opinions really does help. Gaining self-awareness and new perspective on your motivations and weaknesses is always good, but it didn't do a damn thing to fix the physical compulsion that would overcome me when I'd go too long without a drink. Eventually I gave it up. I was tired of talking about being unemployed and my rape experience. The real world was hammering down my door. I needed to concentrate all my efforts on hanging on to my house, along with the sizable emotional and financial investment I'd poured into it.

I couldn't control my compulsion; I acknowledged that. Internally I was out of control, but at least, I reasoned, I had a home. Not a house, a home. My home. I was in control of that, of my immediate physical surroundings. The house was my anchor. I knew that I'd be lost without it.

Eventually I got down to my last salable asset. I'd even run out of my regular stash of party wine. The cellar was dry but for one last, untouchable holy relic—the French wine futures.

But I did the sensible thing; I called up Mutt's wine buddies. Some of them hadn't bought in time to secure the bottles they needed from the 2000 vintage, but I had all of them, every single one worth owning. I'd been storing them for three years by then, and I made them what I thought was a fair and reasonable offer, enough to keep me in my house for another three months. Their counteroffer was such an insulting low-ball figure that I told them to go fuck themselves. They knew I was desperate, and thought they'd try to take advantage of my situation.

The next morning I sat and waited for the phone to ring. After an hour I needed a drink. I walked down to my wine cellar.

I gave the sex swing a push as I walked past. It rocked back and forth like a hypnotist's watch. I sat on the edge of the Moroccan bed and watched it.

You know what would teach those assholes a lesson? If you drank every one of those fucking bottles. That'd show them.

I was a mess, and the monster was taking advantage of that. I could barely think straight. My career was my life. I'd sacrificed all my other dreams—motherhood, a long-term relationship, everything—to be a working actress. And now I'd fucked up. I had nothing but a house, which I was going to lose. And 180 bottles of young French wine.

I'd thought I was indestructible, unstoppable, and now the armor that I'd carefully crafted to protect myself had been ripped away. Imagine you're a turtle that has the shell ripped from its back. Then you're kicked upside down so that you're helpless and can't get back on your feet. You just lie there, waiting to die. That's how I felt.

I'd been sucker punched without even realizing I was in a fight. Alcoholism is a sneaky disease; it takes advantage of human weakness, creeps up on you bit by bit, and breaks down your defenses, so that by the time you realize you're in trouble you're already up against the ropes watching the knockout punch come hurtling toward you in slow motion. Only you can't get out of the way. You can only stand there and watch, knowing that there's going to be pain when you come to.

My career was sinking, and I was going down with it. I was dead broke. The house had to go.

So what? Are you going to sit here and suffer a slow and painful demise? Death by a thousand cuts? That's not the Claudia I know. You show those assholes. You teach them a lesson.

Fuck it, the monster was right.

I picked up a bottle of gold-labeled Cristal, ripped off the anti-UV cellophane wrapper, unwound the wire cage, and popped the cork. I always liked that sound. It was like the starter's pistol fired at the beginning of a race, the sound of something new and exciting. Champagne always made me happy. It had been with me through all the good times—maybe it could help pull me out of the bad times.

What the fuck . . . Why not?

The monster liked the sound of the cork popping, too. It had waited, and its patience was now rewarded. It was the time to celebrate. It had won. Checkmate. Game over.

I raised the bottle to my lips, took a swig, and, for the first but not last time in my life, drank champagne alone for breakfast.

Dick and Liz,
a.k.a. Angus and Claudia

With the lovely Michael York
during the filming of *The
Haunting of Hell House* in
Ireland

With director Richard Martin on the *Highlander* shoot. What a blast!

At my parents' home in Puerto Vallarta, Mexico, with Angus

LEFT: With Lucy before the face-
eating incident
BELOW: With Michael J. Fox, Cree
Summer, Don Hahn, John Mahoney,
Corey Burton, Florence Stanley, and
the creative team at the Hollywood
screening of Disney's *Atlantis*

201

Phillip, my
Lakota lover,
with the sacred
white buffalo
twins

PART

FOUR

ONE LITTLE PILL

13

(LAST) RESORT REHAB

*D*RINKING THOSE YOUNG wines is like raping a virgin! It's a crime against humanity!"

That's what Mutt Cohen said when he found out I'd polished off the entire 2000 vintage he'd sourced for me. It was inconceivable to him. He rubbed his eyes as if he'd suddenly been hit with a migraine from hell.

It took me almost a year to finish them off, and what a year it was! At its end, I was down to nothing but liquor and cooking wine!

⌘

I'D CONSUMED enough of those French wines at my Casa de Claudia parties that people believed my cover story—that I'd drunk them out of spite with my friends because no one would give me a fair price. And like all good lies it was partly true. But

I kept some parties in the dungeon private. Invitation only, just one name on the guest list. I fooled everyone. Except my mom. When she senses I'm hiding something, she's like a German shepherd. She doesn't stop until she's sniffed out the lie and worked me into a corner.

"How did your party go last night, Claudia? Oh, you didn't have a party? But you must have had one this week? No?"

Next thing I knew she was standing at my front door, cell phone in hand, recycling bin beside her, its lid flipped back to reveal a full load of bottles, clusters of glass necks and bottoms sticking out at every angle—my collection of shame.

But the monster was my partner in crime now, and she thinks fast.

"What? My gardener forgets to wheel the bin out for three weeks, and suddenly I'm a drunk? If anyone has the right to be indignant it's me. What are you doing going through my trash?"

I invited her inside to make up. I had to keep her sweet, because I was flat broke and she was lending me money to help me hobble along with my mortgage. I managed to keep the house a little longer by convincing my mom that more work would come, but she was always badgering me about whether I had a job. I knew her charity couldn't last much longer.

We had some tea. I was conciliatory. I told her that I understood how she could have made the mistake, but I'd appreciate it if she could keep her paranoid musings to herself.

She let the matter drop, but I knew it was a close call. After that I started hiding my empties inside a cabinet-model Victrola that movie photographer Robert Zuckerman had given me for my birthday. I used to play 1920s His Master's Voice records on it, while inside its belly it kept Its Mistress's Secrets. But secrets have a way of creeping to the surface. One day while my assistant

Holly was helping me choose the last of my personal belongings to sell, she caught sight of the Victrola.

"What about this old thing?" she asked. "Any special reason you want to keep it?"

She tilted it to test its weight, and her question was answered by a muffled orchestra of teetering glass.

I came clean about my drinking problem; Holly was so understanding. She agreed to help me and, for starters, bought a latch and big brass lock for the cellar door, which she proceeded to secure with military efficiency. She locked it down and took the key with her. The next day, after finishing a bottle of cooking sherry that I'd tucked away in the kitchen cupboard, I had a great idea.

What the fuck am I doing drinking cooking sherry? Is this where I am now? Maybe I should go sit on the sidewalk and drink out of a paper bag. Maybe I should drink proper wine like normal people, or not drink at all. Right. I don't have any money, and I can't get into my cellar, so the only option is to just stop drinking.

I was glad that Holly had agreed to help me. This was progress. As Sun Tzu says, know yourself and know your enemy and in a thousand battles you'll never be defeated.

Ten minutes later I was standing in my dungeon drinking a Château Lafite Rothschild straight out of the bottle, crowbar in hand, the brass lock hanging from a splintered door. There's always another option.

My normal morning started with dry heaves. The previous night's wine was no longer in my stomach, but my body kept trying to cast it out, and like a bad exorcist it failed every time. I'd be left exhausted, my muscles aching from the effort.

I was still getting offers for small roles in movies that my friends were making. There was never any real money on the table, but I took the jobs anyway, because I needed to keep busy and I needed to put on a good show to ensure my mom's continued investment in my life.

I knew she had the money. She'd married a multimillionaire and continued to earn her own income as an interior decorator. My mother is an impossibly generous woman. She's always helped her children out, but this time I was taking enormous advantage of her. I'd told her my mortgage payments were slightly higher than they actually were—to make sure I had enough money to drink on. Don't get me wrong; I was working hard to stay sober between binges. I just never wanted to be caught dry. That was an unthinkable possibility.

And I expanded the development of my detox schedule. I'd have scheduled binges, orderly hangovers, and well-planned detoxes, arriving on set or at auditions disguised as my alter ego: happy, funny Claudia. It must be the German in me; I had the whole routine down to stopwatch precision. I was a highly functioning alcoholic, killing myself with utmost efficiency.

A binge would last anywhere from one to three days, and it would usually take me up to a week to recover.

By the time I'd finished off the last of the French collection (and nearly finished myself in the process) I was starting to behave erratically. I'd usually crave alcohol when I was PMS-ing, and when I satisfied the urge it supercharged my emotional irritability.

That's when the monster came a-knockin', and she had another great idea.

You're very touchy of late, and your mom's becoming suspicious. You need to ramp things up to make sure she keeps helping us. Now's not the time for little lies—they're the ones that catch you out. You need to drop the A-bomb, a nice big lie that'll keep the wheels turning for a long time.

I rang up my mom in tears. Through heartbroken sobs I told her I'd had a bad pap smear. What's more, I could never have children. Even worse, they were going to have to perform some kind of operation on me to cut out the cancer. The other end of the phone was silent for several seconds and then a flood of pity and emotional sympathy followed. Mission accomplished.

I was so fucking clever. That's the addict's brain at work. It convinces you that you're not out of control, that your insane decisions are perfectly logical. It's not a big-picture state of mind. You're so busy covering all the angles, looking after all the little details, that you have no perspective, no idea of just how strange you seem to the people who love you.

It took my mom all of twenty minutes to penetrate my carefully constructed fortress of deception. I forgot she knew that my friend Trish and I shared the same gynecologist. She called Trish, asked for my doctor's number, and got him on the phone. The doctor said he couldn't share any patient information, but my mom countered with a whole "I'm so worried about my daughter, she won't talk to me, I think she might be dying" routine, which led to the doctor basically implying that I was fine.

She appeared on my doorstep like an angry Valkyrie; the "for sale" sign went up in my yard the following week.

I figured this was it, that I'd finally hit rock bottom. I'd been found out, my mom knew that I was a fucked-up drunk, and I knew that after that stunt she'd never completely trust me again. One part humiliation, two parts mortification, one part depression—the Stone Cold Sober cocktail. It was time to clean up my act. I wasn't going to add alcohol to that emotional mixed drink. I needed change. Now I couldn't *wait* for the house to sell—it had come to feel like a giant coffin.

To help pass the time, I'd fill out alcohol tests in the backs of magazines and read up on alcohol addiction. Sun Tzu was right; I knew myself but not the enemy, and that wouldn't win me jack shit. For instance . . .

DEAR ABBY ALCOHOLIC TEST

Do you wonder if you're an alcoholic? Try answering the following questions. If you answer positively to more than three, consider seeking professional advice.

1. *Have you ever decided to stop drinking for a week or so, but lasted only a couple of days?*

A: Never. I'm five days into a week of sobriety right now. Wait. Does drinking after 5 p.m. count?

2. *Do you wish people would stop nagging you about your drinking?*

A: No one is nagging me. (They just gossip behind my back.)

3. *Have you ever switched from one kind of drink to another hoping that would keep you from getting drunk?*

A: Nope, I'm a wino, period.

4. *Have you had a drink in the morning during the past year?*

A: Does a mimosa with friends count? Then yes.

5. *Do you envy people who can drink without getting into trouble?*

A: Not really (those bastards!).

6. *Have you had problems connected with drinking during the past year?*

A: Does sleeping with strangers and passing out at 8 p.m. count as a problem?

7. *Has your drinking caused you trouble at home?*

A: Nope, I live alone.

8. *Do you ever try to get extra drinks at a party because you did not get enough to drink?*

A: I'm usually the one throwing the party, so I can drink as much as I want.

9. *Do you tell yourself you can stop drinking any time you want, even though you keep getting drunk?*

A: I don't really get drunk, just happy . . . a lot.

10. *Have you missed days at work because of the drinking?*

A: What work? I'm an actress!

Interlibrary Loan (ILL) Instructions

- If returning ILL on or before January 11, 2019, please return the book to the Costa Mesa/Donald Dungan Library reference desk.

- If returning ILL after January 11, 2019, please return the book to the Costa Mesa/Mesa Verde Library service desk during open library hours, 2969 Mesa Verde Drive, 714-546-5274.

- Request renewals 2-3 days before the due date. Renewals are not always granted.

- If requesting renewal on or before January 11th, please call the Costa Mesa/Donald Dungan Library reference desk, 949-646-8845.

- If requesting renewal after January 11th, please call the Costa Mesa/ Mesa Verde Library, 714-546-5274, service desk.

www.ocpl.org

11. *Do you have blackouts?*

A: Not that I can recall . . .

12. *Have you ever felt that your life would be better if you did not drink?*

A: Yes. I would be thinner.

13. *Have you ever embarrassed yourself or someone else when drinking?*

A: Possibly. Probably. Alright already—yes!

14. *Do you drink every day?*

A: Nearly. Mostly. Always.

Then at the bottom of the page I'd write things to crack myself up, like: "FUCK! THAT WAS EXHAUSTING. I NEED A DRINK!"

I was still running from myself and the reality of my disease. On the set of *Babylon 5* we played practical jokes on each other all the time. Now I was becoming a big joke and I couldn't even see it. I wasn't working, but if an idle mind is the devil's workshop, then I was at least keeping someone well occupied. When I was working fourteen-hour days on a TV series I never thought about drinking, and when I got home I'd never drink because I was too busy learning my lines for the next day. Now I had oceans of time filled with tiny islands of distraction, but those were slowly sinking as even the freebie jobs started drying up. I reached out for the bottle again, despite my promises to myself. I was too far gone to just stop.

I was sick of the Hollywood youth game, sick of the superficiality of the whole industry, and yet I found that I couldn't wander too far from the phone. It was like some kind of underworld torture—chained to a stool beside an eternally silent phone, wine glass in hand, waiting for it to ring. That fucking phone was cursed. Each day it refused to ring, I'd feel that I was aging a year, slowly transforming into a crone. If only the phone would ring, the curse would be broken.

And then one day it did. It was computer animation studio boss Andrew Dymond, who I'd met a few years before at a convention in London. I was telling him my tales of woe (but not of drunkenness) when he said to me, "Well, I'm putting together a really low-budget sci-fi comedy over here. How would you like to come over and star in it?"

I was stunned, so overwhelmed with happiness that for a moment I was speechless. I think Andrew took my silence as lack of interest.

"Look, before you say anything, let me tell you the name of the character—Belinda Blowhard."

Brilliant. I told him that if he could get me SAG scale there was a good chance I'd be interested. Inside I was the dazzled heroine of a bad romantic comedy proclaiming, "Yes, yes, a thousand times yes!"

This was just the change I needed: A new country, a new starring role, a new sci-fi series, and comedy to boot! This was saving grace in action. With change comes hope.

∞

I ARRANGED to rent out my house short-term while my step father kept trying to make a sale. I was happy to let him manage it. After struggling to keep the house for so long, the finality of losing it was all too depressing, and I didn't want to risk doing anything that might jeopardize my new job.

Unfortunately, the carefully executed system of binge-suffer-detox was not working as efficiently as it once had. I needed to sober up, but first I needed one last round of drinks before the bar closed. By then I only had bottles of cheap sherry and vodka in the cupboard. I could walk clear of the fallout of a wine binge within a week, but a binge on vodka was akin to a death sentence. Yet there was nothing else to drink, so I figured I'd dice with death and keep my fingers crossed. I crashed and burned big-time, and as I sat on my tiled kitchen floor, wasted and leaning up against my seafoam-green cupboards, I estimated that it would take me at least two to three weeks to pull clear of the vodka aftershock.

And then I remembered that I was due to visit my mom in Napa. I had already booked the flight.

You have to go. She'll become suspicious if you pull out at the last minute. You can pull it off. Have another drink. That's the world's best hangover cure.

Shit! Mom was having a ladies' luncheon and had made a big deal about my attending. Forget the silent phone—that was lightweight torment. Sitting through a rich women's tea party while detoxing, that was a fate express-shipped straight from the deepest pits of the inferno right to my door.

But the monster was right. I couldn't risk losing her support, not this close to starting my new life. I needed my mom to help prop me up until I could stand on my own again.

There was still a glass of vodka left in one of the bottles. I threw it down my throat and felt better at once. My nerves steadied; I could do it. That was it, my last drink. I was going to dry out. I'd white-knuckled it before and I could do it again. The women's tea party was a bullet that I meant to dodge.

I couldn't fuck up this visit at my mom's, not after the last one. That had been a disaster of epic proportions.

⚭

ON THAT occasion I thought I'd gone in prepared. I knew I was prone to drinking at my parents' house. Family gatherings are always hot-buttons for me, so to avoid the awkward conversation when they noticed their booze slipping away at an alarming rate I supplemented my consumption with vodka that I'd smuggled in concealed in water bottles. I've never really liked hard liquor, but I needed something to numb me out.

My mom has given me a tremendous amount of love and support over the years, and yet she can be a very judgmental person. I'm no pushover, but all it took was one comment from her about my weight or my career to send me running for the bottle. I never felt that I was good enough in her eyes. I wasn't thin enough or pretty enough or with the right guy or rich or famous enough. She wanted her children to be perfect physical specimens with perfect jobs, complete with perfect little families of their own. I guess it was a kind of German-clockwork fantasy, efficient little dolls popping out of the right window at the right time to hit the right bell, everything running smoothly. Add to that my sensitive nature and there was very little anyone could say that was critical without triggering me to drink.

We'd been sitting around the dinner table, my mom, my step-dad, and his son. I was slicing up my lamb chop, happily munching away, when my stepbrother asked if it was any good. I picked up a piece and fed it to him with no sensual motive in mind; I just wanted him to try some. I felt a sudden, sharp pain in my ankle and turned to see my mom's narrowed eyes staring at me. She'd kicked me under the table.

"Stop that!"

I just smiled and kept on eating but inside the monster had been awakened and was already formulating what it considered an appropriate revenge. When we all went to bed I went and knocked on my stepbrother's door, and I seduced him.

He was my stepfather's adult adopted son, so there were no blood ties, and I didn't break any laws, but just the same, it showed just how poor my judgment was. It turned out that he was an alcoholic, too, so we understood each other just fine. We combined our hidden stash of booze and partied on into the wee hours of the morning.

In the morning, after the shit storm had passed, I realized that I had an ear infection, which ruled out flying back to L.A. I was already legally deaf in one ear from an infection I had when I was a kid, so I was terrified of damaging my hearing even more.

My stepbrother offered to drive me to L.A., but my mom and stepdad commanded him to stay put and told me to get on the plane. Now it was his turn to stage a revolt.

"Screw this. I'm driving Claudia."

He was living in their guesthouse, and they were employing him to landscape their garden.

"If you're not here for work tomorrow then don't bother coming back."

He took me to L.A., and in doing so lost his job and accommodations. I felt guilty and invited him to stay with me. I understood where my stepdad was coming from. He was convinced I was on drugs and was just trying to save his son from getting involved with me.

So alcoholic stepbrother moved in, along with his wart-nosed mongrel called Pepsi. The party continued (stepbrother had some money set aside). I've never hated an animal in my life, not even Lucy, who tried to eat my face for lunch, but for the one exception of Pepsi. Whenever I'd go out she'd shit on my floor and chew my furniture. A collection of valuable Native American antiques that I'd been planning to sell ended up as Pepsi chew toys. Maybe she was the jealous type?

In a bout of sobriety I saw the stupidity of it, the rift this situation was opening up between my mother and me. Her marriage was under stress as long as it continued. So I told stepbrother the party was over and sent him and Pepsi on their way. He went back to doing what he did best—growing medicinal pot.

$$\infty$$

ON THE next visit to my mom's house I was determined not to fuck up again. I was a rock. I was on the goddamn stairway to teetotaler's heaven.

And now it's four o'clock on the morning after the tea party, and my mom's there for me again. She stands over me as I hang over a toilet bowl in her house, riding the last wave of a protracted vomiting fit.

The bullet I'd hoped to dodge had hit me right between the eyes. I drank a whole lot one night after an argument with my stepdad, and the next morning I was really sick. I decided to put myself on a forced detox, hoping I would snap out of it, but instead my body went into shock from the sudden alcohol deprivation. The upside was that I missed the tea party; the downside was that I suffered one of the toughest detoxes of my life. I hadn't realized just how badly I'd poisoned myself. I lost motor functions and part of my vision. I didn't know that by stopping cold turkey I was damaging both my body and my brain.

My mom didn't understand just how bad it was for me. "Can't you clean yourself up? Take a shower and come down to the party. It will do you good to talk to people."

"You've got to be kidding me."

"So, you're not coming down to the party then?"

When the party was over, my mother returned to my side and watched me throw up bile. She was angry and confused, tears in her eyes. I was shaking like a leaf, hallucinating and crying. Shame and guilt aplenty, there was no shred of dignity to try to recover. I couldn't even stand up; I was stuck on all fours like a baby.

"Claudia, I've had enough. I called Holly. She's flying up, and we're taking you to rehab. I've booked you in."

I looked up from the bowl, clinging to it so I wouldn't fall in. I had no fight left in me, no tricks up my sleeve. I could only manage one word: "Okay."

It was that easy. I was desperate.

My mom went back to bed. I doubt she slept a wink. When the fit passed I managed to get up and limp down to the kitchen. You can't sleep when you're detoxing. You're a human ant farm, busy little critters rushing around your body and mind driving you slowly crazy until you have to drink to make them stop.

I found an unfinished bottle of decent champagne and grabbed some chilled orange juice from the fridge. This would be my last drink. Seriously. The last one. So it might as well be a good one. I needed the drink to steady my nerves. I was determined that if I had to go into rehab, then I was going to drive myself, and I would drive myself out as well—out to the airport and off to my new job in merry England.

I mixed a killer mimosa and looked out the window at the view of my parents' vineyards as I waited for the dawn. And I prayed. I prayed that God would heal me, that this really would be my last drink, that I could be set free from the cycle that was destroying not only me but my family.

∞

THE DRIVE to the treatment center was a silent one. Holly and my mom sat in the back seat. All my energy was focused on shutting out the voice in my head telling me to turn the car around. Holly tried making conversation with my mom, who'd started mumbling away, mostly to herself, trying to understand how I'd ended up like this.

217

"You're so beautiful, Claudia, so beautiful. Why do you want to do this to yourself?" And then she'd ask Holly, "Why doesn't someone just make Claudia stop drinking?"

She couldn't understand what I was going through. She thought I was weak. She thought that someone other than me might have been able to stop me. Holly didn't tell her about the splintered cellar door and the crowbar and the French wines.

I said nothing. I was preparing for my latest role as a rehab junkie. I already knew what a rehab center looked like. I'd starred in *Clean and Sober*. It would be grimy, with dusty old couches and smoke-filled rooms. There'd be a Morgan Freeman guy, the supervisor who comes down hard on you when you're tempted to relapse.

I was more than a little surprised when we pulled up to the swanky Bayside Marin rehabilitation center, a beautiful complex surrounded by majestic views. This was a far cry from the cell-block I'd been expecting.

I filled out the paperwork, peed into a cup, had blood drawn, and got a tour on the way to my private room. Someone asked me if I preferred tai chi or yoga in the morning before my organic whole-food breakfast. Fuck. I realized that, far from a place of last resort, this was in fact a resort.

"Mom, how much is this place costing?"

"Thirty thousand dollars, so you'd better get better."

I knew the tests would come back clean. I metabolize alcohol fast, and aside from the mimosa I hadn't had anything in my system for a few days. Perhaps Keith Richards and I share some DNA, I don't know, but my hunch was right. The tests came back clean, and I was pleased as punch to tell my mom to let my stepdad know that I was an alcoholic, plain and simple, that I wasn't on drugs, and that in future he could just shut the hell up when it came to making pronouncements about my health.

Sensible Claudia went in there with the best of intentions. I had a job. I'd always dreamed of living in London. This was a chance to fix things with my family, to prove myself to them, to get good and healthy again. I might even regain some semblance of sanity.

But the addict's brain is wily. It's got more tricks up its sleeves than MacGyver with a Swiss Army knife. Claudia's plan was perfectly sensible, but somewhere in the back of my mind the monster had been making preparations for a jailbreak from the Rikers Island of rehab centers. Now all we had to do was escape from a day spa. I was an actress, a pretty good one if I do say so myself. Mere mortals would fall before my batting eyelids and proclamations of sobriety. I had *played* addicts; these rehab guys wouldn't stand a chance.

I SET up in my room, which was decorated entirely with the same shade of orange they use at Burger King, then headed off to do my downward-facing dogs and breathing exercises with the yoga teacher.

We'd meet once a day for group therapy around a kitchen table, talk about our feelings, and then have our meals. There was no one-on-one therapy except for a one-time psychiatric evaluation when we first went in.

They should have screened educational movies. Some footage of black, bloated livers would probably have done me a world of good. At the very least they should have shown *Clean and Sober*. At least it had something to do with why we were there. Instead, they screened feel-good Disney teen movies.

The food was good, but they had a no-sugar policy, which created problems. You're a heroin addict, what the fuck do you care if someone slips you a Hershey bar? Sugar doesn't trigger addiction, or if it does then it's one of a thousand things that, taken to excess, can tip the scales in the wrong direction. Sex, eating, arguments, walking past a liquor store, being in a car accident, having a miscarriage, getting dumped, having a dog rip your face off, needing a cigarette, someone dying, moving house, and, if you really want to get finicky about the whole fucking thing, sure, eating a Hershey bar could do it, but it's at the bottom of a very long list, right above too many cups of coffee.

The people who came to speak to us had between five and twenty years of sobriety, and none of them believed in anything except the AA system. You had to accept that you were an addict for life, repent to God, and surrender. That was the only choice—abstinence and daily or weekly meetings for the rest of your life. I wondered how atheists got sober. Or what if you were a Hindu? Do their gods manage alcoholism?

The shitty thing was that one girl was a bulimic alcoholic, I was just your plain, garden-variety alcoholic, another was a heroin addict, and another was a crystal-meth addict. Beam me up, Scotty; it just made no sense.

The problems of a hard-core heroin addict are not the same as those of someone with an eating disorder or an alcoholic. Your problems are not their problems. A doctor wouldn't treat a cold, flu, and pneumonia all in the same way. The diseases might seem similar—they're all respiratory diseases—but distinguishing between them and treating each appropriately can make the difference between life and death. It seemed to me that the bulimics needed their own group, to talk about body issues or if they'd been sexually assaulted. They don't need to be hearing about the drinking problem of a thirty-eight-year-old actress with career anxiety.

There was an anorexic-alcoholic woman who kept weeping and saying, "I just want a pepperoncini martini at night. What's so wrong with that?" She must have weighed seventy pounds. She couldn't stop drinking, and that made her feel that she didn't deserve to eat. She had a handsome, healthy-looking husband who'd come and visit her on family days. He'd hold her frail body while she wept from a mixture of shame and withdrawal.

There was this one gal who clearly had once been a real beauty but now was missing teeth from crystal meth use. Her skin was as rough and pockmarked as a pineapple. She couldn't have been older than thirty-five but she looked fifty-five. One night she just climbed over the fence and walked to the nearest 7-Eleven. She came back from the other side with presents, her pockets loaded with candy, a sugar messiah reeking of beer and cigarettes.

I stashed my candy bars in my room along with some cookies I'd found hidden in the kitchen. If the sugar bug hit, then I was set. And if it turned out that rehab was more like prison than I thought, then I had a stash of currency at hand to buy whatever I needed.

Sometimes the lesser of two evils is a good thing. All human beings are addicts to their biology. If we don't eat and breathe we get into serious trouble. Sometimes it's a matter of choosing one addiction over another. Go to an AA meeting. There's no shortage of smoking, and everyone's eating copious amounts of sugar. Some of those guys are forty years sober.

The meth addict had a husband and kids who would come to visit, and my guess was that her $30,000 hadn't come as easily as mine. Addiction possesses you. It takes you over. She'd lost her identity as a mother and wife, and however much she wanted it back, she couldn't even stop herself from escaping rehab to get a smoke and a drink. How long would it be before she went back to the addictions she really craved?

After a few days, I felt great. They didn't have to give me Librium, Valium, or any of the other drugs used to cope with alcohol withdrawal, because I completed most of the detox on my own. I started looking better; after a few days I was back to my old self. I signed up to go to the gym, but since they didn't have one at the center they had to bus us to the nearest one, which was located next door to a liquor store. There's some clear thinking for you. Now and again someone would come in to see who was working out, but there was nothing to stop me from strolling next door when they weren't looking. I stood in front of the window and looked past the display of beer and spirits to the wine rack. I didn't go in. I thought of the face of that young woman, her teeth gone, her skin all messed up. Then I thought of my mom. She'd be able to tell if I'd reoffended, and I couldn't risk losing her again. Did I really want to be Irene from *Clean & Sober*?

It's easy for many alcoholics to resist temptation in the first weeks after going sober. That high can last anywhere up to three months, but then the brain starts to crave what it has been missing, and the trench warfare begins again. And each time you relapse it gets worse. The body can't go without its bad medicine. If I had been in rehab three months sober instead of three days, I'd have been the one sneaking back in, reeking of beer and cigarettes.

So I checked that the coast was clear, headed back to the treadmill, and stayed another week—a total of two in all—before I convinced myself that I was ready to leave.

Here's how that happened.

There was this smug psychiatrist who did a personal evaluation of me during the second week. First, she told me I was highly sensitive. No shit; a grown woman who cries when her mommy tells her to lose weight. You bet I was highly sensitive. Then she told me I was antisocial.

"Antisocial? You wouldn't say that if you'd been to one of my dinner parties."

"I think you're in denial about the seriousness of your disease."

"If I didn't think it was serious then why am I here?"

"I don't know. Why are you here?"

It was like waving a red flag at a bull.

"You're right. Maybe I shouldn't be here at all."

I walked out of there shaking my head.

You've gotta be fucking kidding me. Answering my questions with questions? That's the best she's got?

What does she know? She doesn't know you. You've just hit a bump in the road.

The monster was right. I'd hit a whole string of them: the men in my life, the house, Lucy, and, worst of all, my failed career.

Sure, it's been a bumpy ride, but now you're clean, you're sober. You've got a new job waiting. Why the fuck are you wasting your time in rehab?

And it didn't help that rehab was boring. Rehab was about to beat my New Year's Eve at Charlton Heston's house as the single most boring time of my life. Chuck put on a kilt and made his guests eat Scottish food while sitting through the three-and-a-half-hour uncut version of *Khartoum*. It takes a lot to beat that.

I set about manipulating the staff.

"I have to go to England and start a new life. I need to make calls and find a place to live and coordinate being on a TV series."

In no time at all I had my cell phone and computer access. Then I went into my counselor's office and sat down opposite him.

"Thanks for the two weeks. I feel terrific, but I think I'm done here."

"Why do you think that?"

More circular questions.

"Because I don't want to blow the chance to go to the UK and star in a series. It's not going to wait for me, and if I stay here and miss out then I definitely will start drinking again."

"Well, legally, we can't keep you here . . ."

"Oh. Fine. Well, if I'm not staying the whole thirty days I'd like to renegotiate the bill."

That was it. I was out of there.

I went home and started packing. It didn't matter that the monster kept pushing me toward the bottle. I didn't need a drink. I didn't need rehab. I was going to England, baby! Travel has always had that effect on me. I felt that if I could just get far enough away from my problems I'd be able to start fresh. No one knows you in a new country. The weight of expectation is gone. It's an appealing idea and, as I said before, as with all good lies there's some truth to it. But you can never escape yourself. You're always there, looking back at yourself in the mirror; and when you're dry the face you see there never looks quite right. It always looks like it could do with a good, stiff drink.

14

GOD SAVE BELINDA BLOWHARD

*M*OVING TO ENGLAND felt like something of a home-coming. I've always been an Anglophile; it has to do with leaving Connecticut—its landscape and historical buildings—at a young age to move into tract housing in California. I'd learned to thrive in the new world, but my heart always yearned for the trappings of the old, and in that sense England was a cornucopia of distractions.

I'd arrived just in time to experience London in spring. There wasn't a raincloud in the sky, and buildings that predated Columbus's discovery of America were a dime a dozen. The British Museum became my second home; I soaked in the beauty of the antiquities that England had looted from around the world when they had ruled so much of it.

Old things make me happy, and now I was living in the heart of one of the great old cities of the world. Good old Claudia was back. I'd left that broken, needy excuse for a Claudia back in the land of the free and the home of the brave, a place where I could be neither free nor brave. In England I was the master of my destiny, riding the wagon of sobriety, whip in hand, driving its horses onward to a new and more promising horizon.

It had occurred to me that the UK wasn't exactly the perfect country of choice for an alcoholic. After all, drinking is a national pastime. And I love pubs. I knew that was going to be an issue. I jokingly pondered moving to Saudi Arabia. It'd be much harder to get a drink, but, knowing me, I'd manage somehow and instead of getting stone cold sober I'd just end up getting stoned, literally.

So since the Middle East wasn't an option, and I sure as hell wasn't going back to my life in L.A., I decided that London would either make or break me. It was the battleground where the fight for the new Claudia would take place, and so far I was kicking ass and taking names. I was confident and filled with hope. I was so grateful to have another chance that minor temptations seemed like daisies in a field; I paid them no notice, flattening them as I passed.

After being so sick for so long, I knew it would take my body a long time to forget the experience. It's like being forced to chain-smoke cigarettes until you turn green and throw up. You don't want another cigarette. You don't even want to think about smoking. That's how it was with the monster and me. We'd broken up. She was like a persistent ex-lover who keeps on calling, wanting to get back together, but I wasn't taking her calls. As far as I was concerned we had nothing more to say to one another.

It would take four more months before I worked out that I'd underestimated my disease and that I was dealing with something that was less like a persistent ex and more like a stalker who was willing to take me hostage to make her point.

∞

The year is 3034. We have medically suppressed our emotions to
stop illogical thoughts from interfering with our decisions.
—CAPTAIN BELINDA BLOWHARD

Starhyke was great fun—it was like a Benny Hill movie set in outer space. Aliens called Reptids release a weapon that unshackles the passions of the crew of the dreadnought *Nemesis,* producing unintended consequences. And in the strange way that art mirrors life, I was playing a robotically sober character who struggles to control her unleashed desires.

I've always put acting before addiction, even at the worst of times, and now that I was working I had my armor back. It was slightly tarnished and dented, but it was mine and I was strong again. The monster wisely kept her distance.

The show had a great cast. Jeremy Bulloch, who played Boba Fett in the original *Star Wars* movies, was hilarious. And I got on famously with Suanne Braun, who had played the goddess Hathor in *Stargate SG-1,* and with Rachel Grant, who is an actress and an expert in Filipino martial arts. Everyone was very talented and enthusiastic.

It was a low-budget production. The food cost one pound per day per person, and boy, could you tell. Mystery-meat glop was the main course, and you couldn't get a salad to save your life. But I knew I was in safe hands when it came to alcohol. Andrew Dymond, the director, and the majority of the crew didn't drink, and when I went to the pub to socialize after work no one had a problem with my drinking Diet Coke.

At one point Andrew had some difficulties with the actors depicting the more intimate scenes. He asked me if I wanted to direct, and I jumped at the chance. Andrew directed the CGI and more technical scenes in the adjoining studio, and we developed a method for working in tandem that effectively allowed us to complete shooting on the entire first season. It was a great experience for me. I'd act in one scene and then jump over to the set next door to direct another.

In the storyline, Belinda Blowhard was battling the alien Reptids but failing to maintain control of her impulses, which was great fodder for comedy. By the time *Starhyke* production was coming to an end I could sense my inner monster was working on her own ultimate weapon. I'd have to do a better job of managing my passions than Belinda did. It was one thing to play a slapstick role and another thing to live it. I would not allow my life to become a farce.

When my monster did strike again I realized, too late, that I'd been preparing for the wrong kind of battle. I'd been expecting a frontal assault, something I could resist and perhaps overcome. In the meantime, the monster had been tunneling beneath the fortress walls, preparing a sneak attack.

It started with the affair I was having with one of the show's executive producers. He was a very nice guy who'd lent me his flat in Bath while we were shooting the show. He was also a wine enthusiast. I figured that we had something in common, although I bet that no matter how much he knew, he wasn't as enthusiastic about wine as I was. One day he invited me out to dinner, and I accepted, knowing there would be really, really good wine there and that he would offer it to me. That's when the monster started whispering.

Claudia, you haven't touched a drop in four months. You're not an alcoholic, not even close. And this is an opportunity to prove to yourself that you're not addicted. Just drink small quantities of the best stuff. Trust me, it'll be okay.

I made an attempt to push the voice away, just for form's sake. It knew it had me. It had already slipped past my defenses. It waited until I was sitting opposite my date and had seen just how good the wine was going to be.

Claudia. It'd be a shame to let half of a bottle like that go to waste. Have a little drink. You'll stay on top of it this time.

And I did. For about a week. By the time you realize you've been pushed off the wagon it's too late. You're sitting on your ass choking on dust while life trundles off without you. The insidiousness of the disease makes you honestly believe that if you can stay sober for a few months then you are most definitely not an alcoholic and can therefore drink when you want to.

Sober for six months, drunk for a week, two weeks to recover. Sober for three months, drunk for five days, a week to recover. It's a repetitive cycle, like that of Sisyphus, in the Greek myth, forever pushing that stupid rock up the hill only to have it roll down once it gets to the top.

WHEN *STARHYKE* ended I needed to find another job to earn a permanent work permit in the UK, so Andrew Dymond did me a favor and hired me as a receptionist and tea girl at his CG company.

"Hello, is that Lightworx Media? Can you advise me how to get more renderable data into my texture maps?"

"I have no bloody clue. I just serve the tea."

Needless to say, I wasn't well suited to the job, so I did us both a favor and quit. I sobered up, moved back to London, and rented a room in a friend's flat. If I needed to work to stay in the UK, then it would be as an actress. My inner voice, the same one that had given me the confidence to move to L.A.

when I was a kid, was back and giving the monster a run for her money.

Trusting in myself paid off again when I was introduced to a fantastic agent named Roxane Vacca by my friend Hilary Saltzman.

Roxane entered my life like a shining messenger of the gods, a letter in one hand stating she represented me and in the other a contract for a BBC series called *Broken News*. I'd booked a great job right out of the gate. I had enough documentation for my work visa, and I could stay in the UK. It felt just like when I landed Joan Green as an agent. Good representation is everything.

In the meantime, my stepfather had found a buyer for my home in L.A. and made me a million-dollar profit to boot, which made me feel much better about the loss of my house.

I was winning the battle for my new life. I was happy and confident. So why the fuck was I still stuck in a cycle of binging and detox? I started to see that I didn't have an off button even when I was happy and my life seemed problem-free. When I was at a party I just wanted to keep on drinking and drinking. At dinners I wanted champagne, then wine, then a glass of port, and then another glass of port. I couldn't have just one glass of wine, and I certainly never left half a bottle on the counter. I would see half-finished bottles of white wine in people's fridges and wonder how the heck they did that. I'd find myself staring at people's home bars, recalling the day when I'd stocked my own bar and never took a drop from it except to make other people's drinks at parties.

I realized then that this was more than a matter of will or of emotional highs and lows. I *always* wanted a drink. I thought about drinking all the time. If I didn't have a drink in my hand I'd be planning on how long it would be and what I'd have to do in order to be reunited with a glass of wine or a bottle of beer. I had a full-blown, full-time addiction. For the first time in five years I was able to see myself clearly; I was able to admit that I was an alcoholic.

∞

SINCE I hit the UK I'd been jumping around like a grasshopper, moving more than fourteen times in four years to temporary homes in Bath, Winterbourne Down, the Ladbroke Grove and Westminster areas of London, and many other locations. I was done with moving, but I just couldn't find the right place to hang my hat. The last time I'd been settled was in my home in L.A. where everything went to hell, so now I figured I'd make myself a hard target.

Then I had a series of accidents that forced me to slow down. I was walking around the streets of London, property guide in hand, looking for a place to buy with the proceeds from the sale of my L.A. home when I got hit by a guy on a Vespa. No major damage, just a sprained ankle, a chink in the armor so to speak. A few days later I made the mistake of going out in a pair of three-inch heels. The place I was living in had the steepest fucking stairs I'd ever seen in my life, and just as I was about to take the first step down, the injured ankle gave way, turning me around so that I fell backward down the entire flight of stairs, bumping the edge of every step as I went. It was like something out of a Looney Tunes cartoon, except instead of getting up and brushing myself off while everyone laughed, I found I couldn't get up and that there was a baseball-sized lump bulging out from the back of my neck. I fished out my cell phone, only to discover that I didn't know the UK emergency number. I'm dialing 911, and no one's answering. Eventually one of my roommates found me and took me to the hospital. It turned out that it was a neck fracture. They put me in a neck brace, went over my X-rays, and then sent me on my way.

Alcoholics always overanalyze every minute detail of an incident in the hope of gleaning some insight that will help in the fight against the enemy. You're like a military commander staring down at a map, studying the terrain.

So were the accidents just accidents, or were they my body's way of slowing me down, of letting me know that I needed to stop moving and put down roots before things got really bad? Or was it the monster knocking me out of commission so that I'd be forced to sit still, grow impatient, and have a drink? My previous home had been a mixed blessing. I'd loved it, but it had also been a place of suffering and misery. Should I be looking for my own place? Would it make things better or worse?

You see how you can turn into a raving lunatic? You're at war with yourself, you can't trust yourself, you second-guess every thought and impulse. In short, life sucks.

I trusted my instincts and stumbled across the perfect place, a cute little flat in Notting Hill, and when I saw it I thought, "This is it. This is the place where I can make things right."

I'd finished work on *Broken News,* and there was nothing else in the pipeline, but I knew just the trick to deal with the out-of-work blues—remodeling.

I was back in my element. I could redo the flat and make it look exactly how I wanted. I had some money left over to allow me to live comfortably and fund my pet project. I started building closets and tearing down walls.

And I had another project that kept me busy—devising systems of alcohol regulation to manage my problem. I lived next to a charming pub and I made a rule that this was the only pub I was permitted to drink in and that I'd only be allowed one drink per visit. I never kept wine in the house, so if I had a dinner party I would make the guests take the half-empty bottles home with them. The wagon might have been teetering along on broken wheels, dragging its load behind it, but at least it was going.

Those rules helped me, but they also created a whole new series of problems. Social drinking is so common in London that I found myself coming up with a litany of excuses to explain why I couldn't go out drinking with friends at other pubs. I'd started by saying that I was driving but once people learned that I didn't have a car I had to come up with something else.

"I'm on antibiotics. I'm pregnant. I'm allergic."

I'd say anything to avoid being conspicuous, and in doing so made myself incredibly conspicuous. Keeping to my self-imposed rules was hard. Having a glass of wine with friends is one of my favorite things in the world. Wine loosens the lips and helps people relax and unwind. You laugh more, you confide secrets, hopes, and dreams. I missed that. Then I'd remind myself that the same stuff can turn you into a screaming bitch or a bona fide whacko, and I didn't miss that at all.

I finished the apartment, and as if on cue more roles magically appeared. They were in crappy action films made in Eastern Europe. I was glad to have them, but I just couldn't seem to land any more parts in the UK. There were about a dozen Americans and Canadians in London—like Gillian Anderson and Elizabeth McGovern—who'd lived there for years and seemed to book all the expat gigs.

Not allowing myself to drink also made it hard to make friends in England. I had no work or social life and the flat was finished. I tried working on my social life. People were more formal and reserved than in L.A., so I found it hard to strike up conversations with new people. God knows I tried. I would blabber on and smile like an idiot, but even in the grocery store or in elevators people would ignore me.

I began to feel invisible, a feeling accompanied by a mild paranoia. Was it London or was I going slightly mad from alcohol withdrawal? Self-discipline is all well and good when it comes to drinking, but at the same time life seemed to have lost some of its color. That feeling wasn't helped by the long, wet London winter. I began having dreams about riding my motorcycle down Sunset Boulevard, the warm L.A. wind rushing over my face carrying the smell of orange blossoms and the beach. I wasn't sure how much of my depression was me and how much was the weather, so I actually went and got light therapy at a place where they stick you in a little box and zap you with UVA rays.

I started going stir-crazy. I had to do something, so I jumped on a plane back to L.A. for the family Christmas party.

DURING MY time in the UK I'd travel back to L.A. every year for pilot season.

I'd prepare well in advance, getting totally sober and as fit as I could manage. I'd pack my bags and head back to Hollywood with big expectations. I was going to book something. It was comeback time, baby!

I'd look great and feel great and sit in this Archstone apartment that I was paying $3,000 a month for and wait for the phone to ring. I didn't get one audition, let alone an actual part. I had a shitty manager who promised me the moon and delivered nothing—not one meeting or audition.

One year I stayed in L.A. for four months. The apartment complex was filled with people who dreamed of working in Hollywood, wannabes and stage moms, their heads in the clouds, and at one point I realized that I was no different from them. I couldn't book work, I was back at the beginning, all I had was a dream and an ever-deepening hole in my savings. As I sat by the phone I could feel myself becoming increasingly drawn to the bottle with each passing moment. It would only be a matter of time. I needed to keep moving.

So I started treating Los Angeles as I treated London. I'd do little day trips. I thought that if I took the pressure off waiting for the phone to ring, it might actually ring. Sometimes it works that way; this time it didn't. Then I got a call from London. There was a meeting. A producer wanted me to come in and read for a part.

"I'm in L.A."

"I need you here tomorrow."

"I can't. Christmas is coming. I've just rented a place. I just can't."

It seemed that I just couldn't catch a break.

The year I went back for the family Christmas I was in for a pleasant surprise. It was in Aspen and it was snowing. Everyone made an effort to be nice, there were no fights, and I managed to stay sober. But I was bored, and my dreaded fortieth birthday was bearing down on me like a runaway car. I felt like I'd been possessed by Bridget Jones. I stared out the window at the falling snow. The last five years of my life had rushed by in a blur.

I was due to fly back to London, and I resolved to do something, anything to shake things up and reclaim a social life. I needed distraction, I needed friends, I needed a sex life. And so, like any modern girl who has trouble meeting people, I dove headfirst into the world of online dating.

LONDON WAS a different place from when Dodi was alive. Back then it had been sensuous and classy. My new London was bleak and lonely, so I joined an exclusive dating service for the super rich and those of royal peerage.

To weed out gold diggers the membership fee was $25,000 U.S., but there was a loophole. If you were attractive, were sane, lived in an upmarket area, and had no criminal record you could join for much less, something close to $50. This ensured that rich old men who paid the full fee wouldn't be stuck dating rich, ugly women. I sent in one of my *Playboy* shots, cropped to show me from the shoulders up, and within a few days found myself in the offices of the dating service undergoing a psychological test. They checked my passport to verify my age. I had to sign statutory declarations that I had no criminal convictions. I felt like I was interviewing for a position at Scotland Yard.

What the fuck am I doing here? Am I this desperate?

It was a bizarre experience, but still better than inviting my old dinner date, the monster, out for a good time. No, better to keep her locked safely away. I was so desperate to stay out of trouble with her that I didn't mind stepping into a little trouble when it came to dating real people.

"Claudia, you've passed the initial screening. Now we'd like to conduct a home inspection."

"Seriously? You just photocopied my passport. What more do you need?"

"We like to take every precaution. A member of the nobility has already expressed an interest in you."

"After all this, it had better be bloody Prince Charming."

The home inspection was carried out by a flamboyant Russian woman who bounced around my flat with the energy of a meth head.

"Ure antiques are so lubely. Your garten, it is so beautiful. We are soooo embarrassed to intrude but the gentleman is veddy particular."

They pored over my things. I felt like a Mongolian mail-order bride being checked for fleas.

The prospective date called me the next day. He sounded terribly uptight, the kind of guy Basil Fawlty would have dreamed of welcoming in his hotel.

Fuck it, I'm already in for fifty bucks. I might as well get a free dinner and come out ahead.

He picked me up on time, which was good, but he had a Herman Munster head, the kind that looked like it had gotten caught in an elevator door. As we left my flat and walked toward his Bentley I warned him that he should be careful parking in my neighborhood, because the parking inspectors were brutal.

"Those fucking wogs. Give them an inch and they'll take a mile."

I was not amused. Nor was I amused when he berated the waitress or when he snapped his fingers at the sommelier. Even less amusing was the goodnight kiss, which was delivered with an octopus embrace and a straining erection poking against my leg. I gingerly extracted myself from his tentacles and hurried into the safety of my flat, slamming the door behind me. So much for Prince Charming.

You'd have had a much better night if you'd gone to the pub next door. It's still open. Why not drop in for a quick one?

I told the monster to shut the fuck up.

The next day I got a polite inquiry from the dating service regarding my status: "Still single?"

I could sense the bewilderment of the Russian and her business partner. Why hadn't I fucked the aristocratic pinhead, moved into his castle, and started spending his money?

My reply read: "Still single. The one guy you sent was a putz, and I haven't met anyone else in the last twenty-four hours. Next time send a photo and bio first."

And they did. None of them was young, spiritual, or *sportif*, yet they all claimed to be a combo platter of Lance Armstrong,

Donald Trump, and the Dalai Lama. All in all I went on a half-dozen lame-ass dates. It seemed that having lost one Dodi Fayed, it wasn't so easy to find another.

Then I made the mistake of agreeing to go away with a guy I'd never even met in person. We started emailing and then talked for hours on the phone. He had a northern accent, and I struggled to make out every other word, but he seemed funny and nice.

I was doing a play at the Edinburgh Festival and he offered to travel to Scotland, see my play, and take me to dinner. It sounded romantic, so I agreed to meet up. That night I made the colossal mistake of falling off the wagon and ended up in the sack with him and in the bathtub with him and on the floor with him and hanging over the balcony with him. I apparently did things to him that no woman had ever done before, and now he wanted to take me to Cyprus.

I don't even know how it happened. When I woke up the next morning I had only a sketchy recollection of the night before— my memory was a blacked-out city—nothing. The monster was gathering power, and I was getting a little frightened. It was like something out of a fucking Stephen King novel, the kind where you have an evil-twin personality who takes you over and does stuff without your knowing. Scary shit.

I'd been seeing a talented actor in Edinburgh, a young fellow who performed improvised skits in ancient Sanskrit to drunken highbrow audiences. I liked him a lot but, hey, Cyprus beckoned, so I returned the call.

The good news was that Cyprus was lovely. The bad news was that I couldn't recall a single detail of my lovefest with the northern guy, so I had no idea what he expected or even what he looked like naked. I had a feeling it involved something anal, otherwise the poor guy wouldn't be so bloody excited. And one thing was certain: I wasn't going to touch a single fucking drop of alcohol.

We'd both been dreadfully sick on the flight over. My body just quit after a month of work on the play, and he contracted food poisoning. But now that we were in the five-star luxury resort being massaged and eating fabulous food, things would improve. Right?

Now I'm the last one to judge people's behavior whilst they're imbibing. I've fallen asleep at my own dinner parties and slept with far too many strangers to be the one pointing the finger. But I'm usually a happy lush, never mean-spirited or cruel. This guy wasn't a mean drunk, but he was a whining drunk. After he'd had a few he started complaining about everything. I laughed too loud, the service was dreadful, the pool was too cold, the room smelled. None of this was true; we were in a Cyprian paradise and I was a sober little church mouse on her best behavior. Really.

I figured that I must have been way toasted the night we had sex, because now the beer goggles were off and I could barely stand to look at him. I was struck with horror by his yellowed, crooked teeth, his calloused feet, and his fungus-infected toe-nails. I wanted to scream in frustration at his wardrobe of different-colored but otherwise identical golf shirts. I was back in hell, and I hadn't even had a drink.

Luckily the diarrhea that went with his food poisoning kept on running like Niagara Falls. He hadn't approached me sexually, but as in a B horror movie, you know it's coming. It's just a matter of time until the hand creeps over and goes for the grope.

When the moment came he couldn't get an erection, and I thought the horror flick was over until he leaned in close to me and said, "Maybe if you did to me what you did in the bathtub that night we first met . . ."

He was talking about the night I'd blacked out. What the fuck had I done to him in the bathtub? It didn't bear thinking about; I had to get out of there. I offered my condolences about his inability to perform and locked myself in the bathroom for a few hours on the pretext of secret women's business. When I came out he'd gone to the bar and I made a hasty retreat to the next village, where I booked into a shithole hotel, then flew back to London the next morning.

"Nothing's free, baby," a voice in my head kept on repeating.

Was that the monster or the voice of wisdom? I figured they might as well be one and the same since the fucking voice of wisdom, when it can be bothered raising its head, always does so after you've jumped headfirst into the shit heap.

BY THE time my fortieth birthday came around I'd been dry for almost six months. I was sober as a judge and just about as boring.

Long ago I'd set forty as the goal by which I'd be free of my problem and have my career back in full bloom. My career had wilted and dried up, but at least my disease seemed to have followed suit. I'd been seeing a new guy, and he encouraged me to come celebrate my birthday with him in Ibiza, the Spanish island where Brits go to let loose and party. I went to sunny Spain, stayed stone-cold sober, and had the worst vacation of my life. The travel agent booked us into a hotel on the wrong side of the city. We were supposed to be staying in the sexy party zone; instead I found myself sharing the beach with fat German businessmen and obnoxious Brits who wore black socks and were orbited by screaming, sunburnt kids. I was unemployed, sober, living in a foreign country, and my birthday sucked. Life didn't begin at forty, it damn well ended.

I went back to my flat in London totally miserable only to discover that the annual Notting Hill carnival was taking place right outside my front door.

Claudia, this is your chance to have a real party. You made it to middle age, you survived. You deserve to celebrate. Go and have a good time.

The monster had picked its moment well, because, right then, those words rang with authority. They made such perfect fucking sense!

So I listened. No falling off the wagon this time; I threw myself off the fucking thing, right into a tasty pint of lager at my local.

That's one of the things I fucking hate about the monster. I'd lasted it out. I'd buckled up and ridden the fucking bull for half a year, and then one slip and I was back to square one. It's beyond frustrating; it's a disease that swallows hope.

⟡

WHEN I was finally done with my birthday binge, I looked up the address of the nearest Alcoholics Anonymous and headed on down. I was desperate; I was a mess. The room was filled with cigarette smoke; I sat in the back row and kept quiet.

That wasn't my first time at an AA meeting. During one of my visits back to L.A. I'd gone to the Beverly Hills meetings because I heard there were cute guys there. And one of them came right up to me and said, "We don't shake hands here at AA. We hug."

Something about that sent a shiver up my spine. It was as if they were there as a comfort group, to sugarcoat something that was deadly serious to me. A hug wasn't going to fix the monster. You can't wrap a viper in a knit-wool sweater, give it a hug, and expect it not to bite you. The monster doesn't fuck around; the monster is playing for keeps.

And I'd been to one other meeting with my brother in Lake Arrowhead. That was mainly a bunch of old-timers talking about the shittiest things they'd done to their loved ones when they were drunk.

I hated the idea of AA. I hated getting up there and making my confession to a room full of strangers. The very idea was demoralizing, but this time I was desperate and I was in London, so maybe it really would be anonymous. I'd stick with it this time. I'd reverse my childhood divorce from God and really surrender to Him.

When it was my turn I got up there and said, "Hi. My name is Claudia, and I'm an alcoholic. I've been sober for one day."

After I'd spilled my guts, we had a break and everyone rushed out to smoke some more. I was alone again and there was no relief. I'd hated saying it, it depressed me to say it. I thought, wouldn't it have been great to get up there and say, "Hi, I'm Claudia, and I used to be an alcoholic"?

I returned to my seat and, as I listened to them talk about God, I couldn't help but think that if there was a God, he would want us cured, not eternally suffering. The people I saw get up and talk on the podium were all in pain, all still desperate. I saw myself in them and it occurred to me that this wasn't a cure, this was disease management. I knew management; I'd been struggling with my disease for years, wrestling with the monster, and this was a support group to help continue the struggle. This was a way to kill some time so you don't drink.

I left the meeting. There was nothing uplifting or joyful, and the smoking rubbed me the wrong way. It seemed to me that they were just replacing one bad habit with another.

A week later I was back at AA, this time at the Portobello

Road center. I reasoned that I had to overcome my own disincli-
nation to be there. What if the answer to my problems lay on the
other side of my inherited Germanic pride? I'd do it for real. I'd
get up there at the meeting and do my thing, and afterward I'd
go and work all of the twelve steps. And I did. I even did the one
where you're supposed to make amends to everyone you've ever
hurt in your life. I tried it for half a year, but it didn't change the
disease. It didn't change my genetic disposition toward alcohol.
Some of the reports I read said that AA doesn't work for the
gross majority of the people who try it. The numbers are difficult to track because of their policy of anonymity, but I read one
report that said less than 5 percent of people who rely on AA to
stay sober do so after the first year. The relapse rate for people
in AA is huge.[*]

I came to the conclusion that if some people benefit from it
then great, good for them, but this was not the way for me. I was
tired of fighting, I didn't need support or love or strangers sharing their pain with me. I didn't need hugs and handshakes from
withered-up smokers or sugar junkies with fat bellies. I needed
a cure; I needed my life back.

I went home and started buying books. I read just about every
book I could find on addicts and their struggles. I pored over
the pages of other people's stories trying to find a common link.

There were common stories of trauma, of death and divorce
and rejection, but there was something that none of the material seemed to cover—the change that had taken place in my
body and brain. I'd changed. Everyone who told their stories
in those books had. We all went from partying to becoming
unwitting addicts. Why can some people drink heavily but not
become full-blown alcoholics? Why was it so easy for me to give

* http://www.orange-papers.org/orange-effectiveness.html.

up cocaine? I'd never liked blow, never craved it. But wine, wine was a friend. I liked wine and I loved champagne, and now I'd changed. We had a symbiotic relationship; I couldn't live without them.

I gave up on AA but not on God. I'm not an atheist. I've always had a strong spiritual life; it's one of the things that's kept me hanging in there. I've always felt that God was watching out for me, and when I maintained my prayers I felt strong enough to go head to head with the monster. At the same time though, I discovered that God cannot cure this disease just as He cannot cure cancer or make you grow back a limb.

So I kept on praying, but if God was saying anything back, then I couldn't hear him. I figured it was just like the telephone that wouldn't ring; I just had to hang in there and have faith. Just hang in there a little longer.

AFTER FIVE years in the UK I sat down and re-evaluated my life. It was crunch time. I wasn't booking anything in London, I wasn't booking anything in L.A., but I was hemorrhaging money in both towns. I'd moved to the UK hoping for a fresh start but instead felt like a tightrope walker again, swaying back and forth on a thin line between two lives with the abyss always there below me. If nothing else, my time away from the United States had taught me where my true home was and that I could never really leave it. My fascination with history, with the old world, would always be a part of me, but I was bound up with Hollywood body and soul. I missed the sun, the people, and the wheels of the entertainment industry moving around me, even if I was not an active part of it.

And do you know what the ultimate deciding factor was? I

came to the realization that if I couldn't shake the monster in time, if it broke me and I ended up just like my friend Jeff Conaway, then I had to decide where I wanted to die. That was my final moment of clarity that got me on the plane back to L.A.

I rented out my London flat to a nice American couple and headed home. I was done with optimism. There was no spring in my step. The monster was riding me hard, weighing me down. I didn't know what I had to do to get things back on track. Nothing in my life was stable. I was flailing around, searching for the right combination of choices that would allow me to get my life back. The memory of the old Claudia was strong. The good times were still vivid in my mind's eye, but the means to recover them were elusive. I was like Tantalus in the underworld, the fruit he eternally hungered for hanging just beyond his reach.

15 ✺

BUS STOP

ROM MY DIARY, **November 1, 2008:**

It's 8 a.m., and I'm clearing the dishes from last night's dinner party. My boyfriend David is in the shower. One of my friends brought a few bottles of what appeared to be very good red wine. I didn't read the label or smell the wine, because I've only been sober for three months this time around, and I didn't want to think about what I was missing out on. But now there's half a glass staring at me. A sniff can't hurt. I lift the glass; it smells heavenly. The rich, deep red is still fragrant with tannins and earthiness. It smells like autumn, like Italy, like lamb shanks, like making love in front of a crackling fire. It smells like the good times, the happy times when I was alive, when I wasn't an alcoholic.

If I drink this half glass of wine will it awaken the monster? Will I suddenly have an uncontrollable urge to binge? Will the last six months' worth of therapy prove to be a waste of time?

If I drink this wine, I won't be able to kiss David all day because he'll smell it on me and probably never speak to me again. We have plans to go to the beach and walk around Third Street Promenade, maybe buy that new mouse for him at the Apple Store, and get some fresh fish at Santa Monica Seafood. These plans will be ruined.

I know that if I drink this wine I will be toying with the monster. I'll be presuming that I am powerful when I am not. I am weak. I am a drunk just like the guy I saw passed out on the sidewalk in front of Starbucks. I am no better or worse.

I miss red wine. It's like not being able to dance with your favorite partner. I sound like a battered housewife who keeps making excuses for her husband. I love the wine, despite the fact that it's trying to kill me.

I pour the leftover wine down the sink. It's All Saints' Day. The veil between our world and the spirit world is still thin, so maybe Patrick's watching over me today. But tomorrow it'll just be me, myself, and I. Will I ever feel normal again?

∞

MY DIARY was filled with entries like that one. I wrote hundreds of sorrow-filled pages about my struggle. Tear stains marked pages where I'd fallen off the wagon, coffee stains marked pages where I'd been sober for thirty or sixty or ninety days. There were copious musings about how much better my life would be if I were sober forever, and there were diatribes about how shitty it was that I couldn't even have a glass of wine at a dinner party. There are letters written to my parents apologizing for my behavior and thanking them for their support. There are entries complaining bitterly about inheriting their fucked-up, alcoholic genes. My diary is filled with self-absorbed post-binge musings, manic scrawls, even suicidal rants. I have thick diaries and I like to write—a lot. It's one of the ways in which I try to make sense of things.

⌘

WHEN I came back from the UK I was miserable, still stuck in my sober-binge cycle, so I decided to stop waiting for the phone to ring and start living. I took classes in languages, art, and writing. I started hiking every day.

In the summer of 2008 I met a new man, master photographer and lighting guru David Honl. David was a departure from the kind of guy I normally dated. He was my own age, for a start, and he had a depressive streak, but also a very dry sense of humor that I enjoyed. And man, could he make me look good in a photo! He was very encouraging when he'd photograph me, very complimentary, just the thing I needed at that time in my life. He'd lived in Turkey for years, had spent time in Afghanistan and Iraq during the wars. I liked him—a lot—and I was determined that even if everything else in my life was fucked up, my relationship with David wouldn't be, at least not as much as the last string of guys I'd dated.

The smartest way to do that was to try to stay sober most of the time and hide my disease from him. He couldn't be allowed to see the monster. Our relationship was just budding, and the monster was emotional napalm, enough to wipe out a forest.

When I was recovering from a binge I'd pretend that I had a cold or some other illness. The swine flu epidemic bought me a whole week. He appeared on my doorstep unannounced one day, his brother standing beside him, and asked me to come out to lunch. I kept running into the bathroom to throw up, and I looked like shit. I thought I'd die of embarrassment. I'll never forget the disappointed look he gave me as he left. Non-addicts take offense at all sorts of small inconveniences and slights, because they don't share the same perspective; they don't realize that you're fighting for your life.

I started meditating and read a book a day, even though it killed my eyes. It took my mind off of drinking and guilt and helped pass the time until I was once more socially acceptable.

David liked an occasional drink and was very supportive of my sobriety, but he got confused when I'd suddenly fall off the wagon and overdo it. He could see that something was wrong with me, but his vision was clouded; he was in love, and he just couldn't connect the dots because he'd never known an addict. But I couldn't hide the monster away forever. I knew she'd eventually emerge from her cave and then David would turn and run and never come back.

I was so scared of telling David the truth that I started running around like a headless chicken, trying anything and everything to make me well—anything except drugs. I'd seen where that had taken Jeff Conaway and other friends of mine. What started out as medication to manage one problem could quickly turn into a whole other addiction. What if I failed to beat the booze with drugs and then found myself hooked on both?

∞

I MADE up a to-do list that included every kind of nonmedical solution I could think of and got to work on it:

1. GO TO DOCTOR AND GET LIVER TESTS.
   "Claudia, your liver is ruined! How could you do this to yourself? Don't touch another drop. One more mouthful and your liver will explode, leaving you to die the most horrible of deaths."

That's what I'd been hoping to hear, but the tests showed that my liver was completely healthy.

I amused myself with the theory that I was part cockroach, built to withstand even a nuclear disaster. My other leading theory was that the alcohol had pickled my liver, preserving it in perfect condition.

2. BECOME A VEGETARIAN.

I tried, and when that didn't help, I even went macrobiotic and completely cut out sugar. Maybe those hippie therapists at the rehab resort were right. Maybe sugar lured the monster out of its cave. No such luck. It was nuts. I was poring over my past again like a detective, digging up old cases, revisiting past conclusions in case I'd missed one vital clue that would make sense of everything.

3. GO TO CHURCH AND PRAY—HARD!

I'd decided to get back together with God when I was in England but he didn't seem to be returning my calls. That was understandable. I'd called things off a long time ago, and now here I was suddenly wanting to patch things up. I needed to go to church and make an official effort; then maybe he would take five minutes to come down off the cloud and sort my life out.

I had a very bad Easter in 2008, and I'd heard about a healing ceremony in this Catholic church in the valley. The priest was famous for bestowing blessings on the sick, and there had even been some reported miracles.

When I arrived there were lots of people on crutches and in wheelchairs. My goddaughter came with me and we sat through Mass. Part of the service was in Spanish, part in English.

When it was my turn to stand before the priest he asked me, "Do you need to be healed from something?"

And I just burst into tears.

"Yes. I do. I'm sick."

So he put oil on my forehead and on my chest, and all the while I was weeping, praying for a miracle.

And I did feel something go through my body. I felt some sort of healing, and after that any time I felt like a drink I'd throw myself on my knees and pray for help. I'd pray for strength, pray to get through the day, pray not to have cravings, pray not to think about it. And when the craving passed, I'd give thanks for one more day of sobriety.

It was two months before I fell off the wagon again, and man, did I feel guilty. I haven't felt guilt when I cheated on people or when I stole things as a kid. I always justified everything, but now I felt that I was cheating on God. At the same time, I was reminded just how powerless I was against my disease. If God couldn't help me battle the monster, then what hope was there? Then I got angry at God. Why had He done this to me? Why did He piss in my gene pool? How come my brother Vince got off scot-free?

I put a line through number 3. That was okay, I still had two more options on the list.

4. **TRY ALTERNATIVE MEDICINE.**

I went to Siddha Yoga retreats, got acupuncture for addiction, went to a fasting clinic, and even tried a meditation "doctor" who claimed to have cured members of the Grateful Dead.

All failures. I was down to my last shot.

5. **GET HYPNOTIZED.**

I found an ad on the Internet while searching for "the best hypnotist in L.A." I called the number to make an appointment.

"Claudia, I've worked miracles with every kind of addict. I can help you. Come on over ASAP!"

The hypnotist's apartment building was crumbling and looked as if it hadn't been cleaned since the '70s, but it was the fucking Taj Mahal compared to his apartment, which stank of old cigarettes, cat urine, and boiled cabbage.

"Watch the medal as it swings. See how it catches the light?"

He tried to hypnotize me into a state of past-life regression so that I could try to pinpoint when my alcoholism began. Now, I'm a big history buff, so if you want to charge me $450 to send me back to Renaissance Florence where I get to have some life-changing experience or at the very least a romping good time, then great. But this guy had a clumsy manner, the tape recorder kept jamming, and the chair I was sitting in had broken springs.

I told him I wasn't impressed. He told me that I was a difficult case and needed a series of treatments at $120 a pop.

Fuck. That was it, then. It was all a load of very expensive horseshit, and I was at my wits' end. I'd tried everything. Except the hard-core stuff. The stuff with the list of side effects as long as my arm. And I wasn't ready for that, not yet.

∞

I THOUGHT it would be a good idea for David and me to move in together. It would make it harder for me to binge, and he would be a healthy distraction. A relationship was one way of keeping busy. Surprise, surprise! It turned out to be a very bad idea. By then my compulsion was far beyond my control. I'd have to fabricate arguments, sneak out for binges, come up with all sorts of schemes to get what I could not do without.

And, of course, David finally realized I had a problem. And by then it wasn't so much a problem as it was my entire life. Being an alcoholic was now normal. The problem was the lengths to which I'd have to go to appear normal by the standards of the outside world.

I was scared to commit to David, and he was coming on strong, talking about marriage and the future. I felt hopeless, that there was no future for me, that my struggle with the monster was a full-time career and relationship bundled into one. And David sensed this. He was jealous of the monster, of the hold she had over me.

So, since we were fighting at home, and I was in the middle of a binge, and I couldn't stand the sight of David and wanted to break up, we went on a trip to Tahiti.

Now you might be thinking, "Why the fuck would she do something so monumentally stupid?" Because my therapist told me to.

"You should go to Tahiti. It would be good for you to work on your relationship in a neutral environment."

From the moment we stepped on the plane the trip was a disaster. While David slept I sneaked to the back of the plane to buy little bottles of vodka from the flight attendant. My friends told me that Tahiti was heaven on earth. All I remember is rushing about like a crazy woman, drinking anything I could get my hands on. Rum, beer, vodka, gin. I launched an assault on the minibar and gutted it of tiny bottles in under twenty minutes. I'd buy bottles of liquor from the hotel shop and go through the whole charade of having them gift wrapped, only to tear them open in my room and guzzle their contents while I cried uncontrollably. I was a fucking mess. I'd have drunk mouthwash if I'd had any on hand. Tahiti wasn't heaven for me. It was definitely hell on earth.

At one point I changed hotel rooms to get away from David, and then I sneaked back into his room when he was out and drank his entire minibar.

I'm sure David must have had a moment when he went to get a sip of vodka and realized that I'd cleaned him out and filled up all the bottles with water to cover my tracks.

I lasted half a week and then fled. I have no idea how I managed to travel from the island of Moʻorea, where we'd been staying, to Papeete on nearby Tahiti, then get onto a bus and then an airplane, but somehow I made it. They say a drunk can always find his way home. Well, I found my way home from 4,000 miles away in the middle of the Pacific ocean.

I put my suitcase on my bed and opened it. It was filled with sand and ripped clothing and empty little bottles. Then I realized that I'd left my iPhone on with the data roaming the whole time I was in the South Pacific.

Altered flight charges: $5,000. Cell phone stupidity: $2,000. Memories of Tahiti: priceless.

Before David could get home I went to my mom's place in Napa and went through the worst detox in my life. I was dehydrated and shitting blood and my eyelids were so swollen that I tried using Preparation H on them to reduce the swelling. I'd pass out, then wake up a few hours later and search the house for booze. My poor mom ended up taking me to the hospital. It took me nearly ten days to recover.

Needless to say, the Tahiti trip put some strain on my relationship. David now knew that I was a crazy wino and told me that if he smelled alcohol on my breath again he'd leave me. I was grateful for the second chance and swore I'd go dry. I'd lost twenty-five pounds during the detox, and I looked great, which lent weight to my promise of sobriety.

I was sober for three months before I slipped. I started out on small binges with minor detox flare-ups that I thought I could keep hidden. Those flare-ups quickly spread into a raging fire that consumed me, burning me from the inside out.

The binges ran day and night and didn't stop until I passed out. When I woke up I'd shake and vomit until I was empty and then lie on the bathroom floor, half-conscious, hallucinating all kinds of scary shit.

When I could walk I'd start on chamomile tea and water, then move on to milk thistle and warm milk, anything to calm the thoughts of guilt and self-hate and suicide and help get my body into a state where it could sleep and heal.

Sleep deprivation was a big issue. I raided health food stores for natural sleeping aids because over-the-counter pills made the detoxes even worse. They made the hallucinations more intense and wired me up instead of calming me down. At night I'd take a hot bath and lie down and sweat out the toxins, terrified of what was to come. First the shakes would start, then the hot and cold flashes, and then more shaking. The room would fill with crazy thunder crashes, and I'd hear the voices of the ghosts and ghouls who visited me in my nightmares. Then I'd get hungry, but the nausea would overtake me so that I couldn't eat, not even a cracker. I'd go to the kitchen and force down a banana or some milk and pray I wouldn't puke it up. I knew my body needed sustenance when I'd been living on nothing but beer for five days. I'd go back to bed and just lie there, my mind amped up, filled with horrible thoughts that denied me the sleep I so badly wanted. I'd convinced myself that the monster was in the room, that if I fell asleep she would smother me. The CIA tortures people with sleep deprivation, and here I was doing it to myself.

After a sleepless night I'd get up and hide from the California sunshine like a hungover vampire. This was the same light that I had missed so much in London, the sun that I'd longed for. Now it hurt my yellow eyes and revealed too much of my puffy face. It stole away the shadows and left no doubt in my mind that I was losing. I was turning into the very monster I'd been fighting against.

I decided I had to get out of the house. I told David I was going for a walk. My reflexes were so bad, I knew I couldn't get out of the way of a car if I had to. My eyesight was shot from dehydration. I was afraid to leave the house, but I had no choice. I couldn't drink at home, because I was terrified of David catching me and leaving.

That was how I ended up sitting in a khaki-colored bus stop on Coldwater Canyon Avenue watching the world pass me by.

I felt dirty, ugly, and utterly alone. I had thought I'd reached the lowest point in my life when I clung to the toilet bowl at my mom's house, my secret finally revealed. But I was wrong. Sitting at the bus stop drinking a hastily mixed screwdriver—this was rock bottom. You know when you have those dreams in which you realize you're naked and start scrambling around for clothes? I was so far gone I couldn't make the slightest effort to cover up my addiction. I was on display for the whole world as it passed by.

I was a slave to the monster. She was running the show now. I was strapped into the back seat, right between my mom and Holly on the drive to rehab. I'd been there the whole time. I wasn't driving that car; the monster was behind the wheel. It had let me enjoy my delusions while it gathered more power, preparing for the final siege. I'd lost. Sitting there in that bus shelter, I declared defeat.

Game over. I give up. I've got nothing left to fight back with.

When I was a teenager I won a drama scholarship to the Laguna Playhouse that I never used. They had awarded it to me for playing the Marilyn Monroe character in a scene from *Bus Stop*.

In the movie Marilyn's character tries to travel to Hollywood, where she hopes she'll be discovered. Instead, she gets kidnapped by a cowboy who becomes obsessed with her after she sings "That Old Black Magic" at a rodeo.

I really had escaped to Hollywood and been discovered, but my kidnapper had still managed a successful abduction. The song came to me as I sat there, at my own bus stop, my monster mocking me. That old black magic had me in its spell, and it was a spell that I couldn't break on my own. I needed help to do that, and I knew that if I didn't get it right away I'd keep marching on to the monster's tune until it finally killed me.

SOMEHOW I made it home, locked myself in my room, and called Holly. It took me five attempts to navigate the directory on my iPhone and reach her—hand-eye coordination was a distant memory.

"Holly, I can't let David see me like this. Can you take me to a detox center?"

I was shaking so badly that I thought my teeth were going to crack into little pieces.

Holly arrived calm and in control, my guardian angel. She joked with me as she helped me get dressed; I couldn't even put my pants on. She then started calling detox centers, trying to find a place that would take SAG insurance while I lay on the bed and prayed that my heart, which was beating as hard as if I'd just run a marathon, wouldn't suddenly stop.

She found a place in Tarzana, bundled me into the car, and drove me down the highway, straight to hell.

The lady checking me in was on a go-slow—I guess she'd just had a big lunch. I stood there going through a horrible detox, Holly helping me stand upright, while she yammered on and on about policies and procedures and gave me form after form to sign.

"What if I have a seizure? That's why I'm here. I'm terrified I'm going to have a seizure. Can you give me something?"

"No. We have to complete your paperwork."

My eyesight was fading and I was worried I was signing my life away. Was I giving them legal power to hold me? Or relieving them of liability if they killed me out of incompetence?

They're out to get you, especially this bitch. Get out of here. Go and stay with Holly or Trish until you're better. You'll be okay.

That fucking monster sure picks her moments.

That voice in my head became a new kind of inner compass. I decided that when it told me to do something I would do the opposite. It wanted me to go, so I would stay and detox and work out the next step when I was in a rational state of mind.

The monster was displeased with my attempted rebellion and sent me a sign to remind me who was in charge. I fell to my knees and nearly choked on the amount of vomit I produced.

They took me into a holding area, and Holly had to leave. I sat in a plastic chair for over an hour waiting for someone to come and search my bags. There was only one other person in the room, a large man who seemed to take a perverse pleasure in adding to my misery.

I got up to get a sweater out of my bag, which was in the next room. He stepped in front of me and told me in a scary, whispered tone that I had better sit back down.

"We have rules here. You can't get things from your bags while they're being searched."

When you're going through a detox, your temperature goes from hot to cold and back again. One minute you might as well be standing on top of Mount Everest, the next in the earth's molten core.

"I'm freezing. I've got to have my sweater. You can get it for me if you like."

"I can't do that. I can't break the rules for you. People like you make life difficult for everyone here. We have rules here. You have to follow them."

It was insane. Even in my fucked-up state I could see that this guy was messing with me.

He kept me there for thirty minutes while I shook so hard that I nearly bit through my tongue. Next, a lady came for me and led me to a depressing shared bedroom. She was covered with tattoos and had crazy purple hair, a refugee from the Jim Rose Circus. She was clearly an ex-junkie, her teeth rotted through from crystal meth. She took my cell phone away and left me alone.

That was it. No therapy, no one talking to me, no doctor visiting me, nothing.

I noticed that there was a woman curled into a ball on the single bed across from mine. I sat and watched her for a long time, wondering if she was dead or alive. She finally sat up, a tiny, dark-haired woman who spoke in a language I didn't recognize. She kept rifling through a rumpled plastic bag on her bed with some old withered fruit in it, choosing one and holding it out to me. I'd politely refuse, and she'd nod sagely and go back to the bag, searching for a more suitable offering.

I finally took an apple just to stop the lunacy. I felt like I was trapped in a David Lynch movie.

I was still shaking, so I found a nurse and tried to explain to her what the person who admitted me didn't care to hear—that I was scared of having a seizure, that I wasn't a pill popper but did need medical help.

"Med time is four o'clock. Come back in an hour."

"What if I'm dead in an hour?"

She shrugged and looked at me as if I were a stupid child.

"Med time is four o'clock."

I went back and lay on my bed and waited, resting my head on my little suitcase for fear someone would steal it. I heard the fruit lady rustling around in her bag again.

I lasted thirty-six hours before I checked myself out. Suddenly the staff who had been so unhelpful couldn't have been more fucking charming. The center was getting two grand a night for keeping me there, and they wanted to milk at least another two nights out of my stay. Well, fuck them.

The pills they'd given me had helped, though. I even managed to sleep for a whole hour. Holly picked me up and was amazed that I looked like my old self again. Somewhere in the ether a team of overworked angels was keeping me alive.

Lying on the bed in the detox center I'd had a moment of clarity, one thought that helped me pull myself together: I felt a blinding hatred for my disease. There was no more on-again, off-again with the monster. I fucking hated her. I felt the way I did when I was a teenager in that rapist's van, 110 pounds and unable to fight the bastard off.

I'd taken something else from the detox center—a colorful little flyer for Vivitrol.

"One month of Vivitrol—FREE! Vivitrol—the shot that'll help you stay sober."

I called the number on that flyer a dozen times and left messages with various people and answering machines trying to make an appointment to get the shot. No one ever called me back. I left my cell phone number, home phone number, and email address. I'd finally decided to try medication, and now the fuckers wouldn't give me any.

The shot was $1,000 a month, and although my savings were running out I was willing to pay anything if it would help. The shot was supposed to inhibit cravings. I wanted that shot, and getting that shot suddenly became very important to me. I started researching Vivitrol and found it was an opiate blocker. It blocked all good feelings—everything from sexual feelings to enjoyment of food; emotions, including love; work-out highs; everything. Suddenly I was relieved that no one had returned my calls.

I kept on searching for a medical answer and in the spring of 2008 decided to go on Antabuse. My SAG insurance wouldn't cover it, but I figured it was worth the $350 if it worked. I did my research first and found myself in the same predicament as with Vivitrol. You think the list of side effects you hear rattled off on TV commercials for prostate drugs is bad? Here's the small print on Antabuse:

> *Seek medical attention right away if any of these SEVERE side effects occur when using Antabuse:*
> *Severe allergic reactions (rash; hives; difficulty breathing; tightness in the chest; swelling of the mouth, face, lips, or tongue); blurred vision; changes in color vision; dark urine; loss of appetite; mental or mood problems; nausea; numbness or tingling of the arms or legs; seizures; tiredness; vomiting; weakness; yellowing of the eyes or skin.*

I mean, seriously, who'd put that in their body? Alcohol seemed like a milder poison than that. Good Lord, addicts are a confused lot! And a poor lot. Being an addict ain't cheap: $200 an hour for therapy, $350 for Antabuse prescriptions, $3,500 for detox, $30,000-plus for rehab.

I was half mad with frustration and physically, emotionally, and financially drained.

But those angels must have been watching out for me, because while researching Antabuse, I stumbled on an article in the British newspaper *The Guardian* about something called The

Sinclair Method. I didn't know it then but that article would change my life.

That detox from hell, with all its horrific side effects, would be my last. The monster didn't know it yet, but she was beaten.

263

16

EXTINCTION AGENDA

IN THE TIME leading up to my discovery of The Sinclair Method, I could sense that change was in the wind. For starters, after three years of silence, the phone rang and I booked a job on the TV show *Nip/Tuck*.

But would the coming change be for better or worse? Life is seldom cut and dried. Something that starts out well can turn bad and vice versa.

After my stint in the detox center I'd moved out of the place I was sharing with David. I needed space to save our relationship, space to see whether the wind would turn for or against me. I had an acting job, and that, as always, was my life raft. I clung to it, focusing on getting healthy and staying sober.

I was living with my friend Trish and running laps around Lake Hollywood, working out as hard and as often as my body could take it; I had to appear naked on TV. The anxiety I felt as a teenager about seeing my butt on a fifty-foot-high screen was nothing compared to that of being a detoxing forty-something who was going to bare her all on a popular TV series.

What I failed to keep in mind was that a fortysomething body can't be molded as easily as that of a young woman injecting horse piss on a 500-calorie-a-day diet or even a woman in her thirties doing hundreds of lunges in preparation for *Playboy*. I pounded the pavement so hard it threw my back out. My pelvis and lower back felt like they were swimming beneath my skin, and each time they moved (which was any time I did anything apart from lie on my back) I felt a debilitating pain.

Luckily, that happened toward the end of my training regime, so I looked great, but it meant that I was in extreme pain all the way through the shoot. That would have been fine if we were shooting a period drama and all I had to do was sit in a high-backed chair and look statuesque, but for this particular episode the scriptwriters had come up with some particularly weird shit.

I was cast as a woman who pays Julian McMahon's character to satisfy a bizarre sexual fetish. First, he would throw me into a tub filled with ice and keep me there until my heart stopped from hypothermia, then he would carry my numb body to the bed, throw me on it, and fuck me back to life, the heat from his body kick-starting my heart back into action.

I mean, how fucking weird is that? But it didn't stop me from taking the role. My career was as frozen as my body when the stunt man ripped me out of the bath and threw me on the bed. Maybe this job, so long in coming, would drive the life back into it.

When *Nip/Tuck* wrapped I drove straight to Trish's house and raided her cupboards. The pain, combined with the stress of creating what I hoped would be my comeback performance, had knocked down the last of my defenses. I found a bottle of vodka and drank practically the whole thing in one sitting.

The Sinclair Method has successfully helped moderate alcohol drinking in Finland, where excessive alcohol use is a major national problem, as well as other countries including Israel, Russia, the Netherlands, Italy, Spain, Venezuela and Estonia. A statistical analysis of the data obtained from clinics in Finland shows highly significant reductions in alcohol drinking. The method is successful with more than 78% of alcoholics. In Florida the success rates since 2002 have been more than 85%. During the treatment program when shown on a graph a pattern emerges. It was always a classical extinction curve: drinking and craving became progressively lower with each week of treatment.

That was from a scientific article I read called "Clinical Evidence from The Sinclair Method Clinic in Sarasota, Florida." The Florida clinic was the only one in the United States offering the Sinclair Method. The clinic's website said:

Internationally hundreds of thousands of people have been helped using the Sinclair Method.

More than 80% of all the clients in the program were successful in long term control of their alcohol consumption, some to acceptable levels ("Social Drinking") and others to complete abstinence. For those who desired to control their alcohol consumption, their drinking was reduced to an average of 1 drink per day. These same individuals had at one point consumed anywhere from 24 to 50 *drinks or more a week. Some of The Sinclair Method's successful patients had consumed more than 200 ounces of alcohol a week prior to the program.**

An 80% success rate! Apart from the grim reaper, who has the only 100% guaranteed cure for addiction, I'd never heard of a treatment with such a high rate of success. What's more, the article made an astonishing claim—that The Sinclair Method was a genuine cure for alcoholism.

The word "cure" is a powerful one and can't be used lightly. The Sinclair Method makes use of a drug called naltrexone, which creates a state of pharmacological extinction in the addict's brain. It doesn't block the effect of alcohol; rather, it gradually resets the brain back to the pre-addiction condition, making it a bona fide cure.

But there was one catch: the cure only remained a cure as long as you took the pill, every time before you had a drink, for the rest of your life. Otherwise the endorphins released when drinking would not be blocked by the effect of naltrexone and would lead the brain to revert to a state of craving alcohol.

I researched naltrexone and found that it had been available and FDA-approved for the treatment of alcoholism since 1994. It was nonaddictive, and the side effects were minor and temporary—nausea, headaches, and insomnia. *Sign me up!*

The Florida clinic charged $3,800 for treatment, beyond my budget by that stage. Luckily, I found a book, *The Cure for Alcoholism* by Roy Eskapa, PhD.

The book had an introduction by David Sinclair, PhD, who developed The Sinclair Method, which described alcoholism as a learned chemical addiction of the brain. Sinclair maintains that abstinence only makes the problem worse, and I'd made

* www.28weekrecovery.com/index_files/Page389.htm.

the biggest mistake in the book: I'd gone stone-cold sober after every binge. The sudden deprivation of alcohol only led to stronger cravings. This not only leads to eventual relapse but also damages the brain and internal organs. What no one at rehab or detox centers ever tells you is that you can detox by gradually reducing your alcohol intake. The reason no one thinks to mention this is that most alcoholics aren't capable of doing it. But with naltrexone it's made possible by one amazing, almost unbelievable fact—that The Sinclair Method only works as a cure if the alcoholic keeps on drinking.

You take naltrexone to reduce your consumption, and at the same time it kills off your addiction. My armor was battered and hanging on by its fraying straps, but now I'd have something to fight the monster with that I'd never had before—a weapon. I'd always been on the defensive, on the back foot while the monster attacked at will. If the claims about The Sinclair Method were true I just might be able to obliterate that bitch once and for all.

The Cure for Alcoholism contained all the information I needed to start The Sinclair Method solo. The first step was to find a doctor who would prescribe naltrexone, which costs about $30 for thirty 50 mg pills—about a dollar added to the cost of a night out. Even better, I was able to use my SAG insurance, which brought the cost down even more to $10 for thirty pills.

By taking one pill one hour before drinking I could begin the process of pharmacological extinction.

I was still not turned on by the idea of taking a pill forever, but hell, if it worked it was better than going to an AA meeting and fighting the war every fucking day for the rest of my life. And the other thing that resonated with me was The Sinclair Method's treatment of alcoholism as a disease, like diabetes or high blood pressure. It was a relief to know that someone had devised a safe, medically proven, nonaddictive way to combat it.

Following on from the use of naltrexone, the book encouraged using the beneficial effect of the drug to strengthen healthy, alternative behaviors—eating tasty meals, exercise, sports, even sex.

I went in to see my doctor, armed with a copy of *The Cure for Alcoholism*. I'd been fighting every day for the last ten years. I wanted peace, I wanted my life back, and I wasn't going to take no for an answer.

THE DOCTOR was a nice young guy who a pill-popping friend had recommended, one used to dealing with addicts. I'd seen him once before when I was suffering a combo attack of flu and alcohol withdrawal. He'd prescribed some anti-anxiety pills to deal with the monster and an antibiotic for the flu. The flu went the way of the dodo; the monster didn't bat an eyelid.

I was back and this time asking for naltrexone. I'd also printed out pages of the clinical papers I found on the Internet, and I sat with him and discussed The Sinclair Method. He looked up the drug in his pharmaceutical reference book and finally, with trepidation, he gave me the piece of paper that represented my last hope of recovery, my hopeful stay of execution.

I had to go to a compound pharmacy (one that makes special drugs to order) to fill my prescription. Within fifteen minutes I had fifteen pills. I stopped by Trader Joe's on the way home and bought a bottle of red wine and a steak. I was PMS-ing and David was out of town. It was the perfect time to schedule the first experiment.

I shook the plastic pill bottle at the traffic lights, like a witch doctor rattling bones for good luck. The wine sat next to me in the passenger seat. The way home involved driving right past the khaki-colored bus stop on Coldwater Canyon. I turned and looked at it as I drove past and was overcome with emotion. I had to pull over.

I couldn't believe that the pills could work, that I didn't need to abstain. It was too good to be true.

Nothing's for free, babe.

The very idea seemed to go against everything I'd learned at AA and in rehab and at the detox center. The monster was rattling around in my head. I was shaking, tears streaming down my face. The bus stop, the ride to rehab with Holly and my mom, the back of the rapist's van, the sight of my mom in a bloodstained shirt holding Patrick's bandana in her hand, it was all the same place— the monster's cave, its place of power—and I'd been trapped in it for so long that I didn't know if I had the courage to leave.

Claudia, honey, this is just another dead end. Everything else you've tried has failed and you know you swore never to pop pills. Throw them out the window and go home. We'll enjoy the wine together.

∞

AS SOON as I got home I took the pill. It was 5:45 p.m. on February 22, 2009. I waited until 6:45 before having a glass of wine—I wanted to make sure the pill had time to work. I was nervous, but I'd gotten my courage back after the bus-stop incident. I was so hopeful!

After I drank the wine, I felt a little dizzy and found that I could only eat a little of the steak and spinach on my plate. I also felt a little stoned and not at all clear-headed.

Why are you doing this?

The monster was still posturing, but I noticed that her voice lacked power. *She* was anxious as well. I didn't dignify her with an answer, and she knew why. She knew that, more than anything, I wanted to be normal.

Soon I was struck by a revelation: *It's 7:15. I've only had one glass of red wine and don't feel like having another. By now I should be well on my way to polishing off the bottle.*

It was a week before I touched another drop—this time, three glasses of wine. I slept like crap and woke up tired and thirsty the next morning, but the monster was still silent. The binge that I was sure would overtake me like a tsunami had arrived as only a minor swell and quickly receded.

A month after that, I took my pill before having my first social drink, a glass of wine with people in my writing class. I was hyperaware of how strange it felt to be normal. It was as if I were standing outside my body watching myself laugh and socialize. I kept waiting for something bad to happen. Nothing did. A month earlier I'd have been on my third glass and working out how to sneak the unfinished bottle into my bag when no one was looking.

Another week passed, and I attended my first post-Sinclair dinner party with David. I found that my body was adjusting to the pill. I didn't feel so dizzy anymore.

It had been a month since I'd seen the monster in the mirror, and though she was still running around in my mind, threatening and cajoling, I could sense she was getting desperate.

Then came the real test: a trip to Napa to visit my mom and stepfather. It's feeding time in the lion enclosure and Claudia's on the menu. I took two bottles of red to last the whole trip.

And then the carnage began. My mom questioned my latest attempt to fix my life. My stepfather once again posited his carefully thought-out theory that I was injecting hard drugs. I stayed cool like Fonzie. I drank my wine, a glass a day, and returned to L.A. without going on a single binge, having tamed the lions.

It seemed that while I was on The Sinclair Method nothing could trigger me to drink. I still have cravings when I have PMS or if I have a long, difficult day, but there seems to be a disconnect between the voice of the monster and the dangerous behavior it previously triggered.

I took on another big challenge—a trip to Italy with David. Tuscany, land of the luscious red. I resigned myself to drinking only at night. No repeat of the turmoil in Tahiti. I wanted to *remember* my time in Italy.

I was still thinking like an alcoholic. I obsessively counted my supply of naltrexone, ensuring I had enough, but I was anxious without cause. I took my pill as instructed and only drank too much on one occasion—four glasses with a gorgeous meal of pasta puttanesca—but even that didn't lead to a binge.

I returned from Italy triumphant, a Roman emperor having vanquished the barbarians.

By the time I'd used The Sinclair Method for six months the dizzy feeling was completely gone. I cut out drinking during the week altogether, only imbibing on weekends, and then only on special occasions—a few glasses at a dinner party or on a getaway with David. My desire to consume alcohol steadily declined, taking my abnormal behavior with it. I didn't feel dizzy at all or experience any side effects. My life was back to how I remembered it before the monster came along. Drinking, I could honestly take it or leave it.

But fear is the hardest of human emotions to conquer. I was still reluctant to declare total victory; I didn't want to be like George W. Bush and hang out the "Mission Accomplished" banner before I'd really won the war.

It wasn't that long ago that, when I wasn't thinking about what to drink or where to get it, I'd kill time calculating how many days I'd wasted recovering from binges (165) in the hope that the sheer number would deter me from wasting any more.

But my confidence slowly grew. The bottles of wine in my cabinet were only used at dinner parties. The cooking wine that I used to guzzle desperately could rest easy in my pantry beside the Marsala and Cognac—they'd only ever be used as intended, to make sauces for my recipes.

My brain was changing, and as it did I was reclaiming my life.

It took another year, watching the monster slowly wither and retreat from sight, until I made the call, the official announcement. I'd battled the monster for close to a decade, and now I'd finally won. Print the headline: "Armistice Announced—the Enemy Has Signed the Treaty—Peace at Last!"

IT WAS the spring of 2010, I'd been on The Sinclair Method for a few months, and I was getting a manicure-pedicure at this Korean beautician's place when my phone rang. It was Adam Rifkin, my director friend from the good old days.

"Claudia, I'm working on something right now for Showtime. It's a TV version of my movie *LOOK*, do you want to be in it?"

"You've got to be kidding me!"

"It's a really funny character. Her name's Stella. I wrote her specifically for you. I'd love for you to be in it."

I was so grateful, so happy! By "funny" he meant that she was a paranoid, alcoholic cokehead and, according to the production notes, a fortysomething MILF.

"Claudia, you still there?"

I was so stunned, I'd forgotten to talk.

"I'm still here."

"It's really low budget, so there's not much money in it . . ."

"But I'm gonna be back on TV?"

"Yeah, you'll be on Showtime."

And there it was. My career was back. I felt the world change around me, the final piece fall into place. I knew it was real. It felt just like when I got my first role on *Dallas* all those years before. The drought had been broken.

Then another job came, voice work on a computer game, and after that another. I worked on a sci-fi short film written by an Aussie named Morgan Buchanan, who became my regular writing partner (and co-author of this book). We started writing a series of future-Rome sci-fi novels.

I had my life back. People wanted me to be in their lives. Hollywood wanted to make use of my talents. It was a rebirth in every way.

☙

IN MAY 2011 David and I were back in French Polynesia. Mo'orea was beautiful as I stared at its green and gray volcanic mountains from my over-the-water bungalow. I was the happiest I'd been in over a decade, an alcoholic who had found a cure.

David stood by me through the tail end of my struggle, and although he was incredibly supportive our social life had taken on a dismal atmosphere of early dinners and subdued conversation. Now we enjoyed cooking together, dinner parties, wine, and laughter. We survived the monster together and emerged from that ordeal as stronger, closer friends.

My life had come full circle. I had worked hard, taken risks, and believed in myself at the start of my career in Hollywood. I'd experienced meteoric highs and cataclysmic lows. I'd gone from a smart, attractive woman in her early thirties with a six-figure income, a mansion, and a successful career to someone consumed by addiction, an unrecognizable creature, sneaking out, drinking spirits from a paper bag in a bus shelter. I'd gone from someone who was in love with life to a woman who was humiliated, wracked with suicidal thoughts. And now I'd been given the ultimate blessing, the ultimate miracle—a fresh start. Not the false start I used to have when I'd recover from a binge. This was real; I could feel it in my bones.

The Tahitian water is a bright, azure blue, creating an atmosphere of invigorating peace. I'm halfway through my glass of champagne. When I finish it, I'll get a massage and later go snorkeling with David in the lagoon teeming with tropical fish. I've had my pill, and the monster slumbers in the back of my brain, as if it had never been. I actually see Tahiti this time, the color, the slow pace of life, the beauty. A white seaplane flies overhead carrying passengers back to the main island of Tahiti. I'll be on that plane soon enough, heading back to star in a new film. My friends were right, this is paradise, but so is every aspect of my life now. I'm free from hell; I can finally enjoy heaven.

LEFT: Kilts wil never go out of style! With Damon at one of my McStagger haggis parties.
BELOW: As Captain Belinda Blowhard on the set of the UK series *Starhyke*

The *Playboy* image I used for the Internet dating site in London

Crying at my brother Patrick's grave in Houston, Texas, 2008

Happy and healthy on my second trip to Tahiti

WAS FORTY-FOUR YEARS old and doing an explicit sex scene for Adam Rifkin's *LOOK*. It was six months after he'd called me, nine months since I'd been on The Sinclair Method. I had read the scripts for *LOOK*, and Adam was right—the part of Stella was absolutely hilarious—but I could see that it was going to be a demanding role. I got to do my own wardrobe for the part and had a chance to really build Stella from the outside in.

True to his calling as an experimental director, Adam made sure that the *LOOK* experience was unlike anything else I'd worked on, even the movie we did with Charlie Sheen's freeform poetry. There was no traditional filmmaking; it was all flip cams, nanny cams, closed-circuit cameras, and webcams. *LOOK* was a comment on how many times we're photographed and filmed every day without knowing it. It was a fly-by-the-seat-of-your-pants, run-around-Beverly-Hills-stealing-shots kind of production. I felt as I did back at the beginning, as an eighteen-year-old in Cannes stealing shots beside Clint Eastwood, a twenty-one-year-old taking revenge on her lover by filming in his house. It felt great. I was happy as a clam, except that it's never easy shooting fully nude sex scenes in a stranger's house, let alone at forty-four years of age. That makes for a long day.

We wrapped the last scene of the day, an argument in Stella's kitchen. There was a bottle of wine on the counter. I thought it was a prop filled with water. My character was an alcoholic, so halfway through the scene I picked it up and took a swig.

Fuck! It's real! I didn't take my pill!

It was a scary moment. I couldn't yell "Cut!" I was in the middle of a scene, and I couldn't bring myself to spit out red wine all over the place that Adam had borrowed for filming. I wished Jesus were there to do the reverse of his water-to-wine trick, but he wasn't, so I swallowed. I'd been so fastidious with The Sinclair Method, following the rules to the letter, but what happens now? Would I suddenly go bonkers and turn into my psycho character from *Hexed?* Would the monster leap out of its cave, right back into the driver's seat? I dealt with the problem at hand first. I kept my cool and asked them to replace the wine with water on the next take.

I got in the car and drove home. I knew I wasn't cured yet, that I was still working my way through this thing. I felt the urge to drink. I stopped at a store and bought a big bottle of fancy Belgian beer that I intended to share with David. I took my pill in the car on the way home. I was feeling better by the time I pulled into the driveway. I needed David, needed to tell him about how fate had just rolled me. I needed him to sympathize with the bad end to my day. But relationships by nature are unstable things. Sometimes you're in perfect harmony; sometimes you're coexisting in different dimensions.

The second I got through the door I started telling David about my day. I told the story chronologically and didn't make it to the part about the mix-up with the wine. I'd forgotten that this was the first time he'd heard about the hard-core sex scenes. He went bananas. Fuck, I should have seen that coming, I should have played it smarter. But I'd lost perspective; the world was crumbling around me. I retreated into the bathroom and locked the door, the bottle of beer still in the plastic shopping bag in my hand. I could hear the monster laughing.

I knew we'd get back together. How did you ever think you could get by without me? We were made for each other.

She could talk all the trash she wanted, because I'd taken my pill. I was in a bad place, but once that beer was done it was done. It wasn't going to lead to anything else, because I wasn't back in the monster's cave, just in the shadow-world transit lounge, just passing through.

∞

IT TOOK me about a year to unlearn the behaviors associated with drinking. It takes that long to let go of the guilt and anger, to stop being so defensive. The Incident of the Belgian Beer & the Bathroom was a one-off, but it taught me an important lesson. The biological cure starts working straightaway, but the psychological cure takes longer. I mean, it's all in *The Cure for Alcoholism,* and I had become friends with Drs. Sinclair and Eskapa, so I knew that I had to learn new behaviors with the help of the breathing space created by the naltrexone. But book smarts and street smarts are two different things. It takes a little longer to learn to literally change your mind.

∞

AT CHRISTMAS in 2010 I was back in Napa, back on a dusty street in a Sergio Leone Western where Claudia lives or dies depending on her ability to avoid the hail of emotional bullets. The family stands opposite me, they're all armed, and they have twitchy trigger fingers.

But I'm on it. I'm Clint Eastwood in *The Good, the Bad and the Ugly.* They're shooting, but the bullets don't hit home. I'm untouchable, and all the while I'm in the kitchen cooking food for thirteen people. I'm better than Clint Eastwood; I'm Superwoman.

And then one of my brothers said something that made David feel he had to defend me, and then my sister-in-law weighed in, and the next thing I knew I was screaming and pointing a spatula accusingly. They knew not to mess with me. The kitchen emptied, but it was too late. I realized I was already hit. I saw my kryptonite sitting on the counter right beside me: someone's half-finished glass of wine. I threw it down my gullet without a second thought. I realized what I'd done, rushed to my handbag, and quickly took my pill. It had some effect, but I could feel the monster stirring.

That slip-up instigated a whole week in which I didn't take the pill correctly, an hour before drinking. I started popping them after I'd already started drinking, which didn't make any sense. I knew better, but the monster was still there, whispering in the background. It turned out that it still could subtly pull some strings from the back seat. You haven't met a Stephen King monster as resilient as mine. Just when you think it's dead and buried, back it comes, clawing its way up out of the grave.

I drank nonstop for a week. I hid booze and started lying to family and friends. But I didn't throw up or get alcohol poisoning, and I could feel myself teetering on the edge of the slippery slope. I had learned my lesson and had an important realization. The pill isn't a weapon. It isn't something that lets you crush your addiction. The Sinclair Method is an ally, a partner. You have to work with it. After the Christmas fuck-up I took all of January off from drinking and cleaned out my system. I didn't drink at all. I recreated the same physical and emotional environment as the first time I took naltrexone.

I was back on track and have stayed that way since.

I haven't made that mistake again, and I'm back to where I was in my twenties in terms of my consumption.

When I was married to Gary I'd go out and buy one bottle of wine on a Saturday night. That one bottle would last Gary (6'1" and 190 pounds) and me all night long. One-and-a-half glasses for me and three for him, that was our big party night. I never wanted more than that, never gave alcohol a second thought.

So the cure comes with a warning, like the lesson in a fairy tale—you get Prince Charming and the castle, you get what you desire the most, but you have to follow the rule: you have to take the pill every time, one hour before you drink. Then you don't have the Stephen King experience. Then you can handle the monster like a pussycat, as long as you remember that it still has teeth and claws.

IT'S BEEN over three years since I first started on The Sinclair Method. I've been back to London to run my own fan convention, which unfortunately took place on the same weekend as the August 2011 London riots. Buildings burned down, cars were destroyed. The restaurant a block from my flat had its windows smashed in and its diners robbed by a mob of thugs. And while all that was going on I was thinking about Amy Winehouse. The coroner's report has now confirmed what I (and maybe everyone) already suspected, that she died of alcohol poisoning. Her blood alcohol level had been 0.4 percent. Britain's drunk-driving limit is 0.08 percent. She drank three bottles of vodka after a period of abstinence, and her brain and body overloaded. She passed into a coma. Her breathing stopped. When I heard that, it was impossible not to imagine myself in her situation. It could have been me—it so easily could have been me. I ran my convention successfully, took some guests out to dinner, had a few glasses of wine, and then flew home for my next job. No sweat.

And my career has been going from strength to strength. I had a guest spot on *Grimm*, a fantasy-crime series that's part fairy tale, part *CSI*, and I guest-starred in a comedy pilot produced by John Wells and directed by the very funny Peter Segal. I've done voice work on massively popular video games like *Halo*, *Guild Wars*, and *The Elder Scrolls V: Skyrim* with Joan Allen, Christopher Plummer, Lynda Carter (the original Wonder Woman), and Max von Sydow. I even caught up with my old *Babylon 5* friends at Mira Furlan's house for a reunion party. Bruce Boxleitner and Bill Mumy were there, and Pat Tallman, with her new man, Joe Straczynski. Joe and I spoke for the first time in a long while, and it was great to recapture some of our old camaraderie.

There's a happy ending to the story of my mother and me. She's still the most important person in the world to me, the person I love the most, and I'm forever grateful that we survived the highs and lows. Our relationship has now mellowed into a happy continuum of love and communication.

And I'm single again. David is still very much in my life, we're still very close friends, but they haven't invented a pill that lets me keep a relationship together longer than three years. God doesn't owe me a job or a lover. Being cured is no guarantee of happiness. I had to dig deep to realize that only I could make myself happy. I needed to stand on my own two feet and live my life. I think that you can't really help others until you're able to set your own house in order, and in many ways I think my journey, my battle with addiction, was about growing up, about maturing to the point where my sense of self-worth comes not from how I can meet my own needs, but rather from how I can help serve the needs of others.

That sense of purpose has given me the freedom to try again, to rebuild my life. I've just bought a new home, a gorgeous 1920s Spanish Revival house in the Hollywood Hills. I've poured all my life savings into it, and my mother and father have offered me their love, talents, and even money to help make it a place where I can have a new beginning. I've caused them so much pain, yet they keep coming back, giving their love and support in a way that only parents can. The house is a big step, but I'm not even slightly afraid. I know myself, I know the enemy, and I've learned that the best way to win a war is not to start one in the first place—to treat the symptoms, to address the first causes. And I'm going to redesign the house just the way I want, but this time without the monster on my back. This place will be a reflection of the new Claudia, a more integrated Claudia. This time I'm finally coming home.

I'VE BEEN blessed to build a career doing something I love. Acting is a vocation. By 2013 it will be thirty years since my first television job, and I'm proud to have been gainfully employed in one of the world's toughest, most competitive industries for most of that time.

I'm grateful to have inspired people with my portrayals of strong, intelligent women, but now my mission is to help those who have suffered from the same disease that nearly destroyed me. I want to save people the years I spent looking for a way to reclaim my life.

There's a stigma attached to being an alcoholic, a popular

perception that you're weak or immoral. The simple fact is that it's a physical addiction, a learned behavior that the brain cannot unlearn on its own. If you treat the addiction, the symptoms of the disease disappear.

When I met with Dr. Eskapa, the author of *The Cure for Alcoholism*, he looked over my naltrexone diary and concluded that I have a physiological makeup that's extremely well-suited to The Sinclair Method. Some people will have the same response as I did, while others will take longer. Twenty percent of people won't get any benefit at all, but a near eighty percent success rate is enough to inspire me to get to work.

I'm meeting with friends and fans who have reached out to me. I'm in discussions with a North American Indian tribe about starting up naltrexone trials. That came about through Phillip, my white buffalo medicine man. He introduced me to a man named Bear who's now working in partnership with me and believes The Sinclair Method can make a positive difference. And I'm talking with people in the entertainment industry—fellow actors, celebrities, and creative professionals who are drinking to get through tough jobs, drinking out of despair for lack of work, drinking because they've forgotten life before they needed to drink. The word is getting out there.

There's been such a turnaround in my life—it's nothing short of a miracle. I'd prayed for one that was for sure, I'd asked to be healed, but I didn't think that God was returning my calls. Now I see that something good has come out of my dark days. With my healing has come a new calling, or rather a way for me to realize an old calling. I've become a spokesperson for The Sinclair Method. I'm doing what I always wanted to do—I'm helping people.

*A*LCOHOLISM TOUCHES EVERYBODY'S lives—not just the people suffering from it, but their families and friends as well. It takes a great toll on our society.

If you are afflicted by alcoholism and my story resonates with you, then please look into The Sinclair Method. It might help you as it did me.

If you know of someone suffering alcohol addiction, then please share my story or information about the availability of The Sinclair Method with him or her. Dr. Eskapa's book, *The Cure for Alcoholism*, is available from BenBella Books (also the publisher of this book) and there are countless resources on the Internet.

The Sinclair Method saved my life. It's my sincere hope that it will help many others as it becomes more widely known as a treatment option.

I'd love to hear your stories and help, as best I can, anyone suffering from this disease. You can reach me on my Facebook fan page, at www.claudiachristian.net and at claudia@babylon confidential.com.

We all have monsters to battle, and, if nothing else, I hope this book lends hope to those who are walking a similar path to mine. Have faith, forgive yourself. I wish you every strength and much light on your journey toward peace.

TWO YEARS AFTER publication of my book on The Sinclair Method (TSM), *The Cure for Alcoholism: Drink Your Way Sober Without Willpower, Abstinence, or Discomfort,* I received an inspiring phone call from the bright and talented actress Claudia Christian. While she was introducing herself, I ran a quick Google search and saw there were over seven million references to her. I listened intently.

Claudia told me that she had been losing the battle against alcohol addiction for many years and that my book about the treatment had saved her life. I had already received many emails and calls about how TSM had transformed and saved lives—and this was always immensely gratifying—but there was something different, more urgent, about Claudia. I could tell intuitively that she genuinely cared about others and wanted to share her life-saving discovery with the world.

In her struggle to save her career and her life, Claudia had resorted to all manner of practices, potions, and prayers. She had fervently and repeatedly tried to control her drinking—which she calls her "monster"—on her own and via hypnotherapy, psychotherapy, very expensive traditional detox, abstinence, faith-based inpatient rehabs, and AA.

As with the vast majority (85 percent) of the 18 million Americans who have drinking problems, Claudia's attempts at recovery had failed. However hard she tried to control her drinking, she inevitably relapsed back to heavy, dangerous drinking bouts.

Claudia was determined not to become another statistic—one of the 105,000 Americans who, according to the American Medical Association, die from alcoholism each year. She did not want to join the World Health Organization's figure of 1.8 million worldwide deaths from alcohol—double the number of deaths from malaria and equal to the death rate from lung cancer.

Fortunately, fate intervened when she discovered TSM in the nick of time. She was able to reclaim her life. *Babylon Confidential* demonstrates how resilience, determination, and luck led Claudia to discover The Sinclair Method—a safe and cost-effective cure for her addiction.

No one walks into a bar at eighteen or twenty-one, has a beer, and immediately loses control over his or her drinking. The addiction takes time—many drinking sessions over months and years—to *learn* through a process known as *reinforcement*. Some people are faster learners than others, but once the addiction has taken root in the brain *it remains incurable for life*. Or at least it had been incurable. In the past, Alcoholics Anonymous was right: once an alcoholic, always an alcoholic. Today, however, the situation has changed, thanks to the research of Dr. David Sinclair. Today most cases of alcoholism can be cured.

Dr. Sinclair began his research with the groundbreaking discovery—now widely accepted by alcohol and addiction researchers—of the alcohol deprivation effect (ADE).

The most common treatment for alcoholism has been alcohol deprivation: detoxifying patients and then keeping them for several weeks in a place where they cannot get alcohol. This treatment does remove the physiological dependence on alcohol which the theories previously said was the reason for craving and drinking alcohol. But Dr. Sinclair discovered that alcohol deprivation actually *causes* the craving and drinking to be increased. This was a revolutionary discovery. First, it contradicted the standard treatment of detox and rehab. Second, it meant the existing theory was wrong: something other than physiological dependence was causing alcoholism.

The discovery of the alcohol deprivation effect was followed by many years of research with hundreds of experiments aimed at determining what that "something" really is. The studies first showed that the human body's opioid system was involved. Next, they showed that alcohol drinking is a learned behavior reinforced by the opioid system.

Naltrexone and its relatives nalmefene and naloxone are in a class of medications known as "opioid antagonists." These medications are highly effective at blocking the effects of both opiate drugs (morphine, heroin, oxycodone) and the body's own morphine-like substances known as endorphins. When we drink alcohol our brains secrete endorphins, and, like morphine, these endorphins bind to opioid receptors on nerve cells in the brain, causing reinforcement. As a result, the person is more likely to drink alcohol again in the future, releasing more endorphins, causing more reinforcement, and making drinking still more likely to occur. While the majority of people are born with "normal" opioid systems, it is thought that about 15 percent of the population inherit a particularly sensitive opioid system. This engenders a genetic predisposition to alcoholism. For these people, the vicious cycle of drinking, endorphin release, and reinforcement of further alcohol drinking is likely to proceed to the point where the person can no longer control the drinking.

It is now clear that this learning to crave and drink alcohol takes place unconsciously in the primitive parts of the brain. For most people the conscious higher brain can dominate the primitive parts and block excessive drinking. Alcoholics, however, have had so much reinforcement from drinking so often that the primitive brain's demands can no longer be blocked. The primitive brain demands that the conscious brain think about alcohol, and the alcoholic thinks about it nearly all the time. The primitive brain, especially after alcohol deprivation, demands that alcohol be consumed, and so the alcoholic drinks.

The primitive brain is powerful. Once addicted, few of us—perhaps less than 10 percent—have the ability to use our higher cortical brain, our "willpower," to overcome the biological cravings for food and water. The systems in the primitive brain that drive impulsive and compulsive heavy drinking in the alcoholic have become as powerful as those for the basic drives. For those individuals who can override the impulse to drink and can remain abstinent there is no need for The Sinclair Method.

It is often very difficult for non-addicts to understand addiction. One way of illustrating the overwhelming power of biology driving addiction is to imagine being out in the desert for forty-eight hours without water. The forty-eight hours now become seventy-two hours. In the distance you see a truck driving toward you. All you can think about is your thirst—a drink of water. As the truck approaches, you see that it is refrigerated and surely contains some cool, nourishing liquid. Indeed, when it arrives two people hop out and set up a table on which they place a bucket of ice and water and several types of juices and soft drinks. They now instruct you to resist: "Don't drink," they say. But the biological impulse to drink, to survive, overwhelms you, and of course you cannot resist the deprivation effect. This is what it is like to be an alcoholic—or an amphetamine addict, a cocaine addict, or even someone suffering from non-substance addictions like gambling.* The primitive brain takes over and you relapse.

---

* Gambling, high-risk compulsive behavior, and several other destructive behaviors are thought to be mediated via the opioid or endorphinergic system.

Until the discovery of "pharmacological extinction," which has come to be known as The Sinclair Method, alcoholism and many other substance and non-substance addictions were indeed incurable. The best you could hope for was that you would remain on the wagon as long as possible between relapses. While it is true that around 10 to 15 percent of those addicted to alcohol do manage many years of abstinence, they can never touch a single drink again. Indeed, many traditional detox and rehab centers actually inform their patients that their chances of remaining abstinent are less than 15 percent at one year.

Naltrexone changes that situation, *but only when used correctly*. Claudia read about TSM and the correct way in which to use the medication in *The Cure for Alcoholism*. The book describes the origins of Dr. David Sinclair's thirty years of alcohol research for the National Public Health Institute in Finland and how pharmacological extinction represents a major breakthrough in addiction science.

Instead of the 85 percent failure rates associated with traditional treatments,* TSM achieves *success* rates of around 80 percent. Success in TSM terms means that after treatment, individuals are *biologically de-addicted*. Their craving is dramatically reduced, and they are able to drink within World Health Organization safety limits—or they are able to abstain without craving alcohol.

In most cases the benefits of the treatment take about three to four months to appear. *Babylon Confidential* demonstrates that Claudia was a "fast responder." But, depending on the individual, benefits may take some people up to ten or twelve months. Once patients have successfully reversed the addiction they must follow one golden rule. *The Cure for Alcoholism* constantly

---

* *National Institute on Alcohol Abuse and Alcoholism, National Institute on Drug Abuse, World Health Organization.*

reminds them *never to drink alcohol without first having taken their naltrexone* (or nalmefene); otherwise they remain at risk of relearning the addiction.*

Despite more than ninety clinical trials—many of them conducted to the gold standard of clinical research (double-blind and placebo-controlled)—most doctors have not yet heard about naltrexone and its efficacy in treating alcohol addiction. Unless a medication is covered by a patent, there is no financial incentive to spend the hundreds of millions required to market a new medication. Unfortunately, when a doctor *has* heard about naltrexone but prescribes it according to the manufacturer's implied directions—take a 50 mg naltrexone tablet and abstain from drinking—the result is always failure.† Fortunately, Claudia's search led her to my book *The Cure for Alcoholism,* and she learned how to treat her alcoholism effectively with naltrexone by following the golden rule and not abstaining from drinking.

Alcoholism remains a stigma. Physicians, patients, and their families often mistakenly conclude that the individual is "weak" or "immoral." *Babylon Confidential* bravely describes how Claudia Christian was rescued by TSM from the "monster" unconsciously arising from the super-strengthened opioid system in her primitive brain—and how after years of unnecessary suffering she has been freed of the tormenting, unrelenting imprisonment of the addiction that had become hardwired into her brain.

Tragically there are millions of people like Claudia confined to this biological prison. Since they do not know about

---

* 50 mg is standard, but sometimes, according to reports from readers of *The Cure for Alcoholism* on their Internet forum www.thesinclairmethod.com, a dose of 75 mg one hour before a drinking session in a twenty-four-hour period is required.

† John H. Krystal, MD, et al., "Naltrexone in the Treatment of Alcohol Dependence," *New England Journal of Medicine,* December 13, 2001. This study of 627 alcoholics in Veterans Affairs hospitals proved that naltrexone is ineffective when combined with abstinence.

The Sinclair Method, they remain addicted despite battling the craving and addiction as hard as they can. While their intentions may be noble, mere conscious knowledge of the dangers of compulsive, uncontrolled drinking makes no difference, and most unwillingly relapse back to heavy drinking.

295

One study conducted at the Karolinska Institute in Sweden confirmed that naltrexone also attenuates amphetamine addiction. This is a most convincing and groundbreaking study, proving that naltrexone cuts craving and significantly reduces amphetamine abuse by blocking the reinforcement coming from the amphetamine. It was conducted by Nitya Jayaram-Lindström and a team headed by Johan Franck in the Department of Clinical Neuroscience at the Karolinska Institute in Stockholm.[*,†,‡] Jayaram-Lindström points out that there are an estimated 35 million amphetamine abusers worldwide—more than the total number of heroin and cocaine abusers combined. In its final phase the study used a double-blind, placebo-controlled design and obtained results showing that naltrexone was effective in treating amphetamine addiction. Just think about the wonderful implications of pharmacological extinction for the millions in the grip of amphetamine and methamphetamine addiction.

Now think about the World Health Organization figure of 76.3 million people addicted to alcohol. We know from the science that taking naltrexone or nalmefene one hour before

---

[*] Nitya Jayaram-Lindström et al., "An Open Clinical Trial of Naltrexone for Amphetamine Dependence: Compliance and Tolerability," *Nordic Journal of Psychiatry* (59 (3): 167–171, 2005).

[†] Nitya Jayaram-Lindström et al., "Naltrexone for the Treatment of Amphetamine Dependence: A Randomized, Placebo-Controlled Trial" (2007, submitted).

[‡] Nitya Jayaram-Lindström, "Evaluation of Naltrexone as a Treatment for Amphetamine Dependence," a dissertation from Karolinska University Hospital, presented Dec. 18, 2007. After tests with volunteers and a compliance test with amphetamine addicts, a twelve-week randomized double-blind, placebo-controlled clinical trial showed that naltrexone eventually reduced addicts' craving and produced fewer urine positives for amphetamine.

a drinking session (the Sinclair way) can help around 80 percent of people. Unlike many other approaches TSM is firmly grounded on evidence-based medicine. Dignified, safe, and kind, this alcoholism treatment is by far the most effective now known. Unfortunately, it does not produce the kind of profits associated with the $6.2 billion rehab industry in the United States. The main ingredients—a prescription from a physician in any general medical setting, according to the American Medical Association, and taking the inexpensive generic medication one hour before drinking in a twenty-four-hour period— are not profitable propositions.

Dr. David Sinclair's discoveries are now being tested in a promising phase-two double-blind clinical trial for binge-eating disorder (BED) under the auspices of Lightlake Therapeutics Inc. BED appears to be caused by addiction to foods that, like alcohol, release endorphins; therefore, it should be possible to treat BED with a method similar to TSM. It also should be an effective treatment for bulimia. In this instance the treatment uses a short-acting opioid antagonist called naloxone administered as a nasal spray. Naloxone remains in the brain for only a couple of hours, which is the usual duration for an eating binge.

Finally, there is real hope that a sister medication, nalmefene, which is very similar to naltrexone and especially safe, will receive final approval for the treatment of alcoholism after a large European phase-three trial concludes at the end of 2011. Nalmefene would engender enormous hope for problem drinkers, binge drinkers, and alcoholics in the UK, Europe, and eventually the United States.

Claudia Christian's *Babylon Confidential* is a courageous contribution to the world. It will inform others who have no idea that a scientifically proven medical treatment for alcohol addiction actually exists for moderate, severe, and end-stage alcoholics. Alcoholism and other addictive behaviors need no longer destroy so many lives. Despite the widespread misconception that alcoholism is an incurable lifelong condition, science informs us that now there really is a cure—that for 80 percent of those who try it, the treatment allows for gradual detoxification and de-addiction.

Claudia Christian

FROM CLAUDIA CHRISTIAN: Thank you to my family and friends for sticking by me in the tough times; I love and appreciate all of you very much. Holly, you've gone through it all with me and I can never say "thank you" enough.

To Drs. David Sinclair and Roy Eskapa—you saved my life. How do you thank someone for that? I am forever grateful for your research and dedication in developing and spreading the word about The Sinclair Method.

Thanks also to Neil Gaiman, Kevin Anderson, Rebecca Moesta, Shari Shattuck, and Walter Koenig for reading this book and offering their kind words of support, and to David Honl for his love, friendship, and massive talent.

And to Morgan . . . here's to many more years of collaboration. You are a huge talent with an enormous heart. I don't know how we found each other but I am utterly chuffed that the universe managed to arrange it.

Morgan Grant Buchanan

FROM MORGAN GRANT BUCHANAN: Love and thanks to my wife, Catherine, and sons, Calum and Liam, for their patience and support while I scheduled interviews and phone conferences at all hours from Australia to work on this book.

Sincere thanks to my writing collaborator and friend, Claudia Christian, for asking me to help share her amazing life story.

We'd both like to thank our agent David Fugate at LaunchBooks and the team at BenBella Books for their support and professionalism.